No Cross Marks the Spot

Stella E. Kilby

Best wishes
Stella Kilby,
December 2001

Galamena Press

© Stella E Kilby 2001
No Cross Marks the Spot

ISBN 0 9541016 0 X [Paperback edition]

Published by Galamena Press
108 Barnstaple Road
Thorpe Bay
Southend on Sea
Essex SSI 3PW
United Kingdom,

The right of Stella Kilby to be identified as author of this work has been asserted by her in accordance with the Copyright, Designs and Patents Act 1988.

All rights reserved. No part of this publication may be produced in any form or by any means – graphic, electronic or mechanical including photocopying, recording, taping or information storage and retrieval systems – without the prior permission, in writing, of the publisher.

Design and Production co-ordinated by:
The **Better Book** Company Ltd
Warblington Lodge
Havant
Hampshire PO9 2XH
England

Tel: 023 9248 1160
Fax: 023 9249 2819

Printed in England.

Contents

Introduction	i
Chronology	iii
Notes on Spellings	v

Part One

Chapter		Page
1	England, 1815 to 1839	3
2	Griqualand, 1839 to 1843	9
3	Lekhatlong, 1843 to 1856	25
4	England, 1856 to 1858	59
5	Griqualand, 1858 to 1859	78
6	The Kalahari Desert, 1859	108
7	Linyanti, 1860	150
8	The Zambezi, 1858 to 1863	170

Part Two

9	On the Missionaries' Trail, 1999	197
10	The Linyanti Marshes, 1999	240
	Appendices	273
	Sources	286
	Index	288

LIST OF ILLUSTRATIONS

PHOTOGRAPHS

PART ONE   page

1.	Holloway Helmore – 1839.	87
2.	Holloway Helmore – 1858.	88
3.	Anne Helmore – 1858.	89
4.	David Livingstone – *circa* 1856.	90
5.	Mary Livingstone – *circa* 1856.	91
6.	Robert Moffat – *circa* 1871.	92
7.	Mary Moffat – *circa* 1871.	93
8.	Roger and Isabella Price – 1858.	94
9.	John Mackenzie – *circa* 1858.	95
10.	Olive Helmore – 1858.	96
11.	Anne Sophia Helmore – *circa* 1865.	97
12.	The Moffats' homestead at Kuruman.	98

Photos 1, 3, 4, 6, 7, 8 and 9 by kind permission of the Council for World Mission/London Missionary Society Archives.

Photo 5 by kind permission of The David Livingstone Centre, National Trust for Scotland.

PART TWO   Page

1.	The weir on the dam that Holloway Helmore built on the Harts River at Lekhatlong.	213
2.	Kuruman – Old road alongside the Moffat homestead.	214
3.	A typical Tswana home.	215
4.	Driving across the Ntwetwe Salt Pan, Makgadikgadi.	216
5.	Camping alongside Chapman's Baobab.	217
6.	Helmore's carving on Chapman's Baobab.	218
7.	Looking across the Mababe Plains from the Gutscha Hills, Savuti.	219
8.	Transport old and new – Sangwali.	220
9.	Sebituane's grave, Sangwali.	221
10.	Chief Bornface ShuFu and his council inside the *khuta* at Sangwali	222
11.	Chief Bornface Shufu with his council and invited advisers outside the *khuta* at Sangwali.	223
12.	Site of the Helmore/Price camp at Malengalenga.	224

MAPS

1. South and Central Africa, showing Helmore/Price route and that of the Kilby party. BACK PAGE
2. Southern Africa, 1850 – sketched by James Wyld. 28
3. Detail of above map, showing Griqualand and the mission stations. 29
4. Detail from Livingstone's map of his journey through Barotseland, drawn in 1853. 43
5. Livingstone's Zambezi journey, 1853-1855. 172
6. Detail from above, showing diversion at Kebrabasa Rapids. 173
7. The Linyanti region as it is today. 248

Maps 2, and 3 by courtesy of the Royal Geographical Society
Maps 4, 5 and 6 by courtesy of the Council for World Mission/London Missionary Society Archives.
Map 7 adapted from regional map issued by Government of Namibia.

Sketch of ox wagon, by courtesy of The South Africa Library, Cape Town.

INTRODUCTION
No Cross Marks the Spot

The story of the Makololo Mission is one of the most tragic episodes in the annals of missionary history in Southern Africa, yet up to now it has only been discussed as a passing episode in stories about the other persons involved, or about the region. When, on a visit to South Africa my late cousin Grace Norton gave to me a cache of letters and documents for safe-keeping, I knew that the story warranted a book of its own. Here it is.

This is the story of Holloway's life and work, which ended prematurely and tragically, when he was just 44 years old. It is the story of his successful seventeen years at Lekhatlong, near Kuruman, where he developed a thriving mission station. It publishes for the first time in full Holloway's journal of the party's traumatic journey from Kuruman to the Makololo, when they nearly perished in the hot, dry desert and it provides in detail the tragic end to the mission, when nine of their party of twenty one died in the marshes.

No single person or event can be blamed for the tragedy; it is a catalogue of hasty and disastrous decisions. However, although David Livingstone subsequently exonerated himself from any involvement, it is clear that he must take a large share of the blame.

The purpose of this book is to piece together for the first time all the events leading to the fateful decision to proceed with this venture, despite the setbacks and misgivings. It aims to explain and dispel some of the allegations of previous authors. It also aims to respond to four as yet unanswered questions in the aftermath of the tragedy:

1. How far Livingstone should be blamed for the tragedy
2. Whether the victims died of fever or whether they were poisoned
3. Where the Makololo had their town and where the missionaries had their camp
4. Where the victims were buried

The book includes an account of a recent unique journey by the author, following the same route that the party took, with anecdotes about the region as it is now compared with the nineteenth century. It also includes an interview with the *khuta*, or council of elders for the Mayeyi people who now inhabit the Linyanti marshes.

The material is drawn mainly from original documents in archives and in the personal possession of the author, supplemented by that from other books touching on this episode.

I am deeply grateful to the many people who have helped and encouraged me in the writing of this book. In particular, Pierre Craven of African Getaway Safaris, who became more of a friend than a tour guide to our party. Without his help and support the second part of this book could not have been written. I am equally grateful to my cousin and friend Anne Burgess, in providing me with a large amount of the material and for her help in tracking down documents in Cape Town. I wish to thank also Rosemary Seton and her ever helpful staff of the Special Collections at the School of Oriental and African Studies in London, where the London Missionary Society archive material is now stored. Thanks are also due to Dr Sasha Barrow of Botanical Gardens, Kew; Dr John Frean of the South African Institute of Medical Research in Johannesburg; Dr Leon Jacobson of the MacGregor Museum at Kimberley; Mr Innocent Mahoto, a Makololo now living at Katimo Molilo; Chief Bornface ShuFu of the Mayeyi in the Linyanti region and his Council of Elders; Linus Mukwata, head of the Sangwali Community Conservation Centre, our host and interpreter whilst we were at Linyanti; Dr Andrew Morton of the Council for World Mission; Marion Hough and Gillian Poland for kindly proof-reading and providing some helpful comments. Last but by no means least, I am grateful to my family, especially my husband Cyril for his patience, help and support in the compilation of this work. I hope I have not omitted any specific person, if I have, I apologise and extend a general thank you.

S.E.K.
June, 2001

CHRONOLOGY

1811   May. Anne Garden born, Islington, London
1815   14th December. Holloway Helmore born, Kidderminster, England
1815   Helmore family moved to Stratford-upon-Avon, England
1822   1st June. Emily Sophia Helmore born, Stratford-upon-Avon
1831   September. Holloway enters Mill Hill Grammar School, Hendon, London
1834   September. Holloway enters Homerton Independent College, London
1838   20th December. Holloway ordained at Leamington, Warwickshire
1839   21st January. Marriage of Holloway Helmore and Anne Garden at Islington, London
1839   26th January. Holloway and Anne sail for Southern Africa
1839   3rd May. Holloway and Anne arrive at Cape Town
1839   14th October. Holloway and Anne arrive in Griqualand
1840   22nd June. Holloway and Anne commence work at Lekhatlong, Griqualand
1841   April 4th. Birth of Olive Anne Helmore, Lekhatlong. (Died 14th April 1841)
1841   July. Arrival of David Livingstone at Kuruman
1842   11th May. Birth of eldest surviving daughter, Olive Helmore at Lekhatlong
1842   May. Removal of Helmores to Borigelong, Griqualand
1843   October. Return of Helmores to Lekhatlong.
1844   12th January. Birth of second daughter, Anne Sophia at Lekhatlong.
1845   2nd January. Marriage of David Livingstone to Mary Moffat at Kuruman.
1846   31st May. Birth of son, stillborn, to Helmores at Lekhatlong.
1846   November (abt.) Arrival of Holloway's sister Emily in South Africa.
1847   6th August. Birth of third surviving daughter, Emma Elizabeth (Lizzie) at Lekhatlong
1849   24th June. Birth of fourth surviving daughter, Emily at Lekhatlong
1849   1st August. Livingstone reaches Lake Ngami for first time.
1850   April. Livingstone, with his wife Mary, makes first unsuccessful attempt to reach Makololo, via Lake Ngami.
1850   8th October. Marriage of Emily Helmore to Charles Stuart of Bloemfontein.
1851   June. Livingstone, with his wife Mary, reaches the Makololo at Linyanti.
1851   6th July. Death of Sebituane, chief of the Makololo.
1851   Winter. Construction commences of a dam at Lekhatlong.
1851   9th November. Birth of fifth surviving daughter to Helmores, Selina Mary, at Lekhatlong.
1852   23rd April. Mary Livingstone with her children put on board vessel for England. Livingstone begins preparations for his trans-African journey.
1852   August. Boers attack and destroy Sechele's town of Kolobeng.
1852   December. Livingstone sets out from Kuruman for second visit to Makololo, having sent Mary and children to England.
1853   May. Holloway asked to investigate dispute of Batlapin with Boers at Taung
1853   23rd May. Livingstone arrives at Linyanti for his epic journey across Central Africa. Finds Sekeletu now Chief of the Makololo.
1853   22nd September. Birth of first surviving son and sixth surviving child to Helmores, William Holloway (Willie), at Lekhatlong.
1853   November. Livingstone leaves Linyanti for the west coast of Africa.
1854   February. Orange River Sovereignty ceded by British government to Boers.
1855   September. Livingstone returns to Linyanti having reached the west coast of Africa.

1855	November. Death of Emily's husband, Charles Stuart.
1855	3rd November. Livingstone departs from Linyanti for east coast of Africa.
1855	16/17th November. Livingstone sees the Victoria Falls for the first time.
1856	February. Helmore family, with Emily Stuart, depart Lekhatlong for Cape Town to sail for England for three-year sojourn.
1856	18th April. Birth of second surviving son, seventh and youngest child to Helmores, Henry Charles, on voyage.
1856	22nd April. Livingstone departs from Tete near the east coast of Africa, leaving the 110 Makololo men to await his return.
1856	20th May. Livingstone arrives at Quilimane on east coast of Africa.
1856	9th December. Livingstone arrives in England.
1857	26th January. Board of London Missionary Society approve plan to set up two new mission stations, one amongst the Makololo and the other amongst the Matebele.
1857	4th April. Letter to Robert Moffat requesting him to visit Moselekatsi to obtain permission for new mission station.
1857	July. Moffat sets out for Matabeleland.
1857	December. Three young missionaries appointed for Zambezi expedition.
1858	February. Livingstone appointed Her Majesty's Consul at Quilemane.
1858	February. Holloway requested to lead the expedition to the Makololo, Livingstone having resigned from the London Missionary Society.
1858	10th March. Livingstone sails from England for the Zambezi Expedition.
1858	14th May. Livingstone arrives at mouth of the Zambezi.
1858	13th July. Young missionaries arrive in Cape Town for Makololo/Matebele Expedition.
1858	July. Holloway and Anne with four of their children leave England for Africa.
1858	16th August. Helmores arrive in Cape Town.
1858	8th September. Livingstone arrives at Tete to greet his Makololo men.
1858	November. Livingstone finds that the Kebrabasa Rapids are impassable.
1858	27th December. Livingstone starts on his first trip to the Shire River.
1859	12th January. Helmores arrive at Lekhatlong to begin preparations for new mission to Makololo.
1859	March. Livingstone's second visit to Shire and discovery of Lake Shirwa.
1859	8th July. Helmore/Price Expedition to the Makololo sets out from Kuruman.
1859	August. Livingstone's third trip up the Shire.
1860	14th February. Helmore/Price party arrive at Linyanti
1860	2nd March. First death occurs at Linyanti, that of Molatsi.
1860	7th March. Death of Henry Helmore.
1860	9th March. Death of Baby Eliza Price.
1860	11th March. Death of Selina Helmore and of Thabe.
1860	12th March. Death of Anne Helmore.
1860	19th March. Death of Setloki.
1860	21st April. Death of Holloway Helmore.
1860	19th June. Roger and Isabella Price, with Willie and Lizzie Helmore, depart from Linyanti.
1860	5th July. Death of Isabella Price.
1860	August. Arrival of Livingstone at Victoria Falls and Sesheke.
1860	8th September. Mackenzie finds Price near Lake Ngami.
1861	February 14th. Survivors of Makololo Expedition arrive back at Kuruman.

NOTES ON SPELLINGS

Words have in most cases been left as they were spelt in the original documents, for example waggon and jackall. This also applies to place names and tribal names, where in many instances more than one spelling was used.

The style of spelling has changed for the Bantu tribes. Again, for ease of identification the old spellings were retained throughout the book. The following modern, or correct equivalents are listed:

Bakalagari	Bakgalagadi
Bakwena	BaKwena
Bamangwato	BaNgwato
Barolong	BaRolong
Batlapin	BaTlhaping
Bawangketse	BaNgwaketse
Bechuana	BaTswana
Kalahari	Kgalagadi
Lechulathebe	Letsholathebe
Linyanti	Also known as Dinyanti
Lekhatlong	Likatlong, or Dikatlhong
Lotlakane	Letlhakane
Makololo	MaKololo
Maritsane	Mareetsane
Matabele	MaTebele
Matlaring	Mathlaring
Molopo-oa-Malare	Pitsane Molopo
Moselekatsi	Mzilikazi
Sebituane	Sebitoane
Sechele	Setshele

Part One

CHAPTER ONE
England, 1815 to 1839
Africa calls

"My mind has for a considerable time been drawn involuntarily towards Africa, and lately in consequence of my conversation with Dr Philip, been fixed upon that field of labour."[1] Holloway Helmore wrote this even before he had completed his theological studies. It was his response to a letter he had received from the Reverend John Arundel, the home secretary of the London Missionary Society, instructing him to take up a post in Samoa, then known as the Navigator's Islands. Africa had beckoned to Holloway.

Having been born and brought up in the early part of the nineteenth century, at a time when missionary activity was expanding rapidly, he was only one of thousands who left the shores of their homeland to travel to remote corners of the British empire, filled with fervour to bring the light of Christianity to the heathen. Hundreds of these dedicated men, their wives and families, gave their lives for their cause. In this Holloway and his wife, Anne, were not unique, but the circumstances leading to their last fateful assignment and its tragic consequences was then, and still is, an extraordinary story. At the time, *The Times* called it "an enterprise which we should think and hope must be almost unparalleled, and which only wanted the single quality of success to make it miraculous."[2]

Holloway was born on December 14th 1815, just six months after the Battle of Waterloo, the third son of a dissenting, or non-conformist minister. His father, Thomas Helmore, had been born at Titchfield, near Portsmouth in 1783, where he and his brothers and sister were baptised into the Anglican faith. The family subsequently moved to West Cowes on the Isle of Wight and as Thomas grew into a young man, he came under the influence of a local preacher from a nearby small Independent Meeting House. He was eventually admitted to Dr Bogue's Academy at Gosport, where he trained for the ministry; this same Dr Bogue was one of the founders of the London Missionary Society.

One evening, Thomas and some fellow students were asked to go to Warblington, near Portsmouth, to assist a young lady preacher whose popularity was growing so fast that a special meeting house had been erected for her.[3] Thomas fell in love with this pious and lovely lady, Olive Holloway, the daughter of Joseph Holloway, a captain in the Royal Navy. Soon after Thomas's ordination in 1810, they were married in the old Saxon church at Warblington, where generations of Olive's family had worshipped and lay buried.

The young couple were sent to the Baxter Independent Chapel in Kidderminster, Worcestershire, where they lived for the next nine years.[4] Holloway and his two older brothers, Thomas and Porter, were born in this growing industrial town in the West Midlands. When Holloway was three years old, the family moved to Stratford-upon-Avon, where his father had been appointed to the Rother Street Independent Chapel. Here Thomas Helmore ministered to a thriving congregation until his death in 1845. Two further children were born to the couple, Frederick in 1819, and Emily, Holloway's only surviving sister, in 1822.[5]

Olive Helmore spent many hours visiting the poor and sick in Stratford itself, and in the many small villages and hamlets dotting the surrounding countryside. Thomas, meantime, strongly believed that education was the best way to help the poor to a better life. His greatest achievement was the British School, which he had set up soon after arriving in Stratford and which taught over three hundred young boys and girls the rudiments of reading, writing and arithmetic.[6]

Holloway and his brothers received their basic education in this school from their father's own hands, before going on to Mill Hill in Hendon, Middlesex, a grammar school catering for non-conformist children. Their upbringing was strongly Evangelical. The Calvinism of the Independents, or Congregationalists as they were then being called, was instilled into them from a very young age.

However, Thomas Helmore gave his children, and the boys from his school, far more than the Word of God and their basic schooling. At weekends, when the weather permitted, he took his boys on long walks in the beautiful surrounding Warwickshire countryside, with its gently rolling hills and small villages. These excursions were to be affectionately recalled by Frederick in his memoirs of his eldest brother, Thomas.[7] Their home was a happy place. Frederick also fondly recalled the love and laughter and music, which played such an important part in their upbringing. The four brothers had formed a quartet, with three flutes and a bassoon. Their fine singing voices and exceptional musical talents were much appreciated in Stratford-upon-Avon and they were often invited to perform at recitals, or in private homes.

We begin Holloway's story in the summer of 1838. At the time, he was a young man of 22 years, nearing completion of his studies at Homerton College in Hackney, just east of the City of London. This college had been founded by the non-conformists, its main function being to train young men for the ministry, or for missionary work at home and abroad.

Tall and slender, with a sensitive mouth and dark curly hair, Holloway's brown, languid eyes were set below a high forehead. He looked more suited to becoming a musician than a missionary, but from an early age his heart had been set on following in his father's footsteps and training to become a minister. As the story of Holloway Helmore will reveal, however, behind his sensitive features lay a determination and tenacity which, when occasion demanded, surprised even those who knew him.

It was a time of change in the land of his birth. A year previously, the young eighteen-year old Princess Victoria had inherited the throne of Britain and its vast empire from her uncle, King William IV, thus heralding a new era in its history. In that same year, 1838, the Chartist movement was formed. Doubtless Holloway and his father, Thomas, had much sympathy with their aims; the working classes were beginning to rumble and demand the right to vote and be given a fairer share of the nation's wealth. The greatest impact in the way of social change, however, was from the rapidly growing railway system. People and goods were beginning to be transported greater distances, at a considerably faster pace than ever before. A great migration process was under way, with people moving far away from their close-knit village communities to seek their fortunes, often fruitlessly, in the growing industrial areas.

Holloway Helmore, however, had his own personal problem that year. His predicament was how to persuade the directors of the London Missionary Society that, not only was he reluctant to leave college just yet, but that he did not want to go to some remote islands in the Far East. It was a delicate situation. For the past eighteen months they had been generous in supporting him with a personal grant, in addition to financing his studies at Homerton College.[8]

The London Missionary Society had been founded in 1795 as an inter-denominational body, though it soon evolved into a predominantly Congregationalist organisation, with mission stations scattered throughout the world. They were well established in the British-controlled Cape Colony in Southern Africa, with a small enclave of activity in Griqualand, which lay beyond the Orange River, the northern border of the Colony. Largest and the most successful amongst this cluster of mission stations was Kuruman, under the leadership of Robert Moffat and his wife, Mary, and it is in this area that the first part of Holloway's story is focused.

Dr John Philip was their superintendent for Southern Africa. Based in Cape Town, he had the task of co-ordinating contact and movement between the various missions, which were spread out over a wide area, often with hundreds of miles between. He also often had the unenviable task of maintaining harmony amongst a group of strong-minded men, thrown together and forced to tolerate each other in a remote environment, where there was no other European contact. It was Philip who, on a recent visit to England, had encouraged Holloway's interest in Africa, hence his reluctance to obey the request of the London Missionary Society to join their man in the Navigator's Islands.

Deliberating for a time, seeking the advice of friends and tutors and praying for guidance, in the end Holloway wrote a polite and deferential letter to Arundel, requesting the directors to reconsider their decision. He was not yet ready begin work, he told him. He not only wished to complete his studies, but he would also like to continue and take additional courses on methods of education and medicine, to equip himself for life on a remote mission station. A further complication, he wrote, was that he was engaged to Miss Anne Garden of Islington and it would be impossible for her to leave at such short notice.

Holloway's request was granted and he was able to complete his studies, including the basic rudiments of medicine. He was ordained on the 20th December 1838 at Spencer Street Chapel in Leamington, only a few miles from Stratford-upon-Avon, where he had spent his childhood years and where his parents and sister Emily still lived.

His family had by then gone their different ways. His eldest brother, Thomas, had chosen to pursue a musical career and was studying at Magdalen College, Oxford.[9] At that time music was a fairly recent innovation in church services and Thomas had already contributed considerably towards the music in his father's chapel. Through the family's love of music he had become associated with the Anglican Church, which in turn brought to him an awareness that his sympathies lay more with their liturgy. This, together with his desire to obtain a scholarship to study music at Oxford, had persuaded him to become confirmed into the Anglican faith; no one could yet be admitted to the universities of Oxford or Cambridge without subscribing to the Thirty Nine Articles of the Church of England. It was not long before Frederick, the youngest brother, followed the same course.

Meanwhile, the other brother Porter had earlier that year emigrated to Australia with his uncle, William Helmore. In time, he formed his own colony at Encounter Bay in South Australia, farming a small piece of land. A windmill which he built, and which served the small community of settlers, stands there to this day.[10]

Holloway and Anne Garden were married quietly at the Islington Register Office in London on 21st January 1839. Anne was born in Islington, London in May 1811, the eldest daughter of William and Ann Garden. Her father, who had been a captain in the Merchant Navy, had died in 1825. Nearly four years older than Holloway, she was equally strong-willed. Tall, with brown eyes and a generous mouth, her square face was framed with an abundance of thick, brown hair which she swept severely into a coil on each ear. She dressed modestly, in quiet, neutral colours. She shared Holloway's dedication to spreading the Gospel and with her sympathetic, affectionate nature she was to prove a devoted, supportive and loving wife and mother.

Five days after their marriage the young couple travelled down to

Southampton to embark on the packet *Enismeer*, bound for a new life in Southern Africa. It would be seventeen years before they saw their families and homeland again.

[1] L.M.S. Archives, Helmore to Arundel, 4.6.1838
[2] The Times, 28 May 1861
[3] *Memoir of the Revd. Thomas Helmore*
[4] Dr Williams Library, London
[5] *Memoir of the Revd. Thomas Helmore*
[6] *A Church of the Ejectment - The Story of the Rother Street Congregational Church*
[7] *Memoir of the Revd. Thomas Helmore*
[8] LMS Archives, Helmore to Arundel, 7.1.1837
[9] *Memoir of the Revd. Thomas Helmore*
[10] *Colonists, Copper and Corn in the Colony of South Australia, 1850-1851*, Old Colonist, Adelaide; Editor, 1983.

CHAPTER TWO
Griqualand, 1839 to 1843
The price of independence

The *Enismeer* dropped anchor in Table Bay, Cape Town, early in May 1839. The sight that greeted Holloway and Anne Helmore would have entranced them. As gulls circled overhead, squawking noisily, small boats would have already been pulling up alongside the ship to unload goods and passengers, whilst the local natives employed at the docks called loudly to each other in their own language, as they transferred cases, crates and passengers from the ship to the small rowing boats. Beyond the blue-green mirror of water stretched the shoreline of white sands, whilst nestling into the foothills of Table Mountain lay Cape Town, its white-washed buildings dominated by the grey-stone castle. The mountain's flat top would, most likely, have been enveloped in swirling clouds, beneath a deep blue sky.

Holloway, however, must have wondered what lay beyond this beautiful scene. It belied the stories he would have already heard about heat, drought, famine and disease in the Interior.

The couple were welcomed ashore by Dr John Philip, the London Missionary Society's superintendent or agent in Cape Town, whom Holloway had met in London. Holloway handed to him his letter of introduction from the Reverend William Ellis, the foreign secretary in London for the London Missionary Society.[1]

As a married man, the letter confirmed, his starting salary was to be £100 per year. With regard to Holloway's destination, the Directors had left the choice to Dr Philip, who decided that the greatest need for a new missionary was in Griqualand, beyond the Orange River, which was the northern boundary of the Cape Colony. The Paramount Chief of the Batlapin tribe, Chief Mothibi, had for some time been requesting his own mission station at Lekhatlong. At the time this was one of many outstations of the Griquatown mission station, all under the control of Peter Wright and Isaac Hughes.

Since Wright was expected in Cape Town shortly, Dr Philip suggested that they remain there for a few weeks.[2] Holloway had expected arrangements to have been made for them, but found that he was to be responsible for purchasing his own wagons and oxen to transport them and their goods to the Interior, though the Society, through Dr Philip, reimbursed him.

The couple spent seven weeks in Cape Town. Anxious to get on their way and begin their work in Africa, they found the wait for Peter Wright tedious. In the end, it would seem, the latter changed his plans and did not arrive.

To add to his frustration, Holloway was having difficulty in procuring the necessary equipment. The country was suffering from drought and there were no healthy oxen to be bought. Travelling in Africa, Holloway soon learnt, was "very different from travelling in England."[3] Eventually, at Dr Philip's suggestion, Holloway and Anne proceeded by steamer around the coast to Port Elizabeth, from which point the journey to the Interior would be shorter and easier. Here they managed to purchase wagons and oxen and on 12th July they set out for Griqualand.

The young couple were for the first time experiencing travel by ox-wagon and had to learn how to cope with the team of draught oxen which pulled the wagon. They had to learn the local phrases in order to communicate with the driver and herdsmen; *inspanning*, which entailed harnessing the team of oxen to the *disselboom*, or front pole on the wagon, or *outspanning* them at the end of a journey. The oxen were yoked in pairs with the disselboom between them, attached to a *trek-tou*, or drawstring, made of plaited ox-hide. In the front of the wagon was a large chest on which the driver sat and inside was a wooden frame with a mattress for the bed. Pots and pans were carried under the rear end of the wagon, on a grating made of wood. The wagons had to be packed carefully. Anne would have had to learn how to compress a large amount of preserves into a small space and how to dry their bread into hard rusks, to conserve it on long stretches without stops. They would have had little chance to procure fresh game, as the Cape Colony had already been depleted of wild game. It was therefore necessary to herd a few sheep and goats; it was only when they reached the north that they would have come across large herds of springbok and wildebeest, enabling Holloway to practise his skills with a rifle.

Calling at various mission stations on their route gave them the opportunity to make the acquaintance of some their fellow missionaries, and also to taste the sort of life they would lead.[4] They remained a few days at Philippolis, where they met, and formed a lasting friendship with Gotlab Schreiner, the resident missionary and his English wife, Elizabeth. Their daughter Olive, born in 1855, was to achieve fame with her classic novel *The Story of an African Farm*.

"A missionary leaving England for Africa can form no idea of the hinderances [sic] which will be thrown in his way and of the time that must be spent before he can reach his station," Holloway told his mother in a long letter written on their journey. "It is now nearly six months since we set foot in Africa and still we are not settled."[5]

Eventually, on 14th October 1839, they arrived at Griquatown and were greeted by Peter Wright and Isaac Hughes. Wright had been managing the Griquatown station with its eight outstations for the past twelve years and Hughes, a former blacksmith from nearby Kuruman, had recently come to assist him.[6]

There seemed to be some confusion as to where the Helmores would go, as Wright claimed he was still awaiting official word from Cape Town on this matter.[7] It was also soon clear to Holloway that, despite assurances given to him in Cape Town from Dr Philip that he would be running Lekhatlong as an independent station, Wright and Hughes wanted to keep control.

Finally it was suggested and agreed that Holloway and Anne should remain at Griquatown for a few weeks whilst Hughes went on a planned journey into the Cape Colony. It was hoped that by the time Hughes came back, clearer directives would have arrived. More importantly, it gave Holloway and Anne an opportunity to learn the Dutch and Sechuana languages and become acquainted with the area and its people.[8]

For Holloway, anxious to start his work, these continual delays were frustrating. It could take up to ten weeks for a reply to be received to a letter from Cape Town. Letters were handed to traders or missionaries at various posts along the route and then given to passing travellers, traders, missionaries or hunters, to be taken on their next stage, and so on. Replies to and from England could take up to a year.

Installed in Hughes' house while he was away, the couple had difficulty in coping with the unbearable heat. It sapped their energy and made them feel ill. Anne especially found that the strong glare of the sun affected her eyes, making reading or writing difficult. Under these circumstances it was not easy to learn another language, but they struggled valiantly.

During this time Holloway learnt a few details about the area and the people amongst whom he was to work. He found out that the main groups of people who lived in the area were the Griquas, the Batlapin, the Corannas and the Bushmen.

The Griquas, the dominant group, were of mixed descent. Many were legitimately born of mixed marriages between the early European settlers in the Cape and the indigenous Hottentots. However, most were the result of casual liaisons between the two races. They were shunned and treated as outcasts, and were known as Bastard Hottentots. In the early part of the twentieth century, about five thousand of these people, who had been living as nomads with their leader Adam Kok, moved north of the Orange River, beyond the boundaries of the Cape Colony. They were eventually persuaded by the two London Missionary Society missionaries, William Anderson and Cornelius Kramer, to settle. These two men had already established a station there known as Klaarwater (clear water).

In 1813 the tribe agreed to be known as Griquas, rather than by the debasing term *bastards*, and the name of the mission station was changed to Griquatown. However, there were constant clashes between the various tribes over authority. This was not made any easier by the movement of other nomadic people into the area. Anderson and Kramer tried to help to resolve the disputes, realising the need for some form of administration and leadership in a settled community. Eventually Adam Kok II, who was the grandson of Adam Kok I was appointed leader and officially recognised by the Cape government. His lifestyle of foraging and raiding, however, split the clan and he was persuaded to resign his leadership and to move with his own followers to another region.

After further conflict over leadership, through the influence of the missionaries and Dr Philip, Andries Waterboer was appointed and became leader of the West Griquas in this region, holding considerable power.

At this time dissatisfied Boers, or Afrikaner farmers, were migrating from the Cape Colony into Griqualand West in large numbers, and disputes over land or cattle were becoming commonplace. Waterboer had been appointed defender of the borders and supplied with arms, making him a powerful man. He used this power against the other tribes, causing resentment and ill-feeling, but since he had official backing and the support of the missionaries, no one dared to cross him.

Eight months after Holloway and Anne first arrived in Griquatown, Isaac Hughes returned from the Cape Colony. Wright was still reluctant to hand over the Lekhatlong mission station to Holloway. However, in the absence of any further communication on the matter from Dr Philip or the directors in London, and after consultation with the Batlapin chief, Mothibi, and the deacons at Lekhatlong, Holloway signed an agreement which handed the station over to his care.

The conditions read:-
1. That I, Holloway Helmore, should be the sole pastor and missionary of the church consequently under my superintendence.
2. That the affairs of the mission should be transacted by myself and the church unitedly.
3. That in case of any difficulties arising, myself and the people co-jointly should seek advice from Griquatown.[9]

Eager and excited, their headaches and discomforts forgotten, the couple packed their wagons and stocked up with the necessary provisions from traders, ready for departure. They ensured that there was a plentiful supply of rice, flour, dried beans, peas, raisins and other dried fruit in addition to sugar, tea and coffee, knowing it would be some time before they could return to purchase fresh stocks and that it would take a while to establish their own vegetable garden and fruit trees.

In June 1840 they were escorted to their new home by Thabi, a deacon and teacher at Lekhatlong. He was the son of the Batlapin chief Tyso who lived with his tribe at Griquatown.[10] Chief Mothibi was there to welcome them on their arrival. When Robert Moffat had first arrived in the area in 1817, Mothibi had come under his influence, and became a devout Christian. Moffat was one of the earlier London Missionary Society missionaries in that area. Prominent among his brethren, he built up his station at Kuruman to be one of the most successful and active in Southern Africa. Holloway therefore took on a group of people in whom the seeds of Christianity had already been sown and further nurtured by the Griquatown missionaries.

Four years previously, Mothibi had moved his tribe to Lekhatlong. He had long appealed for his own resident missionary and this was at last being achieved. A very old man now, he felt he could leave his people and retire to spend his last days at Taung with his brother Chief Mahura, leaving his youngest son, Jantjie, to take over leadership of the people at Lekhatlong.

Holloway and Anne were installed in Mothibi's old hut until a home could be built for them. Those first months were to be far from comfortable. The site of the town was unfavourable, situated on a rise of red sand, far from the river. The hut itself was "dark, smoky and by no means waterproof," [11] as Holloway reported. He realised that his first and most urgent task would be try to persuade the people to move to a more favourable location nearer the river, and that it was best to delay building his home and church until this was achieved.

Lekhatlong consisted of mainly Sechuana-speaking Batlapin, a tribe of Bechuana people, now called TaSwana, with a sprinkling of Dutch-speaking Griquas, Bushmen and Corannas. On his first Sunday, Holloway conducted a service for more than a hundred people. He soon realised that if he was to preach to them in a language they could understand, getting to grips with Sechuana was another urgent priority. Under his charge were many smaller villages surrounding Lekhatlong, all of which he found "in the darkest heathen state," as he reported to his directors that July.[12] He found his flock consisted of 190 church members, with a further 45 preparing for baptism.

Anne took charge of the school of 140 children, which had been run by Thabi with five or six assistants, whilst Holloway himself took over the task of teaching the older children to write, also running a class for adults in the evening. All this activity took place either in the open air or in the little church, made in the traditional style of reeds with mud walls and a thatched roof.

Domestic chores were entirely different to those undertaken by a wife in England, as Anne was soon to find. Even with the help of servants, her days were arduous and exhausting. The floor of their hut was laid with well-compressed cow dung, which needed to be renewed weekly.

To Anne this was revolting, but she soon found it was the most effective way to keep the fleas and dust under control.[13] She had to make their own soap and candles from hard mutton fat. She had a primitive hearth with a wood fire for warmth against the chill of the winter evenings and the smoke nearly choked her at times. They longed for fresh produce and for the time when they could have their own more comfortable home. Despite the discomforts, however, both were clearly happy to at last feel able to fulfil their ambition and have their own mission station. It is also clear that Africa, with its inimitable sounds and smells, its wide open spaces, brilliant colours and dramatic contrasts, had already started working its charm on them.

On 4th April 1841 a baby daughter was born to Anne. Alas, she was very weak and lived for just ten days. Before she died she was baptised by her father and given the name Olive Ann. To Holloway this must have been a time of deep inner turmoil. Had his own limited medical knowledge been insufficient to save their infant? He and Anne felt their isolation keenly at this time. They were thousands of miles away from family and friends and had no other European friend to turn to.

Anne, grief-stricken, was very ill for a long time after. However, their faith and commitment to their Lord's work helped overcome any doubts as to the course they had chosen and with their Calvinistic doctrine, they would have accepted whatever they felt God had destined for them.

Within a couple of years of his arrival, Holloway was able to persuade his people to move to a more favourable site and a new town was springing up four miles away, on the opposite banks of the Harts River, a little above its junction with the Vaal River.[14] There were already many other settlements taking advantage of the fertile soil of the Harts River, which came under Holloway's care. Holloway chose a piece of ground a short distance from the developing new town of Lekhatlong and set about building a home for himself and Anne.

"The building is comprised of poles and reeds daubed with mud, the roof is thatched with rushes. It is 50 feet by 12 and contains 5 rooms. It is not quite finished but I am still working at it and when it is finished I shall be able to say that with the exception of some of the windows and two of the doors, it is entirely my own workmanship,"

he proudly told his mother.[15] He and Anne worked together to create their first garden, planting seeds they had brought from Stratford, peas and beans and other local vegetables and fruit trees.

Once the homes were erected, all the people set to work on building a new, larger church, which would also serve as the school room. Holloway and Anne found they had been accepted by the people in the town, who were pleased to have their own "teacher" residing amongst them. They were greeted with smiles wherever they went and, as pupils, they found the people responsive and eager to learn to read.

At this time, the question of how Lekhatlong was to be run re-surfaced under the Reverend Arthur Tidman, who had replaced Dr Ellis as the foreign secretary in London. The directors in London wanted Holloway and Lekhatlong to return to the control of the missionaries at Griquatown, as an outstation.

Lekhatlong could not be run as a component part of the Griquatown mission, Holloway responded.[16] To begin with, he was under the impression that Lekhatlong had been given to him as an independent station. They were eighty miles, or four days' journey away from Griquatown, making communication difficult. In addition, the people of Lekhatlong were of a different tribe to the Griquas in Griquatown. They feared the Griqua leader, Waterboer, who had tried to assert his authority over them and their chief. It would not be in their best interests to return to the control of Griquatown. Holloway's own attitude is expressed in a further letter a year later, when he wrote: "I am independent in principles and while I rejoice to see a union established on the principles of the Congregational Union in England, or to receive the duties or counsel of any or all of my brethren, I am jealous of authority and unsolicited interference."[17]

The response to Holloway's argument was that the matter would be resolved by Dr Philip.[18]

Meantime, Lekhatlong thrived and grew. The school doubled in size and Holloway found that by the end of 1841 he was preparing seventy candidates for baptism. His church services were packed and he was at last getting to grips with the language. However, he and Anne felt their isolation and often longed for the company of fellow Europeans. There was no contact with the missionaries at Griquatown or Kuruman. They begged for magazines and newspapers to be sent to them by friends in England. These were avidly read, even though the news was many months old before it arrived. Anne, pregnant again, continued to find the heat trying and her eyes especially, were often inflamed from the glare of the sun and the dust.

At the beginning of May 1842, at the time when Anne's confinement was imminent, Holloway unexpectedly found himself in trouble over the way he was running his mission station. Some weeks previously, after consultation with the other deacons, he had suspended Jantjie, the Batlapin chief, from his office as deacon over the theft of some cattle and a wagon. Holloway was unaware that Jantjie and Thabi had taken their grievance to Wright at Griquatown. At the time, Dr Philip was conducting a tour of the stations in the area.[19]

Peter Wright arrived at Lekhatlong and said he had agreed to meet Dr Philip there. Holloway had not had any contact with him for two years, but welcomed him and offered him the hospitality of his home. Wright was followed soon after by Waterboer, the Griqua chief. Several days later Dr Philip arrived, accompanied by James Read, who was acting as interpreter. Read, aged 65, was a veteran missionary of the London Missionary Society, having worked in Africa since 1800.

Wright and Waterboer asked for a private meeting with Dr Philip, at which they commenced to lodge complaints against Holloway. Dr Philip cut them short, refusing to listen to their complaints without Holloway himself being present and a meeting was convened for the following morning, with Holloway and all the elders and deacons present. Totally unaware of the purpose of the meeting, Holloway arrived and immediately sensed an atmosphere of hostility towards himself, particularly from Wright and Waterboer.[20]

Charges were made that Griquatown had had no communication from Helmore since his arrival; that he was acting in isolation and against the spirit of the brethren of missionaries in the area and that he had excommunicated Chief Jantjie, a serious disciplinary measure, without reference to themselves. Waterboer accused him of indiscretions against himself and of turning the people of Lekhatlong against him.[21]

Dr Philip, through Read, tried to elicit comments from the elders and deacons. They appeared to be in agreement with Wright and Waterboer. They were not happy with the way Holloway was conducting affairs at Lekhatlong, they said. Holloway got the distinct impression that Read was trying to obtain comments against him. Eventually Holloway offered his hand, first to Wright then to Waterboer. Both refused to take it.[22]

In the end, Dr Philip decided to resolve the matter by removing Holloway and Anne from Lekhatlong and placing the station once more under the control of the Griquatown missionaries. The people were told that Hughes would come and live amongst them. As soon as Anne was well enough to travel after her confinement, Holloway was told, he should make preparations to proceed to Borigelong, about 35 miles to the north of Lekhatlong, an outpost of the Kuruman mission.

This unfortunate incident highlights the difficulties faced by missionaries who got caught up in the internal politics of their people. Waterboer was supported by Wright and Hughes and also by Dr Philip and they appear to have taken a one-sided view of the problem. Whilst it must be admitted that Holloway was still a young man, new to Africa and not yet fluent in the Sechuana language, he was sensitive to the fact that his Batlapin people feared Waterboer and "disliked him for his strong language."[23] It is also a sad indication of the ill feeling amongst fellow brethren which often broke out in these remote areas.

Whether Dr Philip had understood the situation and handled the problem in the correct manner is questionable. As soon as all the visitors had departed, and the people had been told that Holloway and Anne were to leave them, they wept and pleaded with him not to go.[24] To Jantjie it appeared that the Griquatown missionaries and Waterboer had seized the opportunity to slander Holloway and force his removal from Lekhatlong and he repented taking his grievance to them. He would take his people and follow Holloway to Borigelong, he declared. He did not want a missionary from Griquatown.

All these goings on must have caused both Holloway and Anne considerable distress. Anne had built a thriving school and had been a stoic wife and partner in Holloway's endeavours. She had planted a lot of fruit trees and they had enjoyed fresh vegetables from her garden for the first time that summer. Now they had to leave it all behind and start afresh. However, for the sake of her husband she put on a brave face. If it was the will of their Lord that they leave, then they had to accept it.

A few days later, on the 11th May, in the midst of their upheaval a healthy, robust baby girl was born to Anne. She too was baptised Olive, after Holloway's mother, with no second name. Their tiny daughter was a great joy and comfort to the couple at this difficult time. "She is very small, with bright eyes (the people say she has eyes of wisdom), an abundance of dark hair, with the upper lip something like her mama's," Holloway wrote to his sister Emily.[25]

As soon as Anne felt strong enough to make the journey, under a steely blue sky they set off from Lekhatlong early one morning. Staring straight ahead, they would have tried to blot out the wailing of their people, as the ox-wagon jolted across the flat, dry and dusty red plain, where not even a blade of grass gave colour to the landscape. They headed for Kuruman first, a journey of approximately 75 miles. It was early winter and the region was experiencing exceptionally bitter weather. Sixteen years later, in 1858, whilst on long leave in England, Holloway was to recall Olive's birth and that journey, in a letter he wrote to her:

"Many happy returns of the eleventh of May dearest Olive. Only think that you are now in your 17th year. How old it makes me appear. I well remember the morning you were born; what a noise you made sucking your little fist as happy and contented as possible. We started for Kuruman before you were three weeks old. On the road we stuck fast in a quagmire which we called the *Slough of Despond*. We slept there that night, and in the morning it was so cold that the water and mud were frozen and we walked over without sinking. We took out blankets and sheets and I constructed a little tent amongst the bushes, then made a bed on the ground and brought you and your Mama out of the waggon. No sooner were you nicely stowed in the tent with a good fire in front than the snow began to fall and the tears ran down Ganaklismos's face when he saw the plight we were in. A man was sent on to Kuruman for help but the next morning, instead of getting help, we heard that the man who was sent feared the cold and was quietly spending his time at a cattle kraal two miles from us. We then emptied the waggon [*sic*], pulled it out of the bog, loaded it again and got safely to Kuruman, then to Motito. I then left you and Mama at

Mrs Lemue's, and went on to Borigelong, where we got a hut ready, and I soon returned to see after you. When two days' journey from Motito I mounted a horse, hoping to reach Motito in the evening. On I went very well till I got to a wood, there I lost my way. When clear of the wood I saw cattle feeding in the distance and rode on, hoping to find a *morisa*, but there was no one there. I then tied up my horse, crossed a ravine and ascended to high ground and at length found a man who directed me to the nearest village. There I obtained a drink of milk for which I gave some tobacco. The people showed me the road but soon after I reached it, it became so dark that I again lost it. My horse was now so tired that I had to lead it with only a star to guide me. At length I became so wearied that although the wolves were making their disagreeable noises I could have thrown myself down on the ground and slept, had it not been for the thought that you were so near. I pressed on but when I got to Motito I was so worn out that I could hardly look at you. However, I took you to Borigelong, there I made four wooden wheels and with the help of a large Caffre basket made you a carriage…. In this I drew you about, greatly to the delight of yourself and Mama and the astonishment of the Batlapi. I used to draw you out as far as the corn fields and sometimes ran with you as fast as I could. But now you are a great girl of sixteen, a boarding school miss in Birmingham, England….."[26]

At this time Robert Moffat and his family were on long leave in England and in his absence Robert Hamilton, his fellow missionary, was managing the affairs of Kuruman. Having recently completed the arduous task of translating the New Testament into the Sechuana language, Moffat had been unable to find anyone able or willing to undertake the printing task in Cape Town. He and his family were, therefore, granted leave of absence to proceed to England; their first visit to their family and their native country in twenty five years.

The Helmores spent a few short weeks at Kuruman, where they received a warm and sympathetic welcome. It was a pleasure for them to have the opportunity to converse with fellow Europeans about England, such as the marriage of their young Queen Victoria to Prince Albert, which had already produced a daughter and a son and heir. They also learned that the Tories had been returned to power under the leadership of Robert Peel; bad news for non-conformists who, through the Liberals, were pressing for further concessions still denied them, such as burial according to their own rites or to holding any official government or army post.

They were interested to hear that Moffat was taking a complaint against Waterboer to England to lodge with the directors, over interference in the affairs of Kuruman.[27]

They also had the chance to meet two new young missionaries who had recently arrived from England, William Ross and David Livingstone.

Livingstone had qualified in medicine before training to become a missionary. Although destined for China, he had been inspired by Robert Moffat, whom he had recently met in London. He then asked to be sent instead to Kuruman. Whilst waiting for Moffat's return he was spending his time exploring the region and learning the language and customs of the people. Since the Moffats were not due to return for a further year or more, he was becoming restless and impatient; a feeling which must have evoked much sympathy within Holloway.

By August of that year Holloway and Anne, with baby Olive, were trying to settle into their new surroundings at Borigelong with its population of approximately 2,000 people. The old Chief Mothibi, paramount chief of the Batlapin people, who was in residence there, made them welcome and appointed Holloway as his personal adviser. He was a very old man by then and a devout Christian.

Despite this, however, the couple were not happy with the situation of the town. It was unhealthy, standing upon an open plain of loose red sand, with no protection from the relentless heat and glare of the sun. The water for most of the year was stagnant and the soil infertile. They were unable to obtain fresh produce locally, or to grow their own and the people were reluctant to move.[28] Holloway paid a visit to his people at Lekhatlong, who were still anxious to move to Borigelong, and found that it had reverted to an outpost of Griquatown, with no resident missionary, despite the assurance of Wright that Peter Hughes would go there.[29] Jantjie was persuaded by Holloway that it would be best to remain where they were, at their new town on the banks of the Harts River, where the soil was more fertile.

Holloway and Dr Philip had naturally reported the events surrounding his departure from Lekhatlong to the London Missionary Society's directors in London and finally, in January 1843, they received their reaction. The directors expressed support and sympathy with Holloway over Wright's behaviour, in not only accepting his hospitality without informing him that charges were to be laid against him, but in interfering with the affairs of his station. The incident was "greatly at variance with the claim of paternal affection and likely to prove unfavourable in the influence on the future purity and prosperity of Church at that station." A resolution was passed at the directors' meeting to the effect:

"That the Reverend Holloway Helmore be assured of the sincere respect and sympathy of the Directors under the trying circumstances connected with his removal from Lekhatlong and of their entire disapproval of the measures pursued by Mr Wright and others in the accomplishment of that object, and that he should be further assured of the continued confidence of the Directors and of their affectionate solicitude for his happiness and usefulness in the new and enlarged sphere of labour which he now occupies."[30]

Wright was sent a strong letter of reprimand.[31] Prior to its arrival in Griqualand, however, he had unfortunately died, aged just 45 years.

Partly as a result of this incident, it was decided to set up a District Committee in each region, with regular meetings, with the power to co-ordinate the movement of missionaries between stations and to try to resolve any local problems. The committees were to report to London, where any major problems would be resolved by the directors.[32] Although Holloway welcomed this move, it was not generally popular amongst the missionaries.

The Helmores were to spend more than a year at Borigelong, with frequent appeals from Jantjie and Thabi for their return to Lekhatlong. It was a year of hard toil against a hostile and unhealthy environment and both Anne and baby Olive were under-nourished, Holloway complained. They suffered from lack of fresh water, fruit and vegetables and his own digestive system had been affected by their poor diet. Holloway had to travel far to distant settlements of people who had not as yet been touched by Christianity.[33] However, they were rewarded with positive results in sowing the seeds of their faith and Holloway often heard stories of some of his flock slipping away into the bushes to pray. He earned the respect and friendship of Mothibi, who supported him whole-heartedly in his efforts. His greatest achievement at that time was the setting up of a church among the people of the notorious Koranna leader, Jan Bloem. They were also pleased to be in closer contact with other fellow missionaries as the endeavours of the London Missionary Society and the Church Missionary Society expanded.[34]

When Anne became pregnant again, Holloway consulted with both Hughes at Griquatown and Hamilton at Kuruman and it was agreed that the couple should return to Lekhatlong, with Holloway continuing to care for the people of Borigelong as an outstation. In October 1843, therefore, they happily packed their wagons and trekked south, back to Lekhatlong. They were received with joy and a warmth which touched them and the people immediately set about putting a new thatched roof on their home and preparing the soil for planting a garden.

"Formerly you instructed us to carry the word of God to the neighbouring villages, but when you left we ceased to go. Today, however, we have recommenced," said Thabi, with a broad smile.[35]

Building was resumed on the new church, which had been interrupted by Holloway's departure. To Holloway and Anne, this was their home, humble, primitive and remote as it was, and these people were their people.

[1] L.M.S. Archives, Ellis to Philip, 21.1.1839
[2] L.M.S. Archives, Philip to Ellis, 3.5.1839
[3] L.M.S. Archives, Helmore to Ellis, 14.12.1839
[4] Pretoria Archives, A.551, Holloway Helmore to his parents, 27.9.1839
[5] Ibid
[6] L.M.S. Archives, Annotated Register of L.M.S. Missionaries
[7] L.M.S. Archives, Wright to Ellis, 5.11.1839
[8] L.M.S. Archives, Wright/Hughes Report for 1840
[9] L.M.S. Archives, Wright/Hughes Report for 1840
[10] L.M.S. Archives, Helmore to Ellis, 17.7.1840
[11] Ibid
[12] Ibid
[13] Dickson
[14] L.M.S. Archives, Helmore to Tidman, 30.8.1841
[15] Personal collection, Helmore to Mrs Olive Helmore, 12.8.1841 (Original in Pretoria Archives, A.551)
[16] L.M.S. Archives, Helmore to Tidman, 30.8.1841
[17] L.M.S. Archives, Helmore to Tidman, 12.7.1842
[18] L.M.S. Archives, Tidman to Helmore, 24.3.1842
[19] L.M.S. Archives, Helmore to Tidman, 16.5.1842
[20] L.M.S. Archives, Helmore to Tidman, 12.7.1842
[21] L.M.S. Archives, Philip to Tidman, 6.5.1842
[22] L.M.S. Archives, Helmore to Tidman, 16.5.1842
[23] Ibid
[24] L.M.S. Archives, Helmore to Tidman, 12.7.1842
[25] Personal collection, Helmore to Emily Helmore, 29.6.1842 (Original in Pretoria Archives, A551)
[26] Personal collection, Helmore to his daughter Olive, 10.5.1858 (Original in L.M.S. Archives)
[27] L.M.S. Archives, Ellis to Philip, 23.1.1839
[28] L.M.S. Archives, Helmore Report to Tidman, 12.12.1843
[29] L.M.S. Archives, Philip to Tidman, 6.5.1842
[30] L.M.S. Archives, Tidman to Helmore, 25.1.1843
[31] L.M.S. Archives, Tidman to Wright, 28.1.1843
[32] L.M.S. Archives, Tidman to Philip, 28.1.1843
[33] L.M.S. Archives, Helmore Report to Tidman, 12.12.1843
[34] Personal collection, Helmore to Mrs Garden, 6.3.1844 (Original in Pretoria Archives, A.551)
[35] Personal collection, tribute by his sister Emily Stuart

CHAPTER THREE
Lekhatlong, 1843 to 1856
Missionary Trials and Enterprises

Holloway soon found that during his absence many of the Batlapin of Lekhatlong who had been baptised into the Christian faith had reverted to old traditional beliefs and practices, having come under the influence of the *baloi*, or witchdoctors. He suspected that even Jantjie, the chief and his head deacon, Thabi, were involved. Their sleep was often disturbed by the doleful sound of drums, causing the children to scream and the dogs to howl. He questioned them, trying to find out what had caused this lapse.

"It is the voice of our god, who is evil. We are trying to drive him out of the village," [1] was the response. He kept watch on a few occasions and the atrocities that he witnessed horrified him. A man was dragged from his sick bed one night and beaten with mattocks and left to die; pregnant women were trampled on until they aborted and died. Children were strangled. When he confronted the people, most accepted his admonitions in sullen silence, but others told him to go back to his own country, saying: "You have your religion and we have ours."

Holloway consulted first with his brethren and then with his elders and deacons and they agreed he should intervene. The following Sunday he preached a strong sermon, denouncing the atrocities. He expelled five members from the church and accused fifteen further women, including one of Thabi's wives and a wife of his father, Chief Tyso, who had moved into the village. This caused the old chief to "exhibit the most unholy passions" and he removed himself and his family back to Griquatown.[2]

These events brought home to Holloway the long, hard struggle missionaries like himself still had. He realised there would still be conflict for a generation or more between the old traditional beliefs and the new religion that they were trying to instil.

On the 6th January the first meeting of the new District Committee took place at Kuruman. Robert Moffat, recently returned from England, was its chairman and William Ross was appointed secretary. In view of Anne's advanced stage of pregnancy, Holloway was unable to attend, but the committee formally sanctioned his return to Lekhatlong. The definition of an 'independent station' was clarified between the directors in London and the Committee; Lekhatlong would be run on the same basis as Griquatown or Kuruman, with decisions regarding the running of the station being made by the missionary concerned.[3] Major issues affecting the area as a whole, or the movement of the missionaries, would be mutually agreed. The committee agreed that Walter Inglis, a new young missionary who had travelled back with the Moffats, would be assigned to Lekhatlong to assist Holloway. However, Inglis refused to accept this decision and insisted he would await directions from London.[4]

The Helmores' second daughter was born on the 12th January 1844, a healthy and sturdy baby. Without the trauma and ill health of her previous two pregnancies, Anne recovered quickly, though she suffered a severe attack of inflammation of the eyes and could do no reading or writing for several weeks.

Three months later the young family journeyed to Kuruman and first made the acquaintance of Robert and Mary Moffat. There, in the church that Robert Moffat had recently completed, and which still stands, baby Anne Sophia Helmore was baptised.[5]

David Livingstone was also at Kuruman at the time, recovering from a nasty experience. He had been attacked by a lion near his mission station at Mabotsa, 250 miles north of Kuruman and his arm was very badly mauled. It was only through the intervention of his companion and fellow missionary, Rogers Edwards, that his life was saved.[6] It was on this occasion that Livingstone first met the Moffats' eldest daughter, Mary, and started wooing her. Livingstone's temperament and outlook were different to Holloway's. Of a fiery, restless nature, he believed in expansion of the missionary sphere, in the setting up of new stations to the north and west. To Holloway's quieter, more placid nature it seemed that more could be gained by first consolidating and improving those they had, creating continuity with a settled missionary in a stable environment.

Holloway and Anne soon settled to a routine way of life, with the local people taking an affectionate interest in the development of the two little white girls who had been born in their midst. A loyal and devoted wife and affectionate mother, Anne gave Holloway the moral and physical support he needed in his work, never wavering, despite constant headaches, sore eyes and tiredness. The lack of irrigation and unpredictable rainfalls caused a problem in the region and the local population relied mainly on sorghum and ground corn or *mealies,* supplemented with soured milk and game meat. Game, however, was becoming increasingly scarce as herds were being driven northward by big game hunters, necessitating a reliance upon domestic flocks; cattle, sheep and goats.[7] The Helmores would have had to adapt to the diet of the region, but they also managed to enjoy fresh vegetables such as sweet potatoes, pumpkin, peas, beans and cabbage from their garden. They had planted a few fruit trees; peach, fig and apricot. A goat and some cows provided them with milk and a few sheep with meat.

In August 1844 Holloway received a letter from his sister Emily, advising him that their mother, Olive Helmore, had passed away in March after a long illness. Emily, the only one of their family still at home, had nursed her constantly. Just a year later Emily had to convey to her brother the news that their father had died on 18th February, 1845.

Holloway must have felt his isolation from his family most keenly at this time and would have longed to be with his sister and brothers, to share their grief and to share his with them. It is clear from his letters to his parents that he had a very close and loving relationship with them. He would have been comforted by the thought that Stratford-upon-Avon paid homage to his father in a fitting way. On the day of his funeral, all the shops closed as a mark of respect and a large procession followed his coffin, amongst them many respectable businessmen and officials who had been educated at his school.[8] To this day a large stone memorial hangs on the wall in the Rother Street Congregational Church in Stratford-upon-Avon, commemorating Thomas and Olive Helmore.

In February 1845 the second meeting of the District Committee was held at Kuruman. Anne, with their two small daughters, accompanied Holloway. To the Helmores this was a welcome break. Holloway already had a high regard for Robert Moffat and Moffat for his part liked this frank young man, who belied his delicate appearance and was willing to tackle any physical task without complaint. Mary Moffat and Anne had

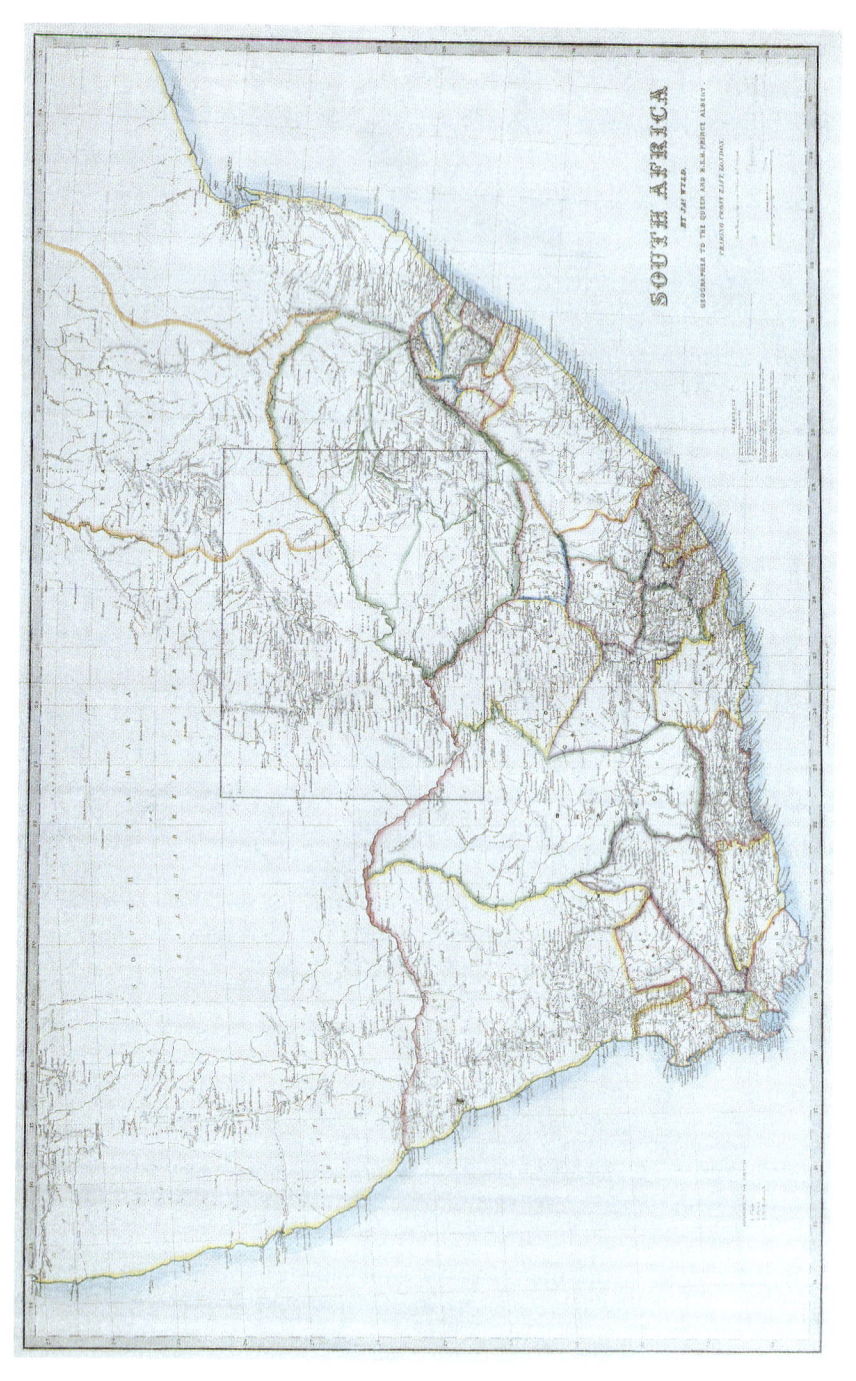

James Wyld's map of Southern Africa as it was in 1850.

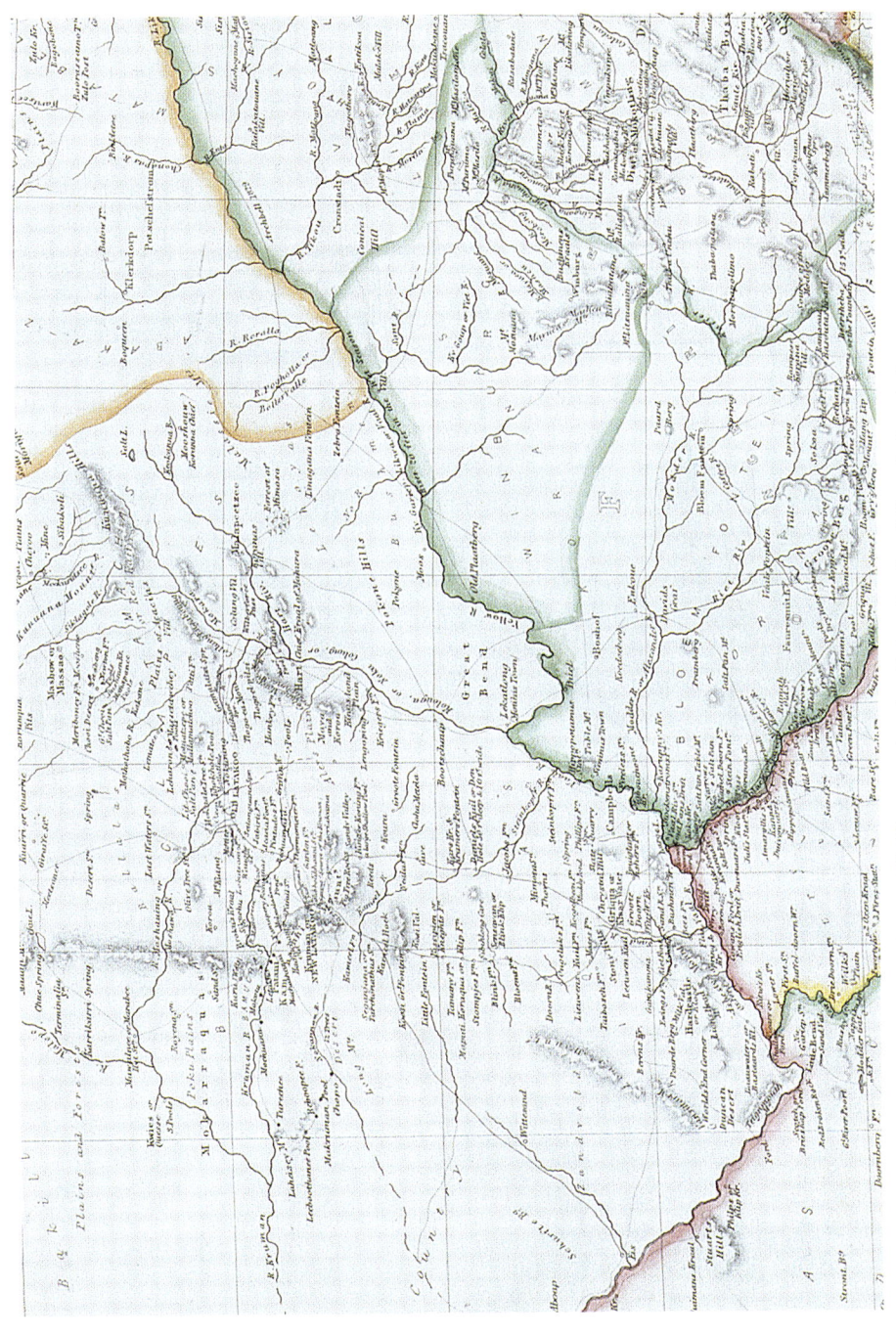

Detail of James Wyld's map, showing Griqualand and the mission stations.

become close friends. Anne was discreet and held herself aloof from the petty squabbles and gossip of the other missionary wives and Mary felt she could confide in her.[9] It was a chance also for little Olive, who was nearly three, and one year-old Anne, or Annie as she was to be called throughout her childhood, to develop companionship with other European children, particularly Elizabeth and Jeannie, the two youngest daughters of the Moffats. David Livingstone and Mary Moffat had been married the previous month and the happy couple were still at Kuruman, where Mary was packing her belongings and eagerly preparing to proceed to Mabotsa, to her new home amongst the Bakatla people.

At the end of October 1845, another death occurred, that of the old Paramount Chief Mothibi. Weak and frail, he had sent for Holloway, who immediately set out for Borigelong. His dying words to his sons and his elders were to exhort them to accept the missionaries and to follow their teachings. [10]

With Holloway's prayers in his ears, Mothibi died peacefully having, according to one of his elders, predicted the exact time of his death. This wise old chief had perceived that the world around them was changing and that his people would have to adapt. When Robert and Mary Moffat had first come amongst the Bechuanas twenty five years previously, he and his wives had welcomed them to Lattakoo.[11] He had converted to Christianity then and spent the rest of his life working hard to get his people to do the same. He was succeeded by his son Gasebonwe, brother of Jantjie.

The church at Lekhatlong continued to grow in numbers, despite the activities of the *baloi*, or witchdoctors. Holloway assisted his people to build a larger brick home for their growing family, which gave them better protection against the heat and rain. Work also commenced on building a larger chapel, to which the directors, despite a huge financial deficit, agreed to grant £45.[12] The Society had to rely solely on voluntary contributions to finance their growing needs, both at home and abroad, and the demands on their resources were growing at an alarming rate; in 1845 they found their expenditure had exceeded their income by approximately £17,000.[13]

Emily Helmore, now left on her own in Stratford-upon-Avon, expressed a wish to join Holloway and Anne and they warmly welcomed the idea.

Emily's strong commitment to the Congregationalists, like Holloway's, had created a closer bond with him than with either of her other two brothers in England. By this time Thomas, the eldest brother, had graduated from Magdalen College with a Masters degree in music and was already becoming well-known in the world of church music, training choir boys in the newly set-up St Marks Training College in Chelsea. Frederick had also graduated and spent a lot of time travelling the country, promoting choral services in churches. The differences in religious doctrine had not affected the strong family bonds that existed and Thomas and Frederick corresponded frequently, often sending funds to support Holloway's missionary work.

On 31st May 1846 Anne was delivered of a baby son. Alas, it was stillborn. One can imagine the desolation and heartache of them both at this second tragedy in their young family. However, their grief was softened by the knowledge that they were soon to have Emily with them.

The Society for Promoting Education in Africa and the East, one of the numerous charitable bodies at that time assisting missionaries abroad, had agreed to sponsor her and paid her passage to Southern Africa. Towards the end of 1846 the Helmores travelled down to Algoa Bay, now Port Elizabeth, to welcome her and escort her to her new home, where she was to take charge of the infants' school at Lekhatlong.[14]

They found the Cape Colony in the grip of drought and war, as Holloway reported to his directors.[15] Men were being taken from work on their farms to defend the borders in the eastern Cape, where raids and retaliations between farmers and the local natives had escalated, causing considerable hardship and the failure of crops.

The abolishment of slavery in the Colony by the British administration in 1838 had caused strong resentment amongst the Afrikaners, or Boers, whose system of farming relied on slavery. Over the previous ten years an estimated six thousand Afrikaners had abandoned their farms and proceeded on their great trek north across the Orange River and east into Zululand. Many went even further north to cross the Vaal River and were settling on the vast plains of the Highveld, almost to the Limpopo River. Here they were frequently coming into conflict with local resident tribes over land rights and borders. Cattle raids and the abduction of the native women and children from the villages to work on Boer farms was becoming commonplace, with retaliation raids, in a continuous cycle.

All this was of considerable concern to the missionaries and relations between them and the Boers were strained. The latter accused the missionaries of inciting the local people, supplying them with firearms and siding with them in disputes. The missionaries had much sympathy with the natives. Land treaties were often obtained through trickery and farm boundaries ignored or extended. The new invaders had strength in firearms, which the natives were not allowed to hold, and this caused further resentment. Despite this conflict, when trying to settle a dispute with another tribe, a chief would often appeal to the Boer for help with his firearms; though in consequence he could be held to ransom for this assistance. With tribal warfare, quarrels amongst the Afrikaners themselves, murder and looting between Boer and native tribes, there was a constant air of tension and unrest throughout the country.

Holloway and his fellow missionaries often wondered where this would all end. When they tried to protect their people, they were accused by the Boers, who were of the same race and religion as themselves, of siding with the local tribes. When they remonstrated with their people over a cattle raid or looting, they were accused of siding with the Afrikaners. Whatever they did, they appeared to be the losers.

Emily adapted to Africa with ease and immediately set about learning the language, whilst Holloway commenced building a small house for her alongside their own. By this time, under Holloway's guidance, Lekhatlong was established as a stable, successful mission station. Many Griquas, Korannas and Bushmen were moving into the town, as Holloway reported to his directors in February 1847.[16] There had been good rains that summer which had alleviated the drought and the crops flourished. Church congregations were growing steadily, as were the number of pupils in the school. The people were becoming cleaner and taking more care with their dress and, to Holloway's satisfaction, they showed themselves willing to spread their new knowledge among the people in the surrounding villages.

In March 1847, soon after Emily's arrival, the annual District Committee meeting was hosted by the Helmores at Lekhatlong, Holloway having taken over as secretary. The main problems for discussion were the independent actions of two of the young missionaries. Walter Inglis, having refused to go to Lekhatlong, had been instructed by the directors to open a new station amongst the Bamaires near Taung, but he again refused. His objections were overruled. Inglis had difficulty in accepting authority. He was self-centred and did not get on well with his fellow missionaries.[17]

David Livingstone, who was also present, was asked to account for his sudden departure from Mabotsa, to which he had been appointed by the directors. He had moved further north to open a new station amongst the Bakwena people of Chief Sechele at Chonuane. The main reason, he explained, was a severe quarrel he had had with his fellow missionary, Rogers Edwards. The circumstances were too complex and the committee decided it was best to drop the matter.[18]

Despite these differences of opinion, the atmosphere was cheerful and friendly. Lekhatlong would have been a hub of activity for a few days, with many wagons stationed around the church, children playing together and wives discussing their particular problems and exchanging tips on how to deal with them.

"The committee meeting did a lot of good. The people were impressed by the unity of the missionaries and seeing many of them meeting to discuss affairs," Holloway commented to his directors in London.[19] After the conflicts of the past, they were pleased to have set a good example, which would benefit their work.

On 6th August 1847 the couple were blessed with another healthy baby daughter. She was baptised Emma Elizabeth and was to be known affectionately throughout her life as Lizzie.

The new Infants' School was completed in time for Emily's 26th birthday on the 1st June, 1848, with Holloway having taken upon himself a major part of its construction. They marked the occasion with festivities, parades and a special dinner. Built of brick and stone, at a cost of £75 to be funded by the Ladies' Society who had sponsored Emily, it was planned to accommodate 200 and it was soon filled to capacity.[20] Holloway took charge of the juvenile school, teaching between 90 and 120 older children. His next target was to have a larger, more substantial chapel built of brick and stone, to accommodate his growing congregation.

Holloway's report to Tidman for 1848 was positive, acknowledging his achievements and looking forward to continued prosperity.

"It is now ten years since I left my native shores to bring the message of mercy to the swarthy children of Africa. Of these more than eight have been spent with the Batlapin. I look back with joy and gratitude to face with pleasure the leadings of Divine Providence.
Since I first came to Lekhatlong the population has doubled [from 600 to 1,200]. The schools have trebled and members added to the church amount to 140,"[21]
he said. He went on to acknowledge that the station's success was due partly to its situation at the confluence of the two rivers, with good grazing and partly to the piety and support of the chief, Jantjie, and his counsellors and deacons.
"During the winter months the church and school are full. The farms are scattered up and down the rivers to a distance of twenty miles each way. Those coming from a great distance come once a month, those near enough come every Sabbath; those very far walk up to twenty miles on the Saturday and return on the Monday. Those who cannot make the journey join together with members of old standing and hold a prayer meeting."
On 24th June 1849 a fourth baby daughter was born to Holloway and Anne, and baptised Emily. During Anne's confinement Holloway's sister Emily, already a firm favourite with Olive, Anne and Lizzie, took on their care and the household duties, as well as her school duties.
The summer of 1849 was to see the start of a long period of drought, which had an adverse effect on the people. It was a year of intense heat and the harvest failed, causing widespread hunger. The people traditionally counted their wealth in cattle and were, therefore, reluctant to sell any to purchase some corn. These matters were of deep concern to the missionaries, as the people wandered many miles away from the mission stations in search of pastures and land to cultivate.[22]

David Livingstone meanwhile had, in the winter months of 1849, set out with his friend William Cotton Oswell and Chief Sechele, to cross the Kalahari Desert in search of the great lake which the missionaries had often heard mentioned. The men endured extreme hardship and severe thirst, but in August they reached the lake, a vast but shallow expanse of water known as Lake Ngami, which lay about 600 miles north-west of Kuruman. There they made the acquaintance of Chief Lechulatebe, who with his Batawana tribe had fled south from the Makololo, to settle on its shores.[23]

Livingstone had strong feelings on the subject of expansion of missionary work. To him it was important to spread the net of Christianity to embrace more distant tribes, and he eventually persuaded his father-in-law, Robert Moffat, to agree with him. The country to the east of Griqualand was being settled by the Boers in large numbers and their hostility towards the missionaries precluded any expansion in that direction. The southern area was already well endowed with mission stations. To the west lay the barren, sparsely inhabited Kalahari desert, therefore there was only one direction in which expansion could take place and that was north.

At this time a director from London, the Reverend Joseph Freeman, was conducting a tour of the South African missions. When he visited Livingstone at his new base at Kolobeng, a considerable distance north of Kuruman, near Kanye, the latter put forward his views on expansion of their sphere of activities. Whilst Freeman agreed in principle, to Livingstone's frustration he made it clear that, due to their difficult financial situation, it was impossible for the London Missionary Society to entertain any ideas of extending their activities. Writing to his fellow directors from Bloemfontein after his visit, Freeman mentioned that Livingstone was contemplating a further trip to Lake Ngami, aiming then to proceed north to Sebituane, who had settled with his Makololo tribe near the Zambezi River. This powerful chief had built up a formidable position on the banks of the Chobe, conquering all the other tribes in the area.

"His object would be to try to introduce missionaries up there in the far distant interior or rather, to open a pathway for them, so that they might enter at some future time, but we have certainly no means of occupying any such new and distant fields of labour at present."[24]

At the District Committee Meeting in December of 1849, it was resolved that Borigelong and Lingopeng be made outposts of Lekhatlong.[25] Borigelong was 35 miles north of Lekhatlong, whilst Lingopeng, a bit nearer, lay on the banks of the Kolong River. Both had been supervised from Kuruman. Holloway agreed to this, but at the same time renewed his request for an assistant and it was decided to raise the matter with Freeman when he arrived. Holloway's days were fully occupied with building projects, preparing sermons, teaching in the school, giving medical attention to those who needed it, counselling and advising and taking Bible classes. He needed to make frequent trips to visit the various towns and outstations. On top of this he would retire to his study when time permitted to work on a commentary on the Revelation of St John, which he hoped to have published. This, however, was never accomplished[26]

Freeman duly visited Lekhatlong in January 1850 and promised to raise the matter of an assistant for Holloway on his return to England. He was impressed with Lekhatlong, regarding it as one of the better stations, able to pay its way and perhaps contribute something, though he found the church was in a dilapidated condition.[27] Holloway had as yet been unable to raise sufficient funds to build a new brick church and no help could be obtained from the directors in London. His personal financial resources were extremely limited; and that of his people at times of drought even less. Without outside help it was, therefore, impossible to make any improvements to the mission station.

From Lekhatlong Freeman, accompanied by Moffat, proceeded to Bloemfontein, the chief town of the Orange River Sovereignty. In 1848 Sir Harry Smith had annexed this territory which, together with Natal and the Transvaal, now came under British jurisdiction. This move had been welcomed by the missionaries and the natives, who hoped to be protected from further Boer incursions onto their land. Lekhatlong lay very near the border with the Orange River Sovereignty and the Helmores had enjoyed regular visits from the British Civil Commissioner based in Bloemfontein, Mr Charles Stuart.

It was not long before Stuart talked to Holloway and told him that Emily had accepted his proposal of marriage. Holloway, no doubt, had to become reconciled to the thought of losing his young sister, but he would have been delighted, rejoicing in her happiness. This tall Scotsman who spoke his mind and showed much sympathy with the missionaries and the Africans, also enjoyed music, therefore they had much in common.

The family took a trip south into the Colony, where on 8th October 1850, Emily and Charles Stuart were married. Whilst Emily proceeded to Bloemfontein with her new husband, to a new life, the Helmores returned to Lekhatlong, having enjoyed the short break and feeling refreshed and improved in health.[28]

In the meantime Livingstone was uneasy about the situation at Kolobeng. The soil was infertile and the water sources were drying up. To add to this, it lay close to the border of the Transvaal. The Boers had already, with Sechele's help, driven Moselekatse and his powerful Matabele tribe further north.

Moselekatse was a despotic and barbaric leader. He had built up a formidable tribe, and terrorised the country for many years, plundering, murdering and conquering the weaker tribes. In 1829 Moselekatse had sent a deputation to Robert Moffat requesting a visit from him, and Moffat had obliged. The Matabele chief took an instant liking to Moffat and an uncommonly cordial relationship developed between these two very different men. Moselekatse's affection and respect for Moffat deepened over the years and Moffat maintained contact with the chief, paying him further visits, in the hope that he could influence him and make him see the evil of his actions.

Now Sechele himself was subject to constant raids and attacks from the Boers. In April 1850, despite Freeman's objections, Livingstone again ventured across the desert to Lake Ngami, aiming to proceed further north to find Chief Sebituane and his Makololo tribe. On this occasion he took his wife, Mary, and their three small children on the journey, even though Mary was well advanced into her fourth pregnancy. Her prolonged absence with no word caused deep anxiety to the Moffats, especially her mother.[29] They reached Lake Ngami, but in the unhealthy swamps the children were soon afflicted with African fever and they were obliged to retrace their steps without venturing further north. Soon after their return to Kolobeng, Mary was delivered of a baby daughter, whom they baptised Elizabeth Pyne. Alas, she lived only a few days before succumbing to a fever. Mary herself was afflicted with facial paralysis and it was many months before she recovered.[30]

At this time it was still believed by all that malaria, then known as African fever, was caused by the vapours of swampy regions. No one had connected the disease to the prevalence of mosquitoes. Livingstone acknowledged that this, plus the prevalence of the tsetse fly, would cause a major setback to his hopes of opening up the Interior further north. He was not deterred, however, and immediately set about planning another venture to the Makololo.[31]

At Lekhatlong, a year after Freeman's visit, Holloway was still awaiting an assistant missionary. The drought, now in its second year, was causing considerable hardship to the people. Cattle and sheep were dying from starvation and the crops were in danger. Unlike Kuruman with its constant supply of water from the underground fountains, the Harts River where they had settled, flowed only in the rainy season. The people of Lekhatlong were, therefore, totally reliant upon rain. If there were good rains in the summer all was well. If there was little or no rain, the crops failed.

Holloway, satisfied four years ago with the well-being of his mission station, was now becoming anxious. In his report for 1850 he wrote: "In outward appearance the present state of Lekhatlong is unfavourable. The majority of the people are wandering with their families and herds in search of food. This disrupts their minds, and being deprived of the usual means of purchasing clothing, their general appearance is not respectable. There is every cause for hope that good will come out of this apparent evil. Hitherto the women have cultivated the soil, but the drought has roused many of the men and induced them to make use of all of the fountains in the country around. They have dug water courses for irrigation, purchased or borrowed ploughs and taken the management of the cornfields upon themselves."[32]

The people of Borigelong, despite their old dying chief Mothibi's entreaties, were still in a heathen state, Holloway reported. Their chief Gasebonwe, son of Mothibi, although professing to be a Christian, still indulged in his old, evil ways.

By the end of the summer of 1851 the situation of the people was desperate. The rains had failed for three successive seasons. A plan had been forming in Holloway's mind for some time past. He decided that the only way he could alleviate the situation was by irrigation of the land and that it was necessary to build a strong dam on the Harts River. He invited Robert Moffat to Lekhatlong to obtain his opinion.

Moffat agreed to Holloway's plan, though both men realised that it was an ambitious project. They would need the help and co-operation of the people in not only building, but maintaining a dam. A suitable site would have to be found on the river. Holloway had already carefully surveyed this stretch of the river and worked out his plans, selecting a spot just four miles from the town where he could sufficiently raise the bank of the river. He sat down and wrote to his directors in London:

"My plan is to build a strong wall, 20 feet broad at the base and 20 feet high and about three hundred paces long, the upper side of the wall being well-packed with clods. The whole will be covered with earth and gravel, 40 feet wide on the upper and 60 feet wide on the lower side of the wall at its base. The embankment will be raised high enough to prevent the water in the reservoir from running over and a weir will be constructed on one side to carry off waste water. We should thus have a large reservoir which will be replenished every summer by the rains which pour down from the neighbouring hills."[33]

The years of toil in a harsh climate, running a large mission station with two satellites and various outposts single-handed, had taken its toll on Holloway's health. He had not as yet received the promised assistant, despite frequent appeals. In undertaking this project, he knew that the major part of the work would have to be done by himself. Holloway showed grit and determination in even contemplating embarking on a construction task of this scale. In this project alone, his commitment to his people, and his duty to them, and to God, is evident.

The plan was explained to Chief Jantjie, who agreed to co-operate in enlisting the help of the people in the construction of the dam and towards the end of February, as they were nearing the end of the rainy season, work commenced.

Holloway's annual salary after eleven years in Africa was still just £100 per year, which, with his growing family, did not leave any excess. Contributions from his people were down due to a drop in their income and he therefore appealed to the directors in London for financial aid.

"The people are hungry and poor and have not the proper implements and will need help. They will give their labour free. I have therefore funded the project myself in the hope that I will be recompensed in due course. I have written to Mr Thompson[*] at Cape Town for help

---

[*] William Thompson had in 1850 succeeded John Philip as the Society's superintendent in Cape Town

with a small sum but hope the Directors will attempt to interest friends in raising money. It will be of great benefit to the station generally. It will consolidate the station and increase it. A settled community means men and women will be able to attend school more regularly; the young men will be diligently employed and the women will gradually quit the fields for the feminine employment of the home. Being more settled means they will not have to recede at the approach of White man; it may confidently be expected that religion, education and civilization will receive a strong impulse from this work. The people are delighted with the prospect before them."[34]

His request was for £100 towards the cost and a further sum for the purchase of about six dozen spades, five or six ploughs and an iron corn mill "so constructed that it may be worked by a water wheel placed in one of the water courses," these implements to be sent out from England.

Eighteen months were to pass before Holloway received a response to his appeal for help and this was most discouraging. Whilst agreeing to the project, the Society could not make any financial contribution; they simply had no funds available. His request for an additional missionary to be sent to Lekhatlong could also not be met.[35] The old church by this time was in a sad state of repair, but the dam was a higher priority; the livelihood of the people depended upon it.

Despite this set-back, work continued on the dam, though this could only be carried out in the dry winter months. Holloway, in addition to his normal duties, was himself actively involved, working alongside his men, supervising and encouraging them.

Conflict with the Boers continued and relations between them and the missionaries worsened. In September 1851 William Ross, a fellow missionary, sought sanctuary at Lekhatlong, having been obliged to abandon his mission station at Mamusa, on the borders of the Transvaal. A dispute had apparently arisen between Mahura, brother of Mothibi and chief of the Batlapin at Mamusa and a party of Bahurutse. Ross was blamed for distancing himself from Mahura's murderous actions and for causing the trouble with the Boers.[36] The Boers themselves took advantage of the situation and sentenced Mahura to pay over 2,000 oxen for shedding blood on their lands. Mamusa was abandoned and Mahura took up residence at Taung, four miles away, whilst Ross eventually went to assist at the Griquatown mission.

In November 1851 Anne gave birth to their fifth baby daughter, who was baptised Selina Mary. At about the same time, Emily and Charles, then living in Bloemfontein, became the proud parents of a baby daughter, Clara Olive. Olive, now nine years old, and Annie, aged seven, joined in the classes at the school and received additional tuition from Anne. Both the girls enjoyed reading but there was a sad lack of new reading material. Their library was limited, with little chance of adding to it. All they had were magazines and old newspapers, sent out by family and friends from England, and these were eagerly awaited, despite the fact that news was quite old before it reached them.

The Great Exhibition in the enormous glass structure specially built for the occasion in Hyde Park was drawing thousands of visitors. Anne must have longed to be in London, where she had been born and brought up, and to be able to take her children to visit this vast display of British achievement. She and Holloway were beginning to realise that the time must come soon when they would have to send the older girls to England to receive a more formal education. They were a very close and loving family and the thought of a separation would have filled them with pain.

Later that same year Anne was grieved to hear from her sister Elizabeth of their mother's death on 24th September, 1851, in London. Such events always left the couple with an empty feeling and an awareness of the distance that separated them from their loved ones.

In April 1851 Livingstone, still restless and looking north to the Makololo again set out with his wife and children, accompanied by his friend William Cotton Oswell.[37] This time, by striking north from Nchokotsa rather than going further west to Lake Ngami, the party were successful in reaching the Linyanti swamps, a journey of 800 miles from Kolobeng. They had to go through the Makgadikgadi Salt Pans and on many occasions the wagons stuck in the deep sand, which necessitated unloading all the contents and inspanning additional oxen to pull them out. After leaving KhamaKhama they and their oxen suffered terribly through lack of water and before reaching the Mababe Plains they had to cut their way through thick bush and forest to force a road for the wagons.

Two months later they reached the Linyanti River, which was then known as the Chobe, where Mary and the children were left on the south bank whilst Livingstone and Oswell crossed into the unhealthy Linyanti marshes. Livingstone finally realised his wish to meet Sebituane, chief of the Makololo. This great chief welcomed the two men warmly and offered to replace the oxen which had been bitten by the tsetse fly. He gave them an ox to slaughter for meat and sent some milk across to Mary and the children. That evening he visited Livingstone and Oswell at their camp and, sitting on his haunches, he started talking to them. In the soft glow of the fire, speaking quietly in Sechuana, the native tongue of his tribe, he related to them the story of his life, his exploits, his battles and his conquests, stopping only when dawn broke, to return to his hut. Through this conversation, which Livingstone recorded in his journal, we have the only primary source record to survive of the story of this man's incredible life, of his march with his followers for more than a thousand miles from the place of his birth.

It all started about thirty to forty years ago, he told them, at the time of the great movement of Bantu tribes, the *Difaqane*. Thousands were fleeing from the Zulus who, under their mighty leader Chaka, had conquered all the land and people east of the Drakensberg and were now venturing further west. Sebituane, only about 20 years old at the time, took ten thousand of his people, then known as the Bafokeng, from their homeland in the foothills of the Drakensberg Mountains, south of the Vaal River, and set out on a long march, heading north.

"I told them," he said, "let us march! Let us take our wives and children and cattle and go forth to seek some land where we may dwell in tranquillity."[38]

Crossing the Vaal, they encountered Moselekatse and his mighty Matabele tribe, whose reign of terror had instilled fear amongst the other tribes over a vast area.

Sebituane had a skirmish with Moselekatse who took all of his cattle. Sebituane then led his people west of the Vaal, raiding, ransacking and enlarging his tribe and livestock as he went.

At this time, in May 1823, Robert Moffat had set out in his wagon to visit Makaba, chief of the Bangwaketse in the north. At Dithakong or Old Lattakoo, where he had first established his mission station in 1816, he was warned of an enormous mass of people heading south, straight

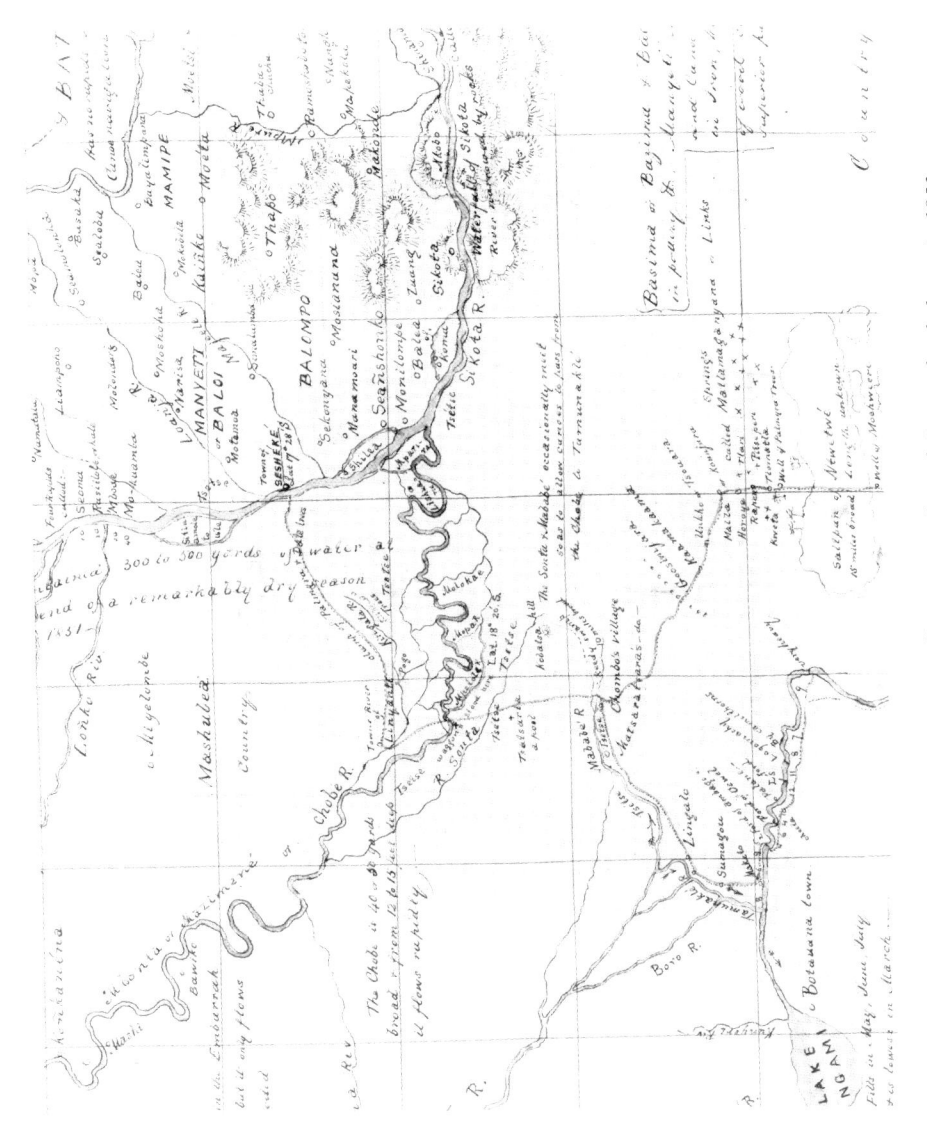

Detail from Livingstone's map of his journey through Barotseland, drawn in 1853.

towards him and towards Kuruman. He retraced his steps as quickly as he could and warned his Batlapin people. Then he hurried south to Griquatown to enlist the aid of the Griquas. The people at the small station at Kuruman waited in fear and apprehension for the attack. The traveller George Thompson, who had been accompanying Moffat, went out from Kuruman to do a reconnaissance at Dithakong. He saw an immense, black mass of humanity heading towards him. They were the Maphuthing, another displaced and marauding tribe. They clashed with Sebituane's Bafokeng, who were hiding in the foothills, and a great battle ensued, in which hundreds were killed.[39] One of the prisoners Sebituane captured from the Maphuthing was a lovely young widow, Setlutlu. He was attracted to her and she produced a son for him, Sekeletu. Setlutlu was one of the Makollo tribe and eventually the Bafokeng became known as the Makololo.[40] [Sekeletu was to become chief of the Makololo upon Sebituane's death. Chapman makes the point, however, that when Setlutlu was captured, she was already pregnant, therefore Sekeletu was not Sebituane's natural son.[41]]

Sebituane then led his tribe north, enlarging it as he went; through the lands of the Barolong, the Bakwena and the Bangwato, fighting and plundering all who stood in his path, still searching for that 'peaceful' spot in which to settle with his people. He eventually reached the banks of the Chobe River where he found the Batawana people living in the swamps at Tshoroga, in the Linyanti marshes with their chief Moremi, father of Lechulatebe. These people fled south to their former land on the shores of Lake Ngami, where Livingstone found them on his visits to that region.

Sebituane soon realised, however, how unhealthy the region was as African fever, or malaria, attacked his men and the tsetse fly attacked his cattle. He proceeded further north with his people, crossing the Zambezi River and subjugated those tribes north of the river, including the mighty Barotse who lived along the banks of the Zambezi. These lands he found were green and fertile, with abundant grazing for their cattle and free of fever.[42]

"This was indeed the paradise I had sought," he told Livingstone and Oswell.

Alas, at about the same time, in 1837, the equally powerful Moselekatse had finally been defeated by the Boers with their superior gunfire and, having been driven north beyond the Limpopo River, was settling his tribe in the country neighbouring Sebituane's domain. Moselekatse well remembered Sebituane and warfare soon broke out between these two mighty chiefs. Livingstone found Sebituane back at Linyanti where, despite its unhealthy marshes, he had retreated and determined to settle.

He was destined never to find the land where he and his people could dwell in tranquillity. He was tired of wars by then and his people were tired of always being on the move. They wanted to settle. Here in these swamps, he was safe from attack by his enemies, but his people were dying from the fever and his tribe was becoming weaker.

By a strange and unfortunate coincidence, on the 6th July 1851, whilst the men were still in his domain, Sebituane died suddenly. According to Livingstone he had insisted upon riding his horse. However, a fall whilst galloping opened an old spear wound and pneumonia set in.[43]

Livingstone was forced to acknowledge that Linyanti was unhealthy and entirely unsuitable for a mission station. Whilst waiting for the new chief to be appointed, he and Oswell left Mary and the children on the south side of the river at Linyanti, whilst they ventured further north, to the banks of the great Zambezi River.[44] They found the terrain there more fertile and healthier, as Sebituane had said, which made missionary prospects more promising. The difficulty, however, would be to persuade the Makololo to venture out of the marshes.

The demise of their great chief was as severe a blow to the Makololo as it was to Livingstone. In a letter to Tidman, the London Missionary Society's secretary for overseas missions, Livingstone talks of Sebituane as being:

"… a man of great ability, he managed to keep his people together and ended his days richer in cattle and with many more people under his sway than any other chief we know in Africa. He had long wished to open up intercourse with Europeans and obtain the weapons he saw used with such fatal effect at Lattakoo, but when he had reached the summit of his wishes, on seeing a path into his country, he was compelled to lie down and die."[45]

In September 1851, on their return journey, on a plain near the banks of the Zouga River Mary was delivered of their fifth child, whom they named William Oswell. Even Oswell, Livingstone's close friend and companion, had been unaware of Mary's pregnancy and was upset at Livingstone's lack of consideration towards her. As he related afterwards: "Again on the Zouga I found him determinedly set on remaining in a grassless locality for eight days. After several fruitless objections eliciting the same obstinate replies, 'I'm going to stay,' I said 'Come out with it! What's the matter?' 'Oh nothing …. Mrs L. had a little son last night.' So I waited eight days very willingly, but I had a deal of trouble to get the reason out of him."[46]

Her confinement left Mary in very poor health, and she suffered a recurrence of the facial paralysis with which she had been inflicted upon their last journey to Lake Ngami. Her mother, Mary Moffat, had been openly critical of Livingstone for exposing his wife to such dangers and prior to their departure had written him a strong letter. Always resentful of criticism, he had copied these extracts into his journal, adding:

"They show in what light our efforts are regarded by those who, as much as we do, desire that the Gospel may be preached to all nations."[48]

Livingstone was single-minded and contemptuous of anyone who hesitated to do what he thought was his duty. If there were dangers one had to accept the risks and, as he proved most effectively, he himself was prepared to risk his life for his ambitions. However it is an ethical debate as to whether he, or Holloway Helmore and the other missionaries at a later date, were right to expose their wives and children to such risks.

Livingstone was inspired by his journey north. He had observed the effects of the slave trade in the area first-hand. He became convinced that opening up the Zambezi River to missionaries and to commerce would counter-act this abhorrent practice. On his return to Kolobeng he wrote to Tidman in London requesting leave of absence from his station for two to three years in order to fully explore the region with the aim of locating an outlet to the sea. Mary, he said, had agreed to go to Scotland with their children and would remain with his parents until his return; "if the London Missionary Society can support them."[48]

At Lekhatlong, the end of the summer of 1852 saw heavy rains which swelled the Harts River. Despite Holloway's warnings and exhortations, the dam had not been properly maintained and the wall collapsed. Now that the drought was broken, they told Holloway, they saw no reason to repair it.[49] Holloway therefore had to carry out the work himself, with the help of some young men and a team of draught oxen. He tried to explain to Jantjie how important it was to maintain the dam, even in a good season. Jantjie talked to his people and they agreed to take over the task of maintaining the dam.

The summer of 1853 was again one of heavy rains, with the walls once more being breached. To Holloway's delight and relief, the directors at this stage finally agreed to make a contribution towards the project, which eased his personal financial burden. In 1854 and again in 1855 the walls were breached during the rainy season and repairs had to be carried out in the dry winter months.[50]

There were further heavy rainfalls in 1856-57, but this time instead of breaching the dam, the river re-routed itself eastwards. Holloway had already left Lekhatlong for long leave in England and unfortunately the dam was not repaired. No further mention is made of the dam, but it is interesting to observe that in 1976, more than 120 years after its construction, the remains of the 6 feet high wall that Holloway had built could still be seen on the Harts River.[51]

In addition to the problems which Holloway and his people had with the dam project, at this time the whole area was in a state of turmoil and uncertainty, with increased Boer activity and rumours that the British government were due to relinquish control of the Orange River Sovereignty. In 1852 there was a change of government in Britain and consequently a change in colonial policy. That same year a treaty was signed at Vereeniging with the Transvaal Boers, to be known as the Sand River Convention. This treaty gave the Boers complete control over the whole area between the Vaal and Limpopo Rivers and enabled them to form their own republic, with the conditions that they were not to keep slaves or interfere in the affairs of the region south of the Vaal River. In return, the British government gave an undertaking not to supply arms or ammunition to the native tribes.[52]

In August 1852, the Transvaal Boers launched a heavy attack on Chief Sechele's town at Kolobeng. His town was destroyed, hundreds of his people were killed or captured and all the crops burned. Livingstone's house was raided and sacked, the Boers' pretext for the attack being that he had been supplying guns to Sechele. Livingstone himself was in Kuruman, making preparations for his prolonged venture into Central Africa.[53] He had just returned from the Cape Colony, where he had put his wife Mary and their children on a boat for England.

As rumours circulated that British control of the Orange River Sovereignty was in turn to be relinquished, tension and concern mounted amongst the missionaries in bordering Griqualand. In January 1853, as secretary of the District Committee, Holloway, whose correspondence with his directors in London was normally polite, moderate and deferential, was sufficiently roused by recent events to pen his emotions to Tidman:

"It is with peculiar feelings that I now sit down to write perhaps the last annual report of this station. The Transvaal Boers are subjugating the Bechuana tribes to their iron yoke. In pursuing their object three things seem to them necessary. First, the means of resistance must be removed; powerful chiefs such as Sechele are therefore attacked. Secondly, the means of independent subsistence must be taken away to render servitude necessary; hence no pastoral tribe, however peaceful is safe from their plundering commandos. Thirdly, the light of liberty must be extinguished; the doom of the missionary is consequently sealed. Mamusa is vacated. The missionaries of Motito* and Mabotsa are driven out of the country and Kolobeng is destroyed. Kuruman and Lekhatlong are the only stations of our Society that yet exist in Bechuana country. Alas! For the tribes beyond us still enshrouded in the black cloud of Heathenism. The Paris Society had once missionaries amongst them, but they were soon forced to retire. The American missionaries left with the Boers. The C.M.S. [*Church Mission Society*] recalled Mr Owen and his companions and now those of our Society are driven out. Shall we quickly retire without using those legitimate means for our return and re-establishment which lie in our power? Much may be done and it should be done promptly and vigorously. The independence of the Boers north of the Vaal River has been acknowledged by the Colonial Authorities subject to certain conditions. A republic is formed and the whole country as far as the confluence of the Vaal and Black rivers is to be subjugated to it. But are the conditions followed? And even if followed, what becomes of the Act of Parliament

* Jean Fredoux, a French missionary and son-in-law of Robert Moffat

proclaiming jurisdiction of the 25th degree of S. Latitude? Will England confirm or annul the Act of the Assistant Commissioners? Let the Aboriginal Protection and Anti-Slavery Societies ask England this question. Let Challis and Miall† commence their Parliamentary career by placing themselves at the side of Buxton and Wilberforce and propose this question in the Senate House. The subject is one of deep and general interest. Let it be fully comprehended and clearly stated and surely the sympathies of all classes will be engaged. Let the politician consider the probable result of a Boer Republic formed of such material, placed in so awkward a position (locally) and related by blood to the majority of the Colonial population. Let the Philosophers and Merchants look at the obstacles which will now be thrown in the way of future discovery and the advance of commerce. Let the Philanthropist consider the misery and oppression inflicted on a mild and inoffensive people by a body of men who till lately stood in the position of rebels against the British Government. And let the Christians decide whether or not the light of the Gospel shall be extinguished and the souls of their fellow men left to perish."[54]

On 22nd May, 1853 Holloway was requested by the Batlapin Chief Matimo to travel to Taung, about 80 miles north of Lekhatlong, to investigate a dispute with the Boers over some allegedly stolen cattle. A meeting was called on 24th May, attended by Chief Matlaba of the Barolong, Chief Matimo with about 50 of his people, four Boers and Holloway. Holloway, in a full report to the directors,[55] stated that the Boers appeared uneasy about his unexpected presence.

A herder claimed that someone had come and driven off some of the cattle he was guarding, Holloway reported. Asked why he had not reported it, the herder responded that he would have been beaten. Some of the herd of 300 had been returned but about 130 were still missing. Matlaba then confessed to having received them and there were counter-charges of the Boers having stolen some of their cattle.

One of the Boers, Jacobs, then read a proclamation from General Pretorius, Commandant General of the Transvaal Republic, proposing a treaty with the Batlapin and disclaiming all intention of taking their country and guns.

† Two recently-elected Liberal MP's who championed the non-conformist cause.

Matimo replied that he had no authority to agree in the absence of the other Batlapin chiefs. A long dispute ensued, with charges and counter-charges over land borders and cattle raids, resulting in messengers being despatched to summon the other chiefs.

On 26th May Gasebonwe, Paramount Chief of the Batlapin, who resided at Borigelong and his brother Jantjie, chief of the Batlapin at Lekhatlong, arrived. The Boers were in conciliatory mood and said they would consider the matter settled if the cattle were returned.

The Barolong chief, Matlaba, then stood up and angrily accused the Boers of treachery. Whilst at Thaba'Nchu, he declared, he was requested by Hendrik Potgieter to aid the Boer Commando against Moselekatse. He helped him, he cried, to defeat the Matabele and drive them north and was encouraged by Potgieter to settle in his territory. He was asked to sign a treaty with the Boers, but refused and then the troubles began. He was driven from his location and constantly harassed. General Pretorius proposed a boundary line, but they could not agree on this. Then the Boers proposed an attack on Sechele and asked him to raise some men. He refused. He was commanded to report to General Pretorius his reasons for refusing. Reluctant to go himself, he sent a messenger, which angered the general. He was eventually persuaded by Mr Ludorf* to move. There was a dispute over some stolen cattle. The Boers fired on them and they fought back. Chief Mahura then advised him to keep his people from further trouble and promised to make an alliance with him and the other Bechuana chiefs against the Boers.

Holloway reported that Jacobs then spoke up and asked Jantjie to give his opinion on Pretorius's proposal of a treaty, adding that if he would unite with Matimo in calling for Pretorius, the latter would come and give land to him, Matimo, Gasebonwe and to Matlaba. Jantjie retaliated with some strong words:

"Your people have come from the Cape. You fought with the English and now you are fighting with the Bechuanas. You have made war with all the Bechuana chiefs."

The meeting broke up with nothing resolved. That evening, Holloway said, he went to Jacobs, who told him that his object in coming to Taung was to make peace.

* Their German missionary

Holloway asked who it was that offered peace. "Pretorius," was the reply. Holloway responded by accusing Pretorius of being the perpetrator of all the unrest in the area. He had done so much to ferment war, Holloway said, if he really desired peace he should prove before God and man that he was a new man. At this, Jacobs got up and walked away.

The following morning, Holloway was told that Jacobs had shown Mahura letters that he claimed had been sent to him by some missionaries, urging the Boers to fight with him, Mahura. Holloway again approached Jacobs and challenged him to produce the letters. Jacobs was unable to do so and backtracked.

This incident is an example of the conflict raging in the area at that time between Boer and Bantu, with the missionaries often caught in the middle; being asked to mediate but then accused of partiality.

In June 1853 news reached the missionaries that Sir George Clerk, a servant of the British government, was on his way to Bloemfontein with the directive to hand over government to the farmers who had settled in the Sovereignty, the majority of whom were Boers; the British had been in control for just five years. Moffat and Holloway convened a meeting at Lekhatlong of all the missionaries in the area, of whatever society or denomination, in order to discuss the deteriorating situation. A memorial was drawn up and agreed by all present and Moffat, Solomon and Inglis travelled to Bloemfontein to present it to Sir George. The memorial read:

"... You have arrived in this country at a most eventful period of its history; a great extent of our country north of the Vaal River is in a very disorganised state and a tone of feeling has been given to the Natives' mind both within and beyond the Sovereignty which we cannot look upon without the deepest regret and the greatest apprehension. A very general impression has been made upon the Native mind that the White man is combining for the destruction of the Black.

The cause of this feeling is principally the events which have recently transpired in the Transvaal country. It cannot be unknown to you that there have been lately much commotion and bloodshed in that quarter; the emigrant farmers have always entertained their low views of the rights and privileges of the Aborigines. ... They have attempted to use their might to bring them into subjection, but since the Convention made between H.M.'s Assistant Commissioner and the emigrant

farmers in 1852, their demands and usurpation have passed all bounds. Since that Convention several native chiefs have been attacked and five mission stations (two belonging to the London and one to the Wesleyan Society) have been destroyed by the Boers.......
We have no hesitation in stating that the attacks were quite unprovoked. The only reason was the love of plunder, lust of power and a desire to obtain constrained, unpaid labour by the Boers.......
In addition to the breaking up of five mission stations and valuable property either taken or destroyed, Messrs Edwards and Inglis were summoned before the Republic Tribunals and on the most flimsy pretexts have been banished from the Transvaal and much of their property confiscated.
Despite Convention terms, many thousands of Natives are held in slavery and servitude in various disguises.
The result of this is the Native tribes are combining to resist the encroachment of the Boers. We behold the dark and gloomy prospect of a long and bloody war between the Black and White races in the Transvaal. We are very concerned about the future, this conflict will go on for many years, hampering progress in every direction, commerce, missionary work and destabilising communities. It is understandable that the Natives regard the Boers with hatred and distrust but they are now beginning to regard the British with suspicion since they think they are combining with the Boers against them.
We beg you to impress very deeply the awful consequences to the British Government of abandoning control of the Orange River Sovereignty.

      Signed: Robert Moffat (Chairman)
      Holloway Helmore (Secretary)"[56]

 Their pleas were of no avail. In February 1854, the Bloemfontein Convention handed the country over to the Boers, with no restrictions or provisos.
 To Holloway and Anne these were anxious days. Lekhatlong lay close to the border of the Orange River Colony, or Orange Free State as it was to become known.
 In the midst of these dark clouds however, there was a ray of sunshine

when on the 2ⁿᵈ October 1853 a baby son was born to Anne. After five daughters and one stillborn boy he was a welcome addition to their growing family. He was given the names William Holloway, William being the name of Anne's father, and was affectionately known throughout his life as Willie.

Livingstone meanwhile, remote from all the difficulties facing his brethren in Griqualand, had reached Linyanti on 23ʳᵈ May, 1853. All his men, he wrote to his father-in-law,[57] were afflicted with the African Fever. In an effort to avoid the tsetse area, he had followed the same route taken across the salt pans, east of the Tamalakane River. He himself did not succumb to the fever until they reached Linyanti, but there, for the first time ever, within a week he suffered his first attack and in all he suffered eight attacks within the next few weeks.[58]

He received a warm welcome from the new chief, the eighteen year old Sekeletu.

"He is not equal in appearance or character to his father, but there is nothing weak or childish in his conduct or conversation … there have been several executions, so he has Sebituane's energy. He is afraid to learn to read, lest it 'change his heart and make him content with one wife,' as in the case of Sechele,"[59]

was Livingstone's assessment of this young man, who was destined to play such an important part in this story.

Was Sekeletu the lawful chief of the Makololo? Before Livingstone left Linyanti in July 1851 Sebituane's daughter, Mamochisane had been appointed to succeed her father. Livingstone wrote in his *Missionary Travels* that she relinquished the chieftainship in favour of her half-brother Sekeletu, saying:

"I have been only chief because my father wished it. I would always prefer to be married and have a family like other women. You, Sekeletu, must be chief and build up your father's house."[64]

However James Chapman in his diaries tells a different story. In his entry for 7ᵗʰ September 1853, when he was in Makololo territory, at the same time that Livingstone was at Linyanti preparing to depart for the west coast, he says:

"Mamutsasanni [*sic*] is the lawful heiress to the throne. Her father, when dying, commanded her never to marry, but to cohabit with whom she pleased. Sekeletu's mother was taken in war by Sebetwane [*sic*] when she was in the family way with him. Mamutsasanni has invested Sekeletu with power over the southern districts, but he seems ambitious and will no doubt soon aspire to something greater. He is a tyrant and is not generally liked. He has killed several chiefs this year because they did not kill enough elephants, and made other chiefs. The Doctor could do nothing in the matter."[61]

A few years later, in 1862, Chapman wrote to his patron, the governor of the Cape Sir George Grey, that Sekeletu, whose leprosy was by then well advanced, had lost the affection and respect of his own people. He was not the lawful heir, he continued. It was widely accepted that Sebituane was not his father. Sebituane had nominated Mamutsasanni to succeed him. However, Sekeletu had attached himself to 'that mysterious person, the White Doctor." By purchasing a few guns from Livingstone he gained power over his half sister. "He held up his guns and exaggerated ideas of the influence of the Doctor, to Sebetwane's friends, amongst whom he made havoc, and forced Mamutsasanni to abandon the command into his hands altogether."[62]

If this is true, was Livingstone, who was on the spot, totally deceived or did he know what was going on, but mislead everyone by painting a better picture of Sekeletu than was actually the case?

Livingstone went on to describe the Chobe River, which was in full flood, as:

"one of great beauty and breadth, often more than a mile broad with islands. The tsetse spoils the most beautiful and healthful spots, but after a laborious search we have not found the spot I could pronounce salubrious. We must brave the fever. It is God not the devil that rules our destiny."[63]

Sekeletu was reluctant to let Livingstone depart. His presence gave them security, not only from the Matebele but other enemies in the region. Discussions had clearly taken place between the two men regarding Livingstone coming to settle amongst them with his wife and family. To be fair, during his stay amongst them Livingstone had become attached to the chief and his people and this affection was reciprocated. However for Sekeletu Mary, as the daughter of Robert

Moffat, the great friend of his enemy Moselekatse, was the key person. Were they to agree to move out of the swamps, she would be their safeguard against attack by the Matebele.

Livingstone had been disturbed to find on his previous visit that the Makololo were caught up in the slave trade, even whilst Sebituane was still alive, and he had been unable to influence the chief against human trafficking. This, more than anything else, persuaded him that it was essential to open the area to mission and commerce in order to counteract this evil.[64]

By November 1853 he was ready to depart from Linyanti, heading for the west coast, following the Zambezi and hoping it would take him to the Atlantic coast. The men he had brought with him from Kuruman were subject to frequent attacks of fever and were too weak for Livingstone to consider taking them any further. He therefore sent them back and took with him twenty seven men from the Barotse tribes. Sekeletu having provided him with four riding oxen for the journey, he left his wagon at Linyanti, planning to return in due course.[65]

Back at Lekhatlong, in February 1855 Holloway was able to report to his directors that the prospects were brighter. There had been no sign of the Transvaal Boers for some time and the Orange Free State Boers were not as belligerent. The local Bechuana tribes had formed an alliance and this too acted as a deterrent. His people had been unsettled for some years due to drought, wars and rumours of war, causing them to scatter. However, the good rains of the past three years, the building of the dam and the more settled state of the country had had a positive effect.

"Travellers new to Africa look with indifference on the mission stations. However, when they travel north and compare with heathens, they can see the effects," he wrote.[66] In the fifteen years since his arrival, his church membership had grown to 1,400, with 4,000 regular worshippers. When compared to 1840, when Wright reported 190 church members and a congregation of 350,[67] these figures reflect the success of Holloway's missionary efforts at Lekhatlong. Holloway was one of only six missionaries who could preach in the Sechuana language. He had achieved this without help; and he was still on his original annual salary of £100, on which he had to keep his ever-increasing family.

He was by then, however, suffering from exhaustion and his nerves were shattered. In April 1855 he wrote to Tidman, requesting permission to visit England with his family early the following year. He had already spoken to Robert Moffat, who had agreed to take charge of Lekhatlong during his absence. Despite his poor state of health, he expressed his main concern as being the welfare of his children:

"… My children are now of an age which render it desirable that the older ones should not be kept longer from our native country. The eldest is now thirteen years old and the second eleven.

The situation and principles of our relatives in England are such that I deem it my duty as a parent (if practicable) to accompany my children and make suitable arrangements for their guardianship during their stay. Sixteen years of missionary labour, during which both mind and body have been tolerably worked, might perhaps be pleaded as a reason why my request should be favourably received, but as I have no wish for my own sake to leave my post, even for a short period, I will plead only what weighs with me in mind, namely my duty to my children.…

I wish to start from my station in the month of January next."[68]

Although the bonds of affection were strong and relations cordial, Holloway was clearly reluctant to allow his children to come under the influence of the religious doctrines of his two brothers, Thomas and Frederick.

The belated response from London, dated 8th February 1856, was curt and lukewarm and indicative of the lack of understanding and support which the missionaries had to endure from their directors in London. Tidman wrote that:

"The Directors are not very pleased with your wish to come to England with your family of seven. You should send your children only. They query your Christian duty to your work. However, they have agreed to leave it to your conscience. Had you applied on the grounds of ill health they may have agreed to your request."[69]

A tragedy had in the meantime hit the family. In November 1855 Emily's husband, Charles Stuart, took ill whilst on his way to a Court session and died soon afterwards. The shocked and grief-stricken Emily, pregnant and with two small daughters, became once more the responsibility of Holloway and Anne. Stuart's financial situation was found to be far from favourable, adding to the family's anxiety to leave for England as soon as possible.

Early in 1856 they all departed for Cape Town, leaving Lekhatlong in the care of William Ross. Soon after their arrival Emily was confined of a baby son, whom she named Charles, after his father. Holloway hoped to find a response to his request on his arrival at Cape Town, but nothing had yet been heard from London. Nevertheless, with William Thompson's support and agreement, at the end of March 1856 the party embarked for England.[70]

During the voyage, on 18th April 1856, another son was born to the couple and baptised Henry Charles. He was the youngest of the couple's seven children.

1 L.M.S. Archives, Helmore to Tidman, Report for 1843
2 L.M.S. Archives, Helmore to Tidman, 8.10.1844
3 L.M.S. Archives, Tidman to Ross, 26.8.1844
4 L.M.S. Archives, Inglis to Freeman, 18.9.1844
5 Personal collection, Helmore to Mrs Garden, 6.3.1844 (Original in Pretoria Archives, A.551)
6 Seaver, p.79
7 *The Colonisation of the Southern Tswana*, p.4ff
8 *Memoir of the Reverend Thomas Helmore*
9 Dickson, *p.152*
10 L.M.S. Archives, Helmore to Tidman, 17.11.1845
11 Dickson, *p.46*
12 L.M.S. Archives, Tidman to Ashton, 29.10.1846
13 L.M.S. Archives, Tidman to Ross, 5.1.1846

14 L.M.S. Archives, Helmore to Tidman, 17.11.1845
15 L.M.S. Archives, Helmore to Tidman, 8.2.1847
16 Ibid
17 Seaver, pp.82/3
18 L.M.S. Archives, Minutes of Meeting of District Committee, 12.3.1847
19 L.M.S. Archives, Helmore to Tidman, 25.8.1847
20 L.M.S. Archives, Helmore to Tidman, 27.7.1848
21 L.M.S. Archives, Helmore to Tidman, Report, 2.1.1849
22 L.M.S. Archives, Helmore to Tidman, Report, 10.10.1849
23 Seaver, p.118ff
24 L.M.S. Archives, Freeman to Directors, 2.2.1850
25 L.M.S. Archives, Report of the District Committee, 10.12.1849
26 Personal collection, Memorial of Emily Stuart
27 L.M.S. Archives, Freeman to Directors, 22.1.1850
28 L.M.S. Archives, Helmore Report, 1.1.1851
29 Personal collection, Mary Moffat to Anne Helmore, 22.7.1850 (Original in L.M.S. Archives)
30 Seaver, p.125ff
31 Seaver, p.129
32 L.M.S. Archives, Helmore Report to Tidman, 1.1.1851
33 L.M.S. Archives, Helmore to Tidman, 9.4.1851
34 Ibid
35 L.M.S. Archives, Tidman to Helmore, 14.8.1852
36 L.M.S. Archives, Ross to Tidman, 4.8.1851
37 Seaver, p.134ff
38 Northcott, p.92
39 Smith, p.371ff
40 Smith, p.372
41 Chapman Part I, p.115
42 Smith, p.402
43 Seaver, p.138
44 Seaver, p.140
45 L.M.S. Archives, Livingstone to Tidman, 1.10.1851
46 Seaver, p.143 (quoted from Blaikie's Autobiography of Livingstone)
47 Seaver, p.131
48 L.M.S. Archives, Livingstone toTidman, 1.10.1851
49 L.M.S. Archives, Helmore to Tidman, 4.9.1852
50 L.M.S. Archives, Helmore to Tidman, 23.1.1854 and 2.2.1855
51 *Putting a Plough to the Ground*, Shillington, p.315
52 Northcott, pp.192/3
53 Seaver, pp.153/4
54 L.M.S. Archives, Helmore to Tidman, 25.1.1853
55 L.M.S. Archives, Helmore to Tidman, Journal of visit to Taung, May 24-28, 1853
56 L.M.S. Archives, Helmore to Tidman, 12.7.1853
57 L.M.S. Archives, Livingstone to Moffat, 16.9.1853
58 Seaver, p.176
59 L.M.S. Archives, Livingstone to Thompson, 17.9.1853
60 *Travels and Researches*, p.50
61 Chapman, Part I, p.115
62 Chapman, Part II, p.216
63 L.M.S. Archives, Livingstone to Thompson, 17.9.1853
64 Seaver, p.141
65 L.M.S. Archives, Livingstone to Tidman, 8.11.1853
66 L.M.S. Archives, Helmore to Tidman, 2.2.1855
67 L.M.S. Archives, Wright/Hughes Report for 1840 to Ellis
68 L.M.S. Archives, Helmore to Tidman, 5.4.1855
69 L.M.S. Archives, Tidman to Helmore, 8.2.1856
70 L.M.S. Archives, Thompson to Tidman, 28.3.1856

CHAPTER FOUR
England, 1856 to 1858
Focus on the Zambezi

When Holloway and Anne returned to England in the spring of 1856, after an absence of seventeen years, they noticed many changes. Queen Victoria and her family of eight children had been affectionately accepted after the instability and extravagances of the monarchy in the early part of the century. Even Prince Albert, whose German roots had not endeared him to the British, found his standing had improved since the Great Exhibition, for which he was primarily responsible. This exhibition in 1851 was a great success, displaying Britain's achievements to the world. Mixed with pride was anger over the war in the Crimea which had ended in February of that year. Debates were still raging about the unsatisfactory conduct of the war, the conditions for peace and the terrible plight of the wounded soldiers.

The most significant change was the growth in speed and availability of transport. The railway lines that now scarred the countryside linked the remotest villages to the industrial towns and cities, which themselves had increased in size. This was enabling individuals and families to migrate far from the place of their birth in search of work. The religious scene was as turbulent as ever. The schisms within the non-conformist movement had resulted in the growth of a large number of breakaway sects, whilst the Anglican Church itself was divided over liturgy, resulting in the High, Low and the Broad church.

To the children, however, these events were of no significance. They would have only noticed how green the grass was, even in the fields, and how big and crowded London was.

Upon arrival, the family proceeded directly to Stratford-upon-Avon for a short while. Emily Stuart took lodgings there, in Ely Street, with the intention of running a small private school in order to make a living for herself and her three small children. She was warmly welcomed back into the fellowship of the Rother Street Congregational Church. Having settled Emily, Holloway and Anne moved on to London and found lodgings south of the river, in Commercial Road, Peckham.

The family reunions were exciting and happy occasions. Anne's sister Elizabeth Garden, or Lizzie, was happy to move in with the family. Aged forty, she had never married. After the death of her parents, with no legacy, she had taken various positions as governess, but had often been thrown upon the charity of their extended family. They were warmly and affectionately welcomed by Holloway's brother, Thomas Helmore and his wife Kate and paid many visits to their home in Chelsea. The children soon formed a close relationship with their five cousins, also with their Uncle Frederick, who was a frequent visitor to Cheyne Walk. Thomas Helmore, who had developed a renowned boys' choir at St Mark's Chapel, Chelsea, was now Master of the Children of the Chapel Royal, St James's.[1] He played a large part in the re-introduction of medieval plainsong into church music in the mid- nineteenth century. He had also, with John Mason Neale recently published the *Hymnal Noted*, a compilation of hymns and carols. Thomas could not have then known that one of his hymns in particular, *O Come, O come, Emmanuel* would still be sung at Christmas-time in churches throughout the world at the end of the twentieth century.

One of Holloway's first calls was to the London Missionary Society's offices in the City, where he was welcomed by the Foreign Secretary, Arthur Tidman, who introduced him to the Board at their regular meeting on 11th August, 1856. Holloway "furnished them with much interesting information relative to the present state and prospects of the Society's missions among the Bechuanas."[2]

At the same meeting, the Board were informed that letters had reached London from Livingstone, one written from Linyanti on 12 October 1855 and one from Tete, near the east coast, dated 2nd March, 1856. This was the first news they had received of Livingstone since he had set out from Linyanti for the west coast in November 1853. He had sent despatches and letters from Loanda in Angola, but these were lost when the ship carrying them was wrecked off Madeira. By a strange twist of fate Livingstone, whose poor state of health and exhaustion gave cause for concern, had declined to return to England aboard this ship, despite pressure from the local Portuguese consulate. This decision clearly portrays his tenacity and determination to accomplish his goal, regardless of the difficulties. His wife Mary, meantime, had not got on well with her in-laws in Scotland and had soon moved to England with her children to await the return of her husband. It had been more than two years since she had last heard from him. Not knowing if he were alive or not, desperately unhappy and home-sick, constantly begging the London Missionary Society for a grant to sustain herself and her children, the wait must have seemed interminable and her relief can be imagined when she heard that her long wait for her husband's return was near an end.[3]

Holloway spent the next eighteen months travelling the country, giving talks on his missionary work, and attempting to raise funds. He found he had little time to relax. Nevertheless, he and Anne were happy to be back in England and enjoyed the society of family and old friends. Olive, Anne and Lizzie, however, were finding it more difficult to adapt to a different way of life and a different climate and Olive especially was not happy at the thought of being left behind at school when her parents returned to Africa. Lizzie suffered frequent chest colds, which caused considerable anxiety.[4] It would seem Anne and Holloway were already hesitant over leaving her in England when they returned to Africa.

Whilst the family were enjoying their sojourn, they were following with interest events surrounding Livingstone's return to England. Little did they realise how dramatically these events were to alter their own destiny.

On 9th December 1856 the steamer bringing David Livingstone back to England sailed into port, where his wife Mary and their children were waiting on the quayside to welcome him back. Livingstone had last seen them on 23rd April 1852, four years and seven months previously, when he had put them on board a steamer at Cape Town. For whatever reason, Mary was disinclined to write, or maybe by some misfortune her letters never reached him. His correspondence constantly complains to others of having had no letters from his wife. Nevertheless, despite his sad neglect of herself and their children, her love and loyalty to him remained constant and she was overjoyed to have him back, safe and well, after years of loneliness, unhappiness and uncertainty.

Livingstone soon found that he was a celebrity. In May 1856, when he arrived on the east coast of Africa, at Quilimane on the mouth of the

Zambezi River, he sent his various detailed geographical observations of the regions he had traversed to Sir Roderick Murchison, president of the Royal Geographical Society and these in particular had been made public. He and Mary were obliged to travel to London immediately, where he was officially welcomed back at a special reception by the Royal Geographical Society on 15th December. His name soon became a household word. Honours were conferred upon him, tributes were paid to him and he was invited to attend civic functions throughout the country and to give talks on his travels.

The Directors of the London Missionary Society gave him their own formal welcome at the Freemasons' Hall and again many speeches were delivered in praise of his achievement. These honours were justified. Livingstone had opened up the Dark Continent; he had explored regions as yet unknown to Europe and he had travelled from the west coast to the east, covering 4,300 miles, mostly on foot or on the back of an ox given to him by Sekeletu. He had endured frequent bouts of malaria, an attack of rheumatic fever, dysentery and threats of attack from hostile natives, yet he had never wavered in his determination to complete his expedition.

Of considerable interest to the British Government was his assertion that he had opened up Central Africa for communication and trade; that he had followed the Zambezi River from the heart of Africa to its source on the east coast, and that it was navigable.[5] The terrain was unsuitable for travel by ox-wagon, he claimed, but people and goods could be brought to Quilimane by ship and transported up the river; it was no longer necessary to make the long and hazardous trek through the Kalahari Desert from South Africa. Trade would be possible with the tribes living along the banks of this great river as far as the Chobe, where the Barotse and the Makololo lived. Livingstone was convinced that by introducing alternative means of livelihood, together with Christianity, the hold that slave-traders had on the tribes in the area would be loosened. His comments and ideas found fertile ground with the British Government.

There has been a long-standing debate as to how far Livingstone could be held responsible for the tragic consequences of the Makololo Mission. It may be an appropriate point in the story to consider his involvement.

When Livingstone first arrived in Makololo country with his wife Mary in 1851, his objective was to settle amongst them. This is clear from his letter to Tidman, written on the banks of the Zouga whilst he was waiting for Mary to recover from her confinement.

"... Conversation with the people Sebitoane [sic] sent out to Kolobeng last year, led me to the conclusion that I ought immediately to form a settlement in a hilly part of their country, and to the important ends, which I still hope to see accomplished, I shall in a subsequent part of this letter more particularly refer- Having been rather sanguine in my hopes of effecting a settlement, I resolved to obviate the necessity of a wearisome journey back for my family by taking my whole establishment with me, and though now obliged to return to a certain extent unsuccessful I think I erred on the right side in attempting, much. Those who may view it as a mere journey of exploration, ought perhaps to remember that we bring to view a large section of the human family, and others who have tried to discover only rivers &c &c have not accomplished so much, though quite unencumbered with 'impedimenta'. The people too whom we visited were wonderfully well pleased with the children, and the presence of the little ones playing merrily among them, was of itself sufficient to dissolve all suspicion..."[6]

In 1853 when he arrived at Linyanti on his own from Kuruman, he wrote to Thompson in Cape Town: "I have just returned from a nine weeks tour through the country in search of a suitable location for a mission."[7] The major obstacle, he said, was the unhealthy region in which the Makololo had settled. Alas, fever in the marshy swamps would make any settlement in that area impossible, and danger of attack by their enemies the Matebele, made Sekeletu reluctant to leave the marshes, as Livingstone explained to Tidman in a letter written at the same time.[8]

He returned from the West coast in March 1855, bringing back the men he had taken to assist him. Whilst preparing for the second stage of his journey to the east coast, he again wrote a long letter to Tidman in October 1855, with detailed observations on the subject of missionary, trade and geographical features of the region. Amongst many comments, he said:

"I may have dwelt too long on the foregoing topic, but you will at once perceive it has a most important bearing on our prospects. The great humidity produced by quick evaporation from such a vast expanse of water and marsh - the exuberant vegetation caused by fervid heat, and a perfect flood of light in a rich moist soil, and the prodigious amount of decaying vegetable matter annually exposed, after the inundations to the fervid rays of the torrid sun, with a flat surface often covered with forest, and little wind except at one season of the year, all combine to render the climate far from salubrious for any portion of the human family. I really do not desire to deepen those dark colours in which the climate of certain parts of Africa have been portrayed, but in dealing even prospectively with that sacred thing, human life, it is necessary to be conscientiously explicit. Take the experience of the Makololo, who are composed of Basutos, Bakwains and the Bamamgwato, they came from a dry climate than which there are few more salubrious in the world, they have not been twenty years in this quarter, but so great has been the mortality among the men of the tribe, that it presents all the appearance of being destined at no distant day to extinction. I have heard Sebituane and many others complain of the numbers of children who have been cut off by fever, the women are less fruitful than formerly and ascribe the difference to the excessive operation of a natural phenomenon (menstruation) produced by the climate. This may explain why they are generally less subject to fever than the men - the Barotse, Batoka, Bashubea, etc., who belong to the true Negro race now constitute the body of the Tribe. Those who can boast of being pure Makololo are considered the aristocracy and are a mere handful. ..."[9]

He went on to expound the positive advantages of sending other missionaries to this area in which, he declared, despite its unhealthy characteristics, Europeans could cope with the remedies he had developed and which had proved effective on himself and his men. Of his own personal plans, his concluding comments are relevant:

"... Commerce has the effect of speedily letting the tribes see their mutual dependence. It breaks up the sullen isolations of heathenism. It is so far good, but Christianity alone reaches the very centre of the wants of Africa and of the world. The Arabs, or Moors, are great in commerce, but few will say they are as amiable as the uncivilized Negroes in consequence. You will see I appreciate the effects of commerce much, but those of Christianity much more. Theoretically I would pronounce the country about the forks of the Leeba and Leeambye, or Kabompo and rivers of the Bashukulompo, as a most desirable central point for the spread of civilization and Christianity. And unfortunately I must mar my report by saying I feel a difficulty as to taking my children there, without their own intelligent self-dedication. I can speak for my wife and myself, we will go whoever remains behind."[10]

Livingstone had certainly discussed with Sekeletu the prospects of his coming back amongst the Makololo as a missionary.

"Sekeletu says he will go to live in the Barotse country when you come and we all wish very much for your presence …"[11] he wrote to his wife Mary from Linyanti on the 14th September 1855.

It is clear that at this stage the seeds were sown, both in Livingstone's and Sekeletu's minds, that Livingstone's presence amongst the Makololo with his wife Mary would enable the tribe to move to healthier ground. As we know, Mary was the daughter of Robert Moffat and the high esteem with which Moselekatse regarded Moffat would ensure that he did not attack the Makololo whilst Mary was amongst them. His tribe was weakening in the unhealthy marshes, making them more vulnerable to attacks from not only the Matabele but the Barotse and other tribes in the area who had been made subjects of the Makololo by his father Sebituane.

There is no doubt that Sekeletu liked and trusted Livingstone, but his acceptance of Livingstone as a missionary was not so much due to his desire to convert to Christianity, as for political and practical reasons. He welcomed Livingstone's efforts to procure a route to the coast as a means of increasing his trade in slaves and ivory in exchange for guns. Chapman gives an insight into the reception Livingstone's sermons to the Makololo received at this time. He was in the Chobe area in September 1853, at the same time as Livingstone:

"They laugh at Livingstone telling them about God, mimic him preaching and singing, and the chief and his councillors fill the air with shouts and yells. Last year they asked the traders if Livingstone was coming to bring guns. "No." "Well, then, he had better stop away. We are tired of Jesus. Jesus has killed us."[12]

Naturally, any plans discussed by Livingstone and Sekeletu would have needed to be approved by the directors in London. These are important points and relevant to the subsequent tragic events.

On 3 November 1855, at the time that Holloway and Anne were making preparations to leave Lekhatlong for their journey to England, Livingstone set out from Linyanti on his search for a route to the east coast. He was accompanied by 110 Makololo men, including a headman Sekwebu who was familiar with the Zambezi River and was to act as his guide. Sekeletu, who had given him ivory with which to barter for necessities along the route, escorted him on the first leg of the journey.[13]

Before departing from the area, he decided to see for himself the large waterfall on the Zambezi River, which lay approximately sixty miles or 100 kilometres to the east of Lake Leeambye. Since first entering Makololo country four years previously, he had been interested in the stories of this waterfall, which the locals called *mosi-oa-Tunya*, 'the smoke that thunders.' Thus it was that on the 17th November, 1855, Livingstone became the first European to bring to the notice of the world the existence of this incredible natural wonder. The Zambezi, which at that point is about 6,000 feet or 1,700 metres wide, pours through a deep cleft in the earth's surface, forcing a sheer cascade of water to tumble down to the gorge, about 350 feet or 100 metres below. The force of water, Livingstone had been told, was so great that the spray could be seen ten miles away. He was fortunate to have visited them at the end of the dry season when the water level of the river was low; at the height of the rainy season the volume of water and density of the spray creates a mist over the immediate area, which mars the view. We can only imagine his excitement and elation as he gazed upon this gigantic force of water. He spent three days there, taking measurements and making surveys in his usual precise way for his reports, giving them the European name 'Victoria Falls.'[14]

Upon Sekwebu's advice, they set out on their long march following the Leeambye River for a short distance before joining the Zambezi. This diversion, to the north of Sesheke, avoided the tsetse region, and also enabled Livingstone to see if there was an alternative river route to the Makololo by-passing the falls. They plodded on alongside the river for many weeks, enduring rough terrain, fever and tsetse, scorching heat and drenching rain, wild animals, reptiles and rats; and occasionally a hostile reception from a suspicious tribe.

Some miles east of Tete, as they were entering Portuguese territory, they encountered the tribe of Mpende, a chief notorious for his belligerence and brutality. Livingstone was at first mistaken for one of the hated Portuguese, but Sekwebu's diplomatic negotiations persuaded the chief that Livingstone and his party travelled in peace. At this stage the terrain had become very difficult, with rough hills covered with dense trees and bush and infested with tsetse. Taking Mpende's advice they crossed to the south side of the river in canoes, their route taking them for a considerable length away from the river.[15] As we shall see later, this detour was to be a disastrous mistake.

On 3rd March the party arrived at Tete, the furthest point inland of the Portuguese colony of Mocambique. They were warmly welcomed by the resident commandant Major Sicard, with whom Livingstone remained for some weeks to recover from his exhaustion; and from his first bout of fever since leaving Linyanti.[16]

Through all his travels Livingstone was prolific with his pen. Most of the outpourings of his discoveries, his scientific and geographical notes, his impressions and ideas have survived, if not in their original form in archives, in transcriptions into the many books on his life and work. Amongst the many letters which he wrote from Tete was one to Tidman on 2nd March, in which he said:

"It will be gratifying for you to hear that I have been able to follow up without swerving my original plan of opening a way to the sea on either the East or West coast from a healthy locality in the Interior of the continent....... And now I can announce not only a shorter path for our use but if not egregiously mistaken a decidedly healthy locality. By this fine river flowing through a fine fertile country we have water conveyance to within 1° or 2° of the Makololo. The only impediments I know of being one or two rapids (not cataracts) and the people in some parts who are robbers. ..."[17]

On this positive note, on 22 April 1856, taking Sekwebu with him and leaving the 110 Makololo men still with him in the care of Major Sicard, he set forth on the last short stage of his journey to Quilimane. These men had been his companions and helpers for five months.

He had brought them nearly one thousand miles from their country and it would have been impossible for them to have made their way back in safety without his protection against slave traders and his remedy for fever. In any event, their chief had instructed them to await Livingstone's return from England with Mary, and to escort them back to Linyanti. This he promised them he would do.[18]

When Livingstone arrived at Quilimane, on 20th May 1856, amongst a batch of letters awaiting him was one from Tidman dated 24th August 1855, which was to change his relations with the London Missionary Society. It was in reply to his various despatches since 1853, discussing the possibilities and advantages of opening up the Central African region to missionary work and commerce. Tidman wrote:

"The Directors, while yielding to none in their appreciation of the objects upon which, for some years past, your energies have been concentrated, or in admiration of the zeal, intrepidity, and success with which they have been carried out, are nevertheless restricted in their power of aiding plans connected only remotely with the spread of the Gospel. Of the important bearing of your researches upon the interests, not only of science, but of general humanity, we have the most entire confidence and we would also cherish the hope and belief that they will ultimately tend to the diffusion of Christian truth among the populous but yet uncivilised tribes inhabiting the districts to which you have obtained access. But your reports make it sufficiently obvious that the nature of the country, the insalubrity of the climate, the prevalence of poisonous insects, and other adverse influences, constitute a very serious array of obstacles to missionary effort, and even were there a reasonable prospect of their being surmounted - and we by no means assume they are insurmountable - yet, in that event, the financial circumstances of the Society are not such as to afford any ground of hope that it would be in a position, within any definite period, to enter upon untried, remote, and difficult fields of labour."[19]

It is easy to imagine Livingstone's anger, frustration and disappointment at receiving this communication at the end of a journey of over four thousand miles, much of it on foot, or uncomfortably on the back of an ox. He had been in danger of his life on many occasions from hostile tribes, or slave-traders to whom his presence in the region was unwelcome. The London Missionary Society had, albeit reluctantly, granted him leave of absence to make his journey but he had received little additional funding and was on a salary of just £100 per year, with grants from this being made to Mary in England. It was tactless of Tidman to have written in this vein. To be fair, however, from the start the London Missionary Society had not been happy about Livingstone pushing the boundaries of missionary work so much further afield. Their funds were limited and the effects of the Crimean War meant that in 1855 the Society faced a deficit of £13,000; a fact of which Livingstone was well aware.[20] This letter set Livingstone wondering what his future would hold. He would hardly have felt inclined to go back to his old life as a missionary in Griqualand.

He had to wait six weeks before being able to leave Quilimane on the *Frolic*, bound for England. It was to be a long voyage home. At Mauritius he took ill with a recurrence of fever and an enlarged spleen and was put ashore to recover, residing as the guest of the Governor-General. Meantime, poor Sekwebu was completely overwhelmed and distressed at sea on such a large vessel. He became mentally deranged and just off Mauritius he leapt overboard and was drowned.[21]

From Mauritius Livingstone wrote to Thompson in Cape Town, saying he was resigned to severing his connection with the London Missionary Society rather than be sent to "some of the tried, near, and easy fields where I may wax fat and kick like Jeshuruh."[22] When, after further frustrating delays Livingstone finally arrived in England, he was still bitter over the letter from Tidman. He found the London Missionary Society, however, happy to bask in the glory and publicity that their honoured member had brought their way.[23] They had already been put under pressure from Thompson in Cape Town to support and follow up his endeavours, rather than to risk not only losing Livingstone but tarnishing their reputation as the primary Christian missionary society in Southern Africa.

The nation hailed Livingstone as a hero and he lost no time in propounding his ideas on missionary work and commerce in the regions he had opened up, his words falling on fertile ground. Within weeks of his arrival, having agreed to write a book of his travels and being feasted and feted throughout the land, he realised that his return to Africa would have to be delayed.[24] The 110 Makololo men left at Tete would have to wait a while longer.

With pressure on all sides, including Livingstone himself, the directors of the London Missionary Society found themselves obliged to re-think their decision on new missions. Within a month of Livingstone's return home, a special Board meeting was held on 12 January 1857, to receive communications from him with regard to the establishment of a mission "in the newly discovered regions of Southern Africa." The minutes further record that:

"The Doctor stated in his opinion the most healthy and eligible position for the establishment of a mission... was upon the high ground stretching along the north bank of the Zambezi, between 400 and 500 miles west of Quilimane. That this was the country from which, a few years since, the Makololo had been driven by the Matebele, whose country lies south of that river. He believed the former would readily re-occupy, if they could do so without being molested by their neighbours and further, in his judgement the result would be promoted by the residence of Mr and Mrs Livingstone amongst them. The Board further recommended that Mr Moffat be asked to commence a mission at the town of Moselekatse, chief of the Matebele."[25]

The second mission to Matabeleland would, it was envisaged, help to keep the peace between the two tribes.

It was further resolved that the matter be referred to a special committee to be drawn up to confer with Dr Livingstone as to the best method of implementing the project. The seeds were thus sown for a venture which was clearly beyond the resources of the London Missionary Society, financially and physically.

Meantime, Holloway and Anne and their young family, oblivious to the effect these events were to have on them personally, had their own problems. At this same meeting, the Board sanctioned a grant of £50 to Holloway, to "provide suitable clothing for his family and necessary furniture for his house during his stay in this country." Holloway was not getting the much-needed rest he had hoped for. Invitations to talk on missionary work in Africa often obliged him to travel long distances.

Olive and Anne were still not happy at the prospect of being left behind at a boarding school. They were a close-knit, loving family and the thought of a long separation filled them all with sadness. However, such decisions could be put off for another year.

The first meeting of the London Missionary Society's new committee lost no time in coming up with some recommendations, which they submitted to the Board on 26th January 1857. It was recommended and duly approved:
1. "That the new mission stations be opened, the one among the Makololo north of the Zambezi and the other to the south of that river among the Matebele under the chief Moselekatse.
2. That as Mr Moffat has now completed the translation of the Sechuana Scriptures and Mr Ashton may be left in charge of the Kuruman Station, Mr Moffat be invited to commence the proposed new mission station among the Matebele, should the state of his own health and that of Mrs Moffat appear to be such as to justify the undertaking.
3. That a missionary be appointed to assist Dr Livingstone in the organisation of the intended mission among the Makololo, and that two missionaries be sent out to unite with Mr Moffat on the foundation of the proposed mission among the Matebele.
4. That a meeting of the Town and Country Directors be convened at the earliest practicable period to consider the proposals contained in the preceding resolutions… with a view to obtain the necessary funds for effectually carrying out the objects contemplated.[26]"

There was a large gathering for this special meeting of the Town and Country Directors, which was held on the 10th February 1857. Holloway went along, his interest naturally aroused in these plans for new missions far to the north of their own cluster of stations. Dr Livingstone, the directors said, had "sent a letter expressing objections to the course which he had erroneously supposed the Directors designed to take for the establishment of the missions." When sent for, he accepted an explanation, expressing his "entire concurrence in the recommendations of the Committee."[27] No record appears to have survived which explains Livingstone's concerns. In the light of subsequent events, one can merely conjecture that it was either to do with his own personal involvement, or the route which they were to take to get to their destination.

The meeting agreed that it would be difficult to fund this venture without jeopardising their existing commitments and it was resolved that a special appeal would be made to the Friends of the Society for contributions.

With great enthusiasm the special fund was launched, in May 1857 at the Society's Annual Meeting. Immediately money came pouring in and within a year £7,000 had been accumulated. The target was £10,000, which it was hoped would set up the stations and contribute towards running costs for the first four years.[28]

On 4th April 1857 a letter was sent to Robert Moffat requesting him to pay a visit to Moselekatse and to report back to the Directors on the feasibility of the plan. The success of the undertaking, Tidman stressed, would initially depend upon Moffat's co-operation and in this Livingstone concurred.

"… we are desirous before the initial steps are taken, to ascertain your feelings and views on the subject and how far the state of your health and other circumstances may enable you to sustain the important part it would devolve upon you…"[29]

Moffat was by this time aged sixty and feeling the effects of his long hard toil amongst the Bechuanas. He was proud and delighted with his son-in-law's achievements, he had agreed with him that the way forward was north. However, he had reservations about the practicalities of having two missions with a thousand miles' distance between them and their nearest brethren. Communication was slow and uncertain, with chiefs at war with one another and often not forwarding mail. More importantly, on his three previous visits to Moselekatse he had been unable to persuade the wily chief to agree to a mission. Would it be any different now? It had already been suggested that their son, John Smith Moffat, who was completing his studies in England, would be sent back to Africa to accompany his father as one of the new missionaries for the Matebele.

Despite his reservations, Moffat packed his wagon and, at the end of July 1857, set off on the long road north on his mission.[30] The Matebele had settled to the east of the Makololo, in what is now Zimbabwe. They were in healthier country and the road from Kuruman followed the eastern edge of the Kalahari Desert. Although a long and difficult journey, Moffat did not need to face the hazards which made the journey to the Makololo so treacherous.

Caught up in the atmosphere of public enthusiasm and urged on by Livingstone, without waiting for Moffat's report the Society went ahead with the project. In addition to John Smith Moffat two further young missionaries, Roger Price and John Mackenzie were officially appointed in December, 1857.[31] 24 year old Price, fresh from college, had previously applied to the Society. Born in the Welsh valleys and speaking no English until he entered college at Plymouth, he was a shy young man and he showed no particular talents at college. However, he was in time to prove one of the steadiest and most able of the nineteenth century missionaries in the Northern Cape. In March 1858 he married Isabella Slater, aged 28, the daughter of the pastor of the congregational church at Plymouth.[32] Isabella's journal and some of her letters are in the archives of the London Missionary Society, a poignant portrayal of a brave and lovely young woman whose life was brought to a premature end in heartbreaking circumstances.

John Mackenzie was a young Scotsman of 22 at the time of his appointment, and a new missionary. Mackenzie too was destined to carve his name on the history of Griqualand, both as a missionary and, from 1884, as Resident Commissioner for the Cape government. His good organisational skills and rational assessment of a problem were to be of great value to the London Missionary Society on this expedition and in the remainder of his time in Southern Africa until his death in 1899.

These two men were assigned to the Makololo Mission, whilst John Smith Moffat was to go initially with his father to the Matebele, together with William Sykes, appointed in January 1858.

The year 1857 therefore was one of hectic and enthusiastic preparation, not only by the London Missionary Society but by the Geographical Society and the British Government, all focusing upon opening up Central Africa, lured by the vision of mission, exploration, trade and colonisation.

Livingstone was extremely busy. His first book, *Missionary Travels and Researches in South Africa* was written and ready for publication within a few months, but the demands on his time obliged a delay yet again on his departure for Africa.

It is clear that as early as April 1857, he had distanced himself from the Society's project, finding no time in his full schedule to offer assistance or advice.

The rebuff he had received from the directors at Quilimane still rankled, even though they had accepted his recommendations on mission and implemented his plans. Moreover, his friend and admirer Sir Roderick Murchison, president of the Royal Geographical Society, was using his influence with Lord Clarendon, the Foreign Secretary, to persuade him to take advantage of Livingstone's talents and knowledge of that region by appointing him as a government emissary. In his biography of Livingstone, Seaver reveals that as early as January of that year, within weeks of Livingstone's arrival in Britain, approaches were being made to the British government and Livingstone personally wrote to Lord Clarendon, at Murchison's instigation, in May 1857.[33]

He had now begun to see himself more as an explorer than a missionary. Moreover, a salary of £500 was alluring, compared to the £100 he was getting from the London Missionary Society. His speeches emphasized his having not only opened the country for Christian endeavours, but for commerce and trade, for encouraging the growth of cotton, groundnuts and sugar cane. In a memorable speech which he delivered in Cambridge on 3rd December 1857, he stressed the importance of men taking up the challenge, despite the hardships. He ended his speech with a ringing challenge:

"I beg to direct your attention to Africa. I know that in a few years I shall be cut off in that country, which is now open. Do not let it be shut again! I go back to Africa to try to make an open path for commerce and Christianity. Do you carry on the work which I have begun. I Leave It With You!"[34]

Cambridge did take up the challenge and the Universities' Mission was formed in 1860. A party led by Bishop Charles Mackenzie arrived on the east coast of Africa in February 1861, to open a new mission in the newly-explored area of the Shirwa.[35] Alas, this mission also ended in tragic circumstances.

No trace of an official letter of resignation from the London Missionary Society can be found in their archives, but it was evident from a Board meeting on 27th October 1857 that Livingstone had resigned. Tidman reported that he had received a letter from Livingstone expressing satisfaction at the course taken by Robert Moffat. He went on to say:

"Dr Livingstone has been compelled to defer his departure for Africa until next spring, but prior to this time it is his purpose to visit Portugal with a view to obtaining the concurrence and aid of the government of that country in the object he has in view, and further, although he declines to receive pecuniary support from this Society and will probably in future sustain some relation to the British Government, there is every reason to believe he will render the Directors his best assistance in the establishment of a mission north of the Zambezi."[36]

The Society merely assumed that Livingstone would help establish the mission amongst the Makololo, and, at this advanced stage, not yet having received Moffat's report, that Moselekatse would accept the other mission amongst the Matebele, without which it would be difficult to persuade the former to move out of the swamps.

Early in 1858, Livingstone's official appointment as "Her Majesty's Consul at Quilimane for the Eastern Coast and Independent Districts of the Interior, and Commander of an Expedition for Exploring Eastern and Central Africa, for the promotion of commerce and civilization, with a view to the extinction of the slave-trade" was announced in The Times[37] Livingstone's input to their project having been scant, the directors of the Society acknowledged that they would have go to ahead without his assistance.

Holloway Helmore received a summons to Bloomfield House and was asked if he would head the mission to the Makololo.

We can imagine the turmoil in Holloway's mind. He had not the same pioneering spirit of Livingstone. He and Anne had made their home at Lekhatlong and had anticipated returning there. He was now being asked to take his wife and family and venture into a wild, unknown region, hundreds of miles away, with no proper line of communication. It would mean cutting short his stay in England by a year and returning to Africa as soon as possible.

Holloway was forty two at the time, though he looked much older. His eyes had lost their sparkle, his face was thin and haggard. He had arrived in England exhausted and overworked but had not rested to regain his strength and health. Although not a trailblazer, he was steady and reliable and had an even temperament and had built Lekhatlong into one of the most successful mission stations in Griqualand.

Moreover, he was the only one available with a sound knowledge of the Sechuana language. His standing with the directors, his peers and his people was high. Having been in Southern Africa for seventeen years he was one of their most experienced missionaries. Holloway did not want to go, but he realised, as did his directors, that he was the only person capable of seeing this project through.[38]

At this stage, many questions still remained unanswered. Would the Makololo accept strangers? They had agreed to have Livingstone and were expecting him to return from the east coast with his wife Mary, escorted by the men Sekeletu had sent with him, and who were still at Tete, awaiting his return. Would they agree to move out of the marshes without Livingstone, and without any proper guarantees as to their safety? Moffat's report on his visit to the Matabele chief was still awaited. Why this haste in proceeding with this expedition, with all its uncertainties, without first obtaining Robert Moffat's advice, which they had already acknowledged was necessary? Communication was so slow in Africa and decisions were never taken without much lengthy deliberation amongst the chief and his elders.

Tidman, however, was an autocratic man, with no first-hand knowledge of Africa and little understanding of the conditions of travel. His decision to go ahead was ill-judged. Livingstone had clearly distanced himself from their activities. Although he had had no firm commitment from Livingstone, Tidman worked on the theory that if the new missionaries, travelling north overland from Kuruman, arrived at the Linyanti at the same time as Livingstone, who would be coming by launch on the Zambezi from the east coast, with thousands of miles of bush separating them and with no lines of communication between them, Livingstone would be able to introduce Holloway and his party to the Makololo chief, Sekeletu.

Possibly Tidman felt he had been driven into a corner. Four young missionaries had already been appointed and were awaiting further instructions. £7,000 had been collected for the mission, with money still coming in. Equipment had been purchased. They had gone too far down the road now to pull out.

Holloway, dutiful as ever to God and his directors, agreed to head the Makololo expedition. He was duly appointed and asked to make arrangements to return to Southern Africa as soon as possible. Arrangements had already been made for the other young missionaries to depart in June. However, it was impossible for Holloway and Anne to make their final preparations and to settle their three older daughters in a boarding school at such short notice and it was agreed that they would follow in the August.

1 *Memoir of the Revd. Thomas Helmore, M.A.,* Frederick Helmore
2 L.M.S. Archives, Board Minutes, 11.8.1856
3 Seaver, p.276
4 Personal collection, Lizzie Moffat to Anne Helmore, 25.1.1858 (Original in L.M.S. Archives)
5 Livingstone to Tidman, 2.3.1856, quoted in Chamberlin, p.257
6 Livingstone to Tidman, 17.10.1851, quoted in Chamberlin, p.153
7 L.M.S. Archives, Livingstone to Thompson, 17.9.1853
8 Livingstone to Tidman, 24.9.1853, quoted in Chamberlin, p.202
9 Livingstone to Tidman, 12.10.1855, quoted in Chamberlin, p.240
10 Ibid
11 Livingstone to Mary Livingstone, 14.9.1855, British Library, Add MSS 50184
12 Chapman, Part I, p.117
13 Seaver, p.249ff
14 Ibid, p.250
15 Ibid, p.258
16 Ibid, p.262
17 Livingstone to Tidman, 2.3.1856, quoted in Chamberlin p.257
18 L.M.S. Archives, Livingstone to Thompson, 8.8.1856
19 Seaver, p.269
20 Ibid, p.272
21 Ibid, p.275
22 Chamberlin, p.263
23 L.M.S. Archives, Board Minutes, 15 and 29.12.1856
24 L.M.S. Archives, Livingstone to (unknown), 23.1.1857
25 L.M.S. Archives, Board Minutes, 12.1.1857
26 L.M.S. Archives, Board Minutes, 26.1.1857
27 L.M.S. Archives, Board Minutes, 10.2.1857
28 L.M.S. Archives, Board Minutes, 10.5.1858
29 L.M.S. Archives, Tidman to Moffat, 4.4.1857
30 Matabele Journals, p.5
31 L.M.S. Archives, Board Minutes, 14.12.1857
32 Smith, p.16
33 Seaver, p.296ff
34 Quoted in Seaver, p.292
35 Seaver, p.385ff
36 L.M.S. Archives, Board Meetings, 27.10.1857
37 Seaver, p.308
38 Personal collection, notes of Olive Helmore

CHAPTER FIVE
Griqualand, 1858 to 1859
The difficulties appear formidable

In March 1858 Livingstone was in Liverpool, making preparations for his departure, when he tersely responded to a further letter from Tidman.

"I am happy to be able to inform you that the *Pearl* is now going out of dock and we sail in her on Monday next about noon. We touch on Sierra Leone and at the Cape for coals……. I may repeat, the only thing that should have come under discussion had a meeting taken place, that should they come through Moselekatze's country to the Zambezi to a point above the Victoria Falls where our steamer launch will be of any service to them, my companions will readily lend their aid in crossing the rivers and otherwise, but that part being unexplored and tsetse reported, it might be better to go by the Hill Ngwa, as that is the only known opening northwards. On every point Mr Helmore can be trusted in implicitly."[1]

Livingstone's lack of interest by then, in the expedition which he had urged on the London Missionary Society, is evident. He could have pointed out, as surely he would have known, that the missionaries should not approach the Makololo from Matebele country, which would have immediately aroused the former's suspicions. The route he suggested via the Ngwa Hill was the one which he took in 1853, through the Makgadikgadi salt pans and heading north over the Mababe Plains from KhamaKhama. No other advice or assistance was offered, other than assisting the wagons across the Zambezi.

The *Pearl* sailed from Liverpool on 12th March 1858. On board with Livingstone was his wife Mary, who was determined not to be left on her own again, and their six-year-old son Oswell. Their other children remained to complete their education under the guardianship of Livingstone's parents. Also on board were five men who were to accompany Livingstone on his expedition; his brother Charles, who was to act as general assistant, Richard Thornton, a geologist, the renowned artist Thomas Baines, Dr John Kirk a botanist, George Rae, ship's engineer and Commander Norman Bedingfield, a naval officer, who was to take charge of the river steamer. In the ship's hold was a specially constructed vessel in three sections, the *Ma-Robert*, intended to convey the party along the Zambezi. Heavy and cumbersome, this vessel was to prove totally unsuitable for its purpose. It consumed enormous amounts of fuel before it had sufficient power to move and leaked badly from its various steel joints.[2] They arrived in Cape Town on the 21st April, and spent a few days there before leaving again on 1st May for the voyage around the coast to the mouth of the Zambezi, which they reached on 14th May. When the party docked at Cape Town they were pleasantly surprised to find Robert and Mary Moffat there to welcome them.

Robert Moffat had returned to Kuruman from Matabeleland in February 1858. Although Moselekatse had indicated his willingness to receive missionaries, Moffat had been unable to secure any agreement upon a suitable site for a mission station.[3] He had been home barely two weeks when news came of the expected arrival in Cape Town of the Livingstones.

Unaware that Livingstone had resigned from the London Missionary Society, the couple were still under the impression that they were on their way to settle amongst the Makololo. Mary Moffat doubtless was happy at the thought that at last Livingstone was to provide a settled home for his wife and family.

The realisation dawned on them, however, that they were unlikely to see their daughter again. With the new route opened along the Zambezi, the old dangerous route across the Kalahari would no longer be used. Moffat was also told, to his consternation, that the new young missionaries were also on their way.

The elderly couple hurriedly packed their wagon and made the long trek to Cape Town. The news that greeted them was, to them, deeply upsetting. They were told by Thompson that Livingstone had resigned from the London Missionary Society; worse still, that he had persuaded their son John Smith Moffat, fresh from college, to resign as well. His education and training had been sponsored by the Society, but before they left England Livingstone had offered him independent means, which he accepted. He was still to go to Matabeleland, but not under the auspices of the Society.

Livingstone had become frustrated at the 'trifling' of the London Missionary Society in getting the missionaries on their way. He feared that the directors were considering abandoning the project; and there are grounds for his fears. He had already distanced himself from the mission but, aware that someone from the Moffat family would be needed on the Zambezi to keep peace between the two tribes, he offered John Moffat an incentive. On 12th January 1858 he wrote to his brother-in-law from London:

"Are you youngsters dilly-dallying so that they cannot move you to go, or what is it? …… I would say, take your passage at once and send a note of it to the Mission House …"[4]

He then went on to make a financial offer of £500 down payment plus £150 a year for life to his brother-in-law to secure his release from the London Missionary Society. This was tempting to John Moffat, on a salary of £100 a year. However, seven years later, Livingstone feeling "unable to continue with this agreement," Moffat resumed his connection with the London Missionary Society.[5]

On the voyage to Cape Town Mary Livingstone discovered that she was again pregnant. One can imagine her distress and Livingstone himself confessed: "This is a great trial for me, for, had she come with us, she might have proved of essential service to the Expedition in cases of sickness and otherwise, but it may all turn out for the best."[6] Leaving Mary and young Oswell at Cape Town to return to Kuruman with her parents, Livingstone departed for the Zambezi with the rest of his party. A few days later he wrote to his daughter Agnes:

"Mama was so ill all the way from Sierra Leone that I was obliged to land her at the Cape, but no sooner did I go ashore to look for a room for her at the Hotel than I heard that Grandpa and Grandma Moffat were there, waiting for us. We were very glad to see them again, as you may be sure, after about six years' separation, and now Mama is to go up to Kuruman with them, remain there for some time and then join me by going up through Kolobeng towards the Makololo country…"[7]

Questions have been raised in the past as to whether there was any firm commitment on Livingstone's part to meet the missionaries at Linyanti. Here there was a clear arrangement, made at Cape Town with his father-in-law, that after the birth of her baby, Mary would travel north with the missionaries to join her husband at Linyanti. Livingstone had little time and, no doubt, little inclination for conversation with Moffat on the subject of his own change of plans and his offer to John Smith Moffat and no record exists of their discussions. However, the two did meet and talk[8] and obviously the arrangements for the Makololo mission would have been on the agenda.

Livingstone's plan was to proceed up the Zambezi in the *Ma-Robert*, taking the 110 Makololo men he had left at Tete back to their homeland, and meet his wife. His missive from the British government was to promote commerce in this area, goods being conveyed by river to and from the east coast. He would also, it was assumed, introduce the new missionaries to Sekeletu and persuade him to move with his tribe to healthier ground.

John Smith Moffat arrived in Cape Town a month after the Livingstones with his bride Emily Unwin. The other four young missionaries, Roger Price, William Sykes, Thomas Morgan Thomas and John Mackenzie, all with their brides, were due to leave England on 5th June and the Helmores were to follow a few weeks later. All, like John and Emily Moffat, were to disembark at Cape Town, proceed to Kuruman and then prepare for the long trek overland to the Interior. This news, too, surprised and worried Moffat. Why were they to "wind their weary way through the vast Interior to the Makololo?" Had not Livingstone opened the Zambezi, he asked Tidman.[9] Surely it would have been quicker, easier and cheaper, with less risks to their health, to use this new route to Linyanti? Furthermore, Helmore had told him that they were to go through Matabeleland to the Kafue River, north of the Zambezi. Surely Livingstone would have given advice on this subject. Tidman replied on 5th June 1858:

"On Dr Livingstone's arrival in December 1856, he avowed his intention of returning to Quilemane by the end of April, or latest May, but...... his stay was prolonged in England for nearly a year. This change in Dr Livingstone's arrangements, together with his want of interest in the proceedings of the Society occasioned much uncertainty and no small embarrassment in all our movements."[10]

Regarding the route overland, Tidman told Moffat:

"Dr Livingstone from the first distinctly and positively declared that they could not go through Portuguese dominions of the East Coast to the interior, lest the jealousy of the Catholic priests should be awakened."

Tidman confessed that they had proceeded with the project reluctantly, due to all the uncertainties and expenses and dangers and would have abandoned it altogether had Helmore not stepped in as leader of the Makololo mission.

He went on to detail the financial arrangements. The yearly salary of the missionaries was yet to be decided, by Moffat and Helmore. An allowance of £50 was to be given to each of the missionaries to meet expenses on the journey from Cape Town to the Interior. An extra £100 for each missionary was allowed to purchase articles suitable for barter; beads, woollen goods, calico and articles of hardware. £50 was allocated to each station for a supply of medical equipment. He finished his letter with the request for Moffat's advice and information on:

"everything connected with the establishment of the new missions. In such an experiment our apprehensions may prove very imperfect, especially as we have received so little information from Dr. Livingstone as to the details of the case..."

The Moffat family decided to remain in Cape Town to await the arrival of the other missionaries, and to assist them with the purchase of wagons, oxen and all other necessary equipment. This expedition needed careful preparation. Funds were limited and sufficient supplies had to be obtained for at least three years, due to the vast distance from any source for replenishment. Whilst waiting, Moffat had time to turn over in his mind all the implications of this, to him, hastily-conceived venture. He wrote to Tidman in June: "We must be content with tortoise speed in Africa," he said. He was unhappy about the proposed route.

"Were the Brethren intended for the Makololo to accompany me to Moselekatse, we should after a short stay with him, be obliged to travel about 14 days through a sometimes very dry country in a westerly direction in order to fall into the direct course to this destination."[11]

It would in any event, he went on, be difficult for political and practical reasons. Sekeletu and Moselekatse were hostile towards each other and suspicions would be aroused as to their motives. Moreover the country was infested with tsetse. "an insurmountable barrier to travellers with oxen." He recommended no alternative but to let the Helmore party make their own way north through the Bechuana country, following Livingstone's route through the Kalahari.

He was going to Paarl with Thompson, he said, to purchase suitable oxen and cattle, but there was a severe epidemic of lung disease amongst the cattle and they had trebled in price.

He wrote a further letter to London on 20th July, with the information that Livingstone had reached the mouth of the Zambezi at Quilemane and was proceeding up the river, hoping to have returned to the mouth by Christmas Day.

"Now before that time he may or may not have surveyed the country between the Kafue or Zambezi, the supposed sanatorium of that country. The same may be said with respect to his reaching Linyanti to prepare the Makololo for the probable arrival of the missionaries. Without there be a considerable degree of certainty of their removing to a more healthy situation, the inhabitants of Linyanti will not feel willing to leave their swamps and rivers, and especially until they have been assured that they shall not be molested by the Matebele. This they will require to know from a very reliable source, i.e. either myself or Dr Livingstone. That they will break up their town and remove some hundred miles immediately on the arrival of the missionaries without some such assurance, we can hardly expect.

Now all this makes it rather a serious matter to recommend three missionaries and their wives to proceed at once to Linyanti. This might prove fatal to some, if not all."[12]

He went on to say that had he been nearer at hand in the planning he would have proposed that the brethren for the Makololo defer their departure from England for a year, or remain among the Bechuanas until the removal of the Makololo to the new field be ascertained. He recommended that they remain at Kuruman for a year and set out in about May of 1859, early in winter, in order to reach Linyanti so as to allow sufficient time to remove to the new country, should previous arrangements have been made by the arrival of Livingstone. He had received reports of further skirmishes between the Matebele and the Makololo, he continued, which confirmed his earlier misgivings of the missionaries travelling to their destination from Matabeleland.

Moffat's misgivings were prophetic. He had been in Africa for many years and knew, as he had said, that they "must be content with tortoise speed." He had foreseen the danger of sending the missionaries without awaiting Livingstone's report.

The directors in London agreed to the new missionaries remaining at Kuruman until they had received assurance from Livingstone that the Makololo were prepared to remove to healthier ground.[13]

On 13th July the steamship carrying the young missionaries and their brides sailed into Table Bay, after a voyage of 38 days from England. The new arrivals and all the bustle aroused the interest of the residents of Cape Town and in particular that of the Governor, Sir George Grey. He took a keen personal interest in the venture and donated a team of donkeys to the mission. Since they would be immune to tsetse, it was planned to use them as postal carriers between Kuruman and the Zambezi. Alas, they caused considerable trouble on the journey to Kuruman, refusing even to pull a cart and they were eventually disposed of.[14]

Back in England, when Holloway and Anne knew they were returning to Africa sooner than planned, they immediately set about finding a suitable boarding school for Olive and Annie. The two girls were reluctant to remain in England and it needed gentle coaxing and persuasion to convince them that it was in their best interests. With the aid of a grant from the London Missionary Society, a place was secured for them at Stratford House in Birmingham and in March 1858, whilst Anne spent a few days with Emily Stuart in nearby Stratford-on-Avon, they joined their new schoolmates. Emily Stuart was to act as guardian in their parents' absence. Lizzie and little Emily were placed in another school whilst Willie and Selina spent the next few weeks with their Aunt Emily, attending her day school. Anne reluctantly agreed that Easter should be spent with friends in Warwick and with their Aunt Emily, since the journey to London would have been costly and unsettling. Just before Easter,

Holloway and Anne travelled to Brighton to attend the ordination of John Smith Moffat, at which Holloway gave an address.

The weeks flew by. The couple wrote frequently to their daughters and made excursions to Birmingham to visit them when time allowed, often on separate occasions. Anne's anxiety over her children is evident from her letters; "Will you ask dear Aunt to have your likenesses done at once. I hope they will be good likenesses, I shall look at them with such pleasure when I am in Africa," she wrote.[15] In another letter she gives her daughters a prescription for toothpowder: "Ask Papa to get you 1 oz. of Bark and powdered Myrrh in equal quantities." For Holloway, between preparations there were still many talks and visits to make throughout the country; Southampton, Winchester, Leicester, Lutterworth, Manchester, each necessitating a few days away from home.

At midsummer the family were re-united and for a few precious weeks enjoyed each other's company at their rented home in Dulwich. After considerable debate, it was decided not to leave Lizzie in England and risk further chest infections in the cold, damp winters. Olive, Annie and Emily were to remain at school for at least a year, maybe two, and then return to Africa to join the rest of the family at Linyanti.

At the beginning of July, with tears, hugs and kisses, fond words and the assurance that they would soon be together again, Holloway and Anne bade farewell to sixteen year old Olive, fourteen year old Annie and nine year old Emily and journeyed to Southampton to begin the long voyage back to Cape Town on *The Dane*. With them were their four other children, Lizzie nearly eleven years old, Selina who was six, Willie, four and little Henry, just two years old. It was a long and miserable six weeks on the Atlantic. All suffered from sea-sickness and each day took them further from their children in England.

On the 16th August *The Dane* entered Table Bay and the Helmores were delighted to find Robert and Mary Moffat there to welcome them. The news from the Interior was not good. There had been further skirmishes between the Makololo and the Matebele, and nearer home, further conflict between the Boers and some of the Koranna and Batlapin, though Jantjie had managed to keep his people out of the troubles. After a busy few days packing wagons and making purchases, on 31st August the party of missionaries were ready to set off for Kuruman, the Moffats with their two daughters Mary and Jane having already departed.

The heavy rains had washed away part of the track, causing considerable difficulty in getting the wagons across the mountains of the Western Cape. However, this did not bother the young missionaries and their wives who were entranced with the beautiful scenery as they travelled through Baine's Kloof. Due to drought and lung sickness the condition of the cattle was very poor and they were unable to pull the wagons. Even before they got through the mountains they had lost some of their oxen and their difficulties increased, with progress becoming slower and slower. Having started from Cape Town with five wagons and fourteen oxen for each wagon, by the time they approached Beaufort five weeks later, three of the wagons had been reduced to six oxen each and two to eight. They were forced to abandon the other oxen by the roadside as they became too weak to pull the wagons. The intense heat of the Karroo during the day added to their discomfort. It was impossible to carry on and eventually it was decided that the Helmores, the Thomas's and the MacKenzies would go ahead in three wagons, pulled by the remaining oxen, until more could be purchased. This they were soon able to do and fresh, healthy oxen were sent back to the beleaguered Prices and Sykeses.[16]

A packet of mail awaited them at Beaufort, containing welcome letters from their children in England and Holloway and Anne eagerly read the contents. "You cannot tell, dear Olive what a relief it was to my mind to receive such interesting and satisfactory letters from you all. It removed a heavy load from my mind. My heart was so sad I could seldom trust my feelings to speak of you. But now I feel that our Heavenly Father's arm has been placed around you …,"[17] Holloway wrote back to Olive.

At Hope Town the party split, the new young missionaries heading north for Kuruman whilst the Helmore party went north-east to go to Lekhatlong, where they were to remain until their departure. Christmas was spent on the banks of the Vaal River and the New Year found them still stranded, unable to cross the swollen river. They remained 24 days there and during that time there were only five days that it did not rain.

Eventually, on 12th January 1859, they were able to cross with the wagons and proceed the short distance to Lekhatlong. They had spent

Holloway Helmore, 1839. From a miniature painted when he joined the London Missionary Society.

Holloway Helmore, 1858. Taken in England, just before he returned to Southern Africa to head the Helmore/Price expedition to the Linyanti.

Anne Helmore, 1858. Taken in England, at the same time as Holloway Helmore.

David Livingstone, c.1856. Taken on his return to England after his epic journey across Central Africa.

Mary Livingstone, wife of David Livingstone and daughter of Robert and Mary Moffat. c.1856.

*Robert Moffat, who founded the Kuruman Mission Station, c.1871.
Taken just after his retirement.*

Mary Moffat, wife of Robert Moffat, c. 1871.

Roger and Isabella Price, 1858. Taken just after their marriage and before they embarked for Southern Africa as part of the Helmore/Price expedition.

John Mackenzie, c.1858. The third member of the Linyanti missionary party.

Olive Helmore, 1858, aged sixteen. Eldest daughter of Holloway and Anne.

Anne Sophia Helmore, c.1865. Second daughter of Holloway and Anne.

The Moffats' homestead at Kuruman, which is now a museum.

nineteen weeks on the road.[18] They found their old home in disorder and sadly neglected and the roof leaking, necessitating immediate repairs. William Ross, who had been in charge of the station in their absence, was away and had locked their bedroom door. They noticed many changes in the three years that they had been away. "Everyone looks older," Anne told Olive. "Thabi's wife Sarah has had another baby daughter and Jantjie's wife Sarah has just had her third baby son."[19] In the warmth of the welcome from their people they soon forgot the discomforts of their journey. The joy of Jantjie and his people was short-lived, however, when they learned that Holloway and Anne would be leaving them. Many of their people were anxious to go with them to Makololo country.

Holloway's reluctance to leave his old mission station and his attitude generally, despite the pessimism about their prospects, are aired in a letter to Tidman, written soon after their arrival at Lekhatlong. He found his people very unwilling that he should leave them, he said, and they would not consent to his going unless a new missionary came in to take his place.

"Everyone seems to look despairingly upon our expedition to the Zambezi and certainly the difficulties appear formidable, but not, I think, insurmountable. As far as I am myself concerned I feel that I have given my word to the Directors and if it be the Divine Will their noble purpose shall be accomplished. It is not surprising that people generally condemn the land journey and assert that we should have gone by water but Dr Livingstone, whose judgement in such matters is seldom at fault, recommended this route and has proved his sincerity by sending his wife and child from Cape Town to accompany us."[20]

Difficulties with the length of time between postal deliveries caused much heart-ache in keeping in touch with their daughters in England. The mail ship left monthly and it was necessary to get the letters to Cape Town, or Southampton in plenty of time. "We have had no letters since the middle of November," Anne wrote to Olive on January 15th, "and those were the September and October letters. I am quite heartsick to hear from you again." The November letters lay with a trader en route from the Cape, forgotten for a further three months. A mother's anxieties are reflected in the long, regular letters which Anne wrote to her daughters. "You must tell me how much you have grown," she instructed Olive.

"Who bought Emily's new frocks, are they fashionable?" she wanted to know. They were gratified to learn from letters received that the girls had settled at school and were doing well. Annie had clearly inherited her father's musical talents and Olive had won a prize for French.

It had taken the Moffats three months to get home from the Cape; they had had an equally appalling journey. Mary Livingstone's poor state of health had caused considerable concern on the journey. Just six days after their arrival home, on 16th November she gave birth to a baby daughter, Anna; she was to be nearly five years old before her father saw her for the first time in England. John and Emily Moffat had a baby son at about the same time and Ellen MacKenzie was pregnant. Sarah Ashton, wife of William Ashton who assisted Moffat at Kuruman, died in childbirth, which caused deep sorrow in the small community gathered at Kuruman. Some weeks later William Sykes's young wife died. These deaths must have served as a gloomy reminder to the young women of the dangers surrounding them in remote stations. Added to this, Mary Livingstone was recalling for their benefit the sufferings she had endured on her journeys to Lake Ngami and Linyanti.

The heavy expenses already incurred were causing alarm in London. The biggest problem had been the high price of cattle for the journey from Cape Town. Holloway reported spending £400 for cattle at Beaufort to replace those he had lost through lung-sickness.

Added to these misgivings, there was considerable unrest in the area due to skirmishes with the Boers. In one raid on Borigelong 115 children were rounded up and taken as captive slaves by the Boers. In another the chapel at Taung was destroyed. Feelings were strong amongst the Boers that the missionaries were responsible for the conflict and they threatened to destroy all the mission stations in the area. They alleged that the London Missionary Society was supplying the Batlapin with firearms. A limited number of firearms was granted to the non-European population in order to shoot game for food and this was controlled by the missionaries,[21] but Moffat strongly denied arming his people for warfare.[22]

Soon after their return to Kuruman in November 1858, Robert Moffat received a letter from the Boer Commandant, T.L. Pretorius:

"Sir. We have ascertained through private communication that you are again making preparation for another journey to Moselekatse with other missionaries. Sir, if it is so we would warn you to procure an order from His Honour the President M.M. Pretorius [*of the Transvaal Republic*], otherwise we shall not allow you to pass..."[23]

Moffat immediately wrote to Sir George Grey in Cape Town, requesting him to intervene. Although a clause in the Sand River Convention, signed between the Boers and the British Government in 1852, bound the Boers to keep the road to the north open, Moffat was well aware that the Transvaal president would not grant them leave freely, even though as Moffat pointed out to Sir George Grey:

"The great road to the interior is distant 60 or 70 miles at least from the nearest habitation of the boers of the Republic. It intersects the territories of two independent chiefs, Sechele and Macheng, so that it cannot be said to pass through the possessions of the Republic. It is the only road to the north. To go to the right would bring one nearer to the Boer border and to the left into the waterless Khalaghari [*Kalahari*]."[24]

Sir George Grey acted immediately, sending a message of warning to President Pretorius at Potchefstroom. The messenger was kept waiting four weeks for a reply, during which time he observed preparations for an attack on Kuruman.

These anxieties and gloom over what lay ahead are aptly expressed in a letter which Isabella Price addressed to her parents, Reverend Martin and Mrs Slater. She had, she said, been low-spirited. Moffat, though trying not to discourage them, was angry with the directors in having planned this expedition to go by land. She continued:

"We are thus far on our journey and unless the boers drive us back, of course we shall make the attempt, whatever difficulties present themselves, to go on to Linyanti. The difficulty of getting the people to move to a more healthy locality, I suppose, we shall have to undertake, as from what I can learn from Mrs Livingstone it seems that the consul's movements are very uncertain. The valley to which Livingstone talked of their removing is comparatively near to the Matabele, and as they have once been driven [from there] by the tyrant Moselekatse and since Moffat's last journey to the Matabele have been attacked when going in that direction, it seems very probable that they will not be very soon persuaded to remove there by us. Of course were Livingstone one of our party they might have more confidence, seeing that he is a son of Moffat who has such influence over the Matabele king.

It appears that we shall be unable to journey in the neighbourhood of Linyanti during the summer season on account of the fever. Indeed, Livingstone once took it in May. We are told that few have ever returned from that neighbourhood. Many have perished with their oxen and wagons. I think you will find that Livingstone made the attempt before he could arrive as far as the Makololo, and though Mrs Livingstone did not quite reach their town, she was unable to proceed further - children and servants all laid low. They lost one child and she returned quite a spectacle.

You know that we are well provided for by the directors, they have supplied us with hardware, manufactured goods for barter, various implements,.... Then Mr Thompson at Cape Town let us have goods for three years' use in the shape of groceries, etc. and assisted us to purchase them in the most economical way. These besides our personal outfits, of course, amount to a large number.

We have always comforted ourselves that though we might have to bear a deal of fatigue and even be the subject of disaster, we should have our little supplies to render us comfort. Now, however, we find that we must bid adieu to all that we had been storing ourselves with. We have only our small wagons for everything and these must be lightly loaded. Indeed it is questioned whether we shall even be able to take them on some part of the journey. We shall be unable to purchase any supplies on our way, till we get nearly to the end of our journey, so that even sheep we must take with us.

Now it does seem to me that all these things should have been properly looked into before we were sent here and that we ought to have waited, say a year or two longer to see whether the Zambezi expedition answered or not, and it is probable that if not we, our goods at least might have been sent by water the greater part of the way. As it is we shall have to leave our goods at Hope Town after we have made a selection from them, as it is thought unsafe to bring them here on account of the intended invasion of the boers and, moreover, the impossibility for them ever to be conveyed overland, as there are so very few native wagons to let and the owners of them would think it too great a risk to expose themselves to such dangers. I believe there are only 2 or 3 in this neighbourhood who possess wagons and they will be anxious to go with Moffat to the Matabele. There are frequently hunting expeditions for ivory and if men go with Moffat they will expect to be enriched from being allowed through his influence to hunt in the country.

Mr Price and Mr MacKenzie start with their wagons tomorrow morning for Griquatown and expect to be with us again in a fortnight, bringing the groceries to be divided amongst us. After this we all expect to go to Hope Town to take the quintessence of our personal property. The rest we must leave, hoping that we may get a portion of it some few years hence."[25]

At the end of February, at a meeting of all the missionaries at Kuruman, John Mackenzie proposed that the men make an advance 'bachelor' expedition to the Makololo to persuade them to move to healthier ground. If successful, he said, temporary huts could be built and Paul, the Bechuana teacher who had agreed to accompany them, could be left in charge of the station while the men retraced their steps to bring their wives and children up, together with the remainder of their property. This proposition, however, was not favourably received by most and the ladies especially were entirely against the idea. "Mr Price fully approved of the plan", Mackenzie later wrote and: "Mr Helmore, who had been on a visit to Kuruman, promised to inform us of his decision after his return to his family at Likatlong [sic]. When his letter came, it announced his intention to take with him at once his wife and four children to the Makololo country; and Mrs Helmore at the same time wrote in a tone of quiet determination which showed that she also had carefully considered the matter, and had fully counted the cost."[26]

When Livingstone took his wife and children with him to seek out Sebituane in 1851, the Makololo chief was impressed that Mary had accompanied her husband.[27] It showed good faith, he had said, that she should come all this way, bringing their children. The people were delighted with the children, as most had never seen white children before. These factors influenced Anne and Holloway in their decision. To go herself, with the children, would be a sign to the Makololo of their good intentions and faith in their mission. Another important consideration was her reluctance to split the family even further. 'My place is by my husband's side,' Anne had promised. For better or for worse, they would embark on this mission together.

At the end of March they were still awaiting news of Livingstone's arrival at Linyanti. By April, eight months after their arrival, goods purchased in England and Cape Town for the expedition had not yet come from the Cape. Price and McKenzie were anxious to get on their way and were pressing for an early start. Timing was critical. They needed to wait for the dry season, which commenced in April, to get the wagons through the thick sand without getting bogged down. On the other hand, it was necessary to set out as early as possible once the rains had stopped, before the water holes dried up.

The target date of end of May was set, whether their goods had arrived or not. Surely by then, Holloway felt, word should have reached them from Livingstone. It was also finally decided that the Makololo party should follow the route that Livingstone had taken in 1853, across the Mababe Plains, rather than go through Matabeleland.

Holloway spent those early months of 1859 making preparations, ensuring the wagons were in good shape; building up his team of oxen and selecting the men who would accompany and assist him. He made frequent journeys to Hope Town, loading supplies which were stored there and taking them to Kuruman, where the other missionaries were biding their time.

In April warnings were sent to Moffat of an imminent Boer attack on Kuruman. Clearly preparations for departure had to be delayed until the danger had passed and until a safe passage for the missionaries on the road to the north was ensured. Moffat made preparations to defend against a Boer attack. He himself would not flee Kuruman and his son John remained, as well as Roger Price. MacKenzie moved with his wife to the Cape until danger was passed. Holloway, with "his usual indomitable and persevering spirit" arrived on the scene to render whatever aid was needed.[28]

The weeks dragged on and by the beginning of May it was becoming apparent that the departure of the missionaries would have to be delayed for a further year. Mary Livingstone decided to return to Cape Town, to go round the coast by steamer and then travel up the Zambezi to join her husband.[29] No news had been received from Livingstone and there was uncertainty over his whereabouts. Mary remained some months in Cape Town, awaiting word from her husband that she could proceed. This not being forthcoming, she decided to return to England to visit her children. Travelling up to Scotland, she left Oswell and her baby Anna in the care of their grandparents, and then returned to Southern Africa in July 1861 to join her husband.[30]

By June the threat of an attack on Kuruman had subsided and assurances were given that the missionaries would not be hindered, but valuable time had been lost. To Holloway and Anne the success of the whole mission depended upon Livingstone being there and this feeling was shared by Roger and Isabella Price.[31] Even though assurances had been given that the Matabele would not attack the Makololo, he and Moffat knew that only Livingstone would be able to persuade their chief to remove to a healthier locality. However, still no word had been received either from Livingstone himself, or about his movements.

Despite this and their earlier decision to postpone departure until the following year, Holloway urged an immediate departure; his anxiety not to miss Livingstone clouded his judgement. In addition, expenses were mounting, causing frequent cautionary warnings from the directors in London. Even though the dry season was well advanced, further delay seemed pointless. "It is not my intention to remain at Linyanti," he wrote to his daughter Olive. "If the people remove, we shall probably go with them, but if they are not yet prepared to trek we must cross the Zambezi somewhere about Sesheke and get into the healthy region. We expect to get through in less then three months from Kuruman, unless we are detained long at the Bamangwato."[32] Little did he realise then that in reality the journey would take them just short of seven months.

As Isabella had told her parents, there were difficulties in procuring wagons and even greater difficulties in recruiting men to accompany them. Holloway was criticised afterwards for not taking a water wagon and horses. In fact, due to the heavy expenses already incurred, Holloway decided to take his old wagon for the children. Everybody knew that the risks of surviving a summer in fever country were slim indeed, but setting out so late in the dry season, when most of the water holes would have dried up would, the local men felt, be suicidal. Few were prepared to take the risk, or loan their wagon, and it was with great difficulty that they were able to scratch together a handful of faithful men to accompany them. Amongst these was Thabi and his son Carl. Thabi had escorted Holloway and Anne to Lekhatlong nearly twenty years ago. They had shared a lot over the years. Now, when asked why he wanted to go to near-certain death, his response was: "Surely I must go where my teacher Helmore goes."[33]

Ellen Mackenzie's confinement was imminent and there was much anxiety over her state of health. To add to this, with Mr Ashton away from Kuruman there would be no-one in charge there whilst Robert Moffat conducted the Matabele missionaries to their destination. It was therefore decided that John Mackenzie would take charge of Kuruman in Moffat's absence and journey up the following year to join the Helmores and Prices at Linyanti, bringing with him the remainder of their goods. As it turned out, this was a fortunate decision.

At the end of June, leaving William Ross in charge, Holloway and Anne left Lekhatlong to join the others at Kuruman. They well knew that they were saying farewell forever to the home they had created in a barren stretch of bush, where all but the youngest of their seven children had been born and reared, where they had known joy, laughter and sorrow. Tears flowed freely as they said goodbye to Jantjie and his people, whose wails could be heard above the grinding of the wagon wheels and the shouts of the driver as he lashed his whip to spur the oxen on.

On the 8th July 1859 Holloway and Anne and Roger and Isabella Price, who was six months into her pregnancy, lined their four wagons up on the wide path outside the Moffat homestead. Only the four Helmore children, Lizzie, Selina, Willie and little Henry were excited at the prospect of a long wagon ride and changing scenery. There was a strong sense of foreboding, all were fully aware of the dangers they faced. Anne and Mary Moffat had been close friends for many years and both were aware that they were unlikely to ever meet again. Six days later John and Emily Moffat set out for Matebeleland and two weeks after them Robert

Moffat, with Sykes and Thomas, followed.

Holloway kept a journal of their journey, written on thin, blue writing paper, which he sent to Olive in England whenever opportunity arose to convey post. Olive treasured this journal until her death in 1919, when it was passed to her brother Willie. After his death in 1941 his widow handed these documents to the London Missionary Society for safekeeping in their archives in London, where they are still held. Before parting with them, however, two copies were made to be retained by the family and one copy is now in the hands of the author. In its own words this journal, complemented with that kept by Isabella Price, plus relevant correspondence, tells more aptly of the trauma and trials of that horrendous journey.

1 L.M.S. Archives, Livingstone to Tidman, 6.3.1858
2 Seaver, p.328
3 Matabele Journals P.124
4 Seaver, p.311
5 L.M.S. Archives, Board Minutes, 13.2.1865
6 Seaver, p.320
7 Zambezi Expedition, Vol.I, p.xxxii
8 L.M.S. Archives, Moffat to Tidman, 14.5.1858
9 L.M.S. Archives, Moffat to Tidman, 19.4.1858
10 L.M.S. Archives, Tidman to Moffat, 5.6.1858
11 L.M.S. Archives, Moffat to Tidman, 19.6.1858
12 L.M.S. Archives, Moffat to Tidman, 20.7.1858
13 L.M.S. Archives, Tidman to Moffat, 6.12.1858
14 Public Records Office, Moffat to Sir George Grey, 30.11.1858
15 Personal Collection Anne Helmore to Olive/Annie 30.4.1858
16 Personal collection, Anne Helmore to Annie, 2.10.1858
17 Personal collection, Holloway Helmore to Olive, 9.10.1858 (Original in L.M.S. Archives)
18 Personal collection, Anne Helmore to Annie, 19.1.1859
19 Personal collection, Anne Helmore to Olive, 18.1.1859 (Original in L.M.S. Archives)
20 L.M.S. Archives, Helmore to Tidman, 29.12.1858
21 L.M.S. Archives, Ross to Tidman, 1.11.1858
22 Public Records Office, Moffat to Sir George Gray, 30.11.1858
23 L.M.S. Archives, Moffat to Tidman, 4.1.1859
24 L.M.S. Archives, Moffat to Sir George Grey, 4.1.1859
25 L.M.S. Archives, Isabella Price to her parents, 1.2.1859
26 Mackenzie, p.33/4
27 L.M.S. Archives, Livingstone to Tidman, 17.10.1851
28 L.M.S. Archives, Moffat to Tidman, 22.6.1859
29 MacKenzie, p.35
30 Matabele Journals, p.217
31 Mackenzie, p.39
32 Personal collection, Holloway to Olive, 29.1.1859 (Original in L.M.S. Archives)
33 Personal collection, Mary Moffat to Emily Stuart, 12.11.1860 (Original in L.M.S. Archives)

CHAPTER SIX
The Kalahari Desert, 1859
Thirst, Endurance and Faith

*JOURNAL OF JOURNEY FROM
KURUMAN TO THE ZAMBESI RIVER
FOR THE PURPOSE OF ESTABLISHING
A MISSION AMONGST THE MAKOLOLO
BY HOLLO WAY HELMORE* [1]

Original spellings have been retained.

July 8th 1859
At a quarter to eleven o'clock this morning (Friday) we commenced our journey from Kuruman for the Zambesi. We were commended to God in prayer by Mr Sykes and escorted out of the town by Mr and Mrs Thomas, Mr Sykes, Mr and Mrs John Moffat, the Misses Bessie and Jane Moffat and a train of young people from the Station.

Our company consists of Mr and Mrs Price with one waggon (*Contentment Hall*), 20 oxen and 3 men - Mrs Helmore and myself and four children with two waggons and 28 oxen, 3 cows, a few sheep and 2 goats, 6 men, a servant girl, and a woman with two children. The names of our people are: Carl (son of Thabi) driver of large waggon (*Experience Tower*), Moriegi the leader, Lingkomi, driver of the other waggon (*The Nursery*) and Saboknena the leader. He is husband to the woman with 2 children and will leave her at their home at the Bangwaketse. Setloki is driver of the loose cattle and father of Kionecoe our maid - and Kuisang, a Bushman, has charge of the sheep. The men are all dressed in leather trousers, strong blue shirts, the gift of Colchester friends and waistcoats provided by friends at Weston-super-Mare. Thabi is accompanying us with his son's waggon, but is ill-provided for such a journey. He is, however, a worthy man and will be of such value as a Christian teacher that we shall do our utmost to enable him to go through. Mr Moffat has lent him four of Moselekatse's oxen as far as the Bamangwato.

We outspanned at Maphutheng after travelling about three hours. There was no water. In the afternoon when starting one of the Matebele oxen proved to be so wild - savage as his original owners and managed to break the disselboom* of Thabi's waggon. Having bound it with reims† and a chain we proceeded for two hours when the ox recommenced his pranks, broke loose, rushed in upon the oxen of *The Nursery*, turned them sharp round and away went the disselboom close to the tongue. It was now dark, we were therefore obliged to stop for the night upon a plain with nothing but a bush a few hundred yards from us, which supplied us with firewood. A friend had previously warned us not to start on such an unlucky day as Friday, but we have done it and expect the reward of our presumption.

July 9th
Up at sunrise and out with our tools - saw, adze, auger and chisel have soon done their work. Mr Price assisted. He knows how to use his hands. The oxen however are away. It is nearly 11 o'clock when we start and with two crippled waggons our progress is slow. Early in the afternoon we reached the Matlarine, but determined not to proceed further till Monday. Mr Price has pitched his tent for the first time. It looks well. The Directors have conferred two great boons in supplying each of us with a good tent and rifle.

July 10th
What a blessing is the Christian Sabbath, a blessing to the jaded spirits of an English town and a blessing to the wearied traveller in the wilds of Africa. We laboured hard last week preparing for our journey and on getting out of the waggon this morning everything around spoke of rest, peace and enjoyment. The sun had just risen and its beams even then darted a congenial warmth. The wind which last night was cold had become still. There was pure water behind and before us, fine grass for the cattle, bushes for shelter and wood for fuel in abundance.

We had a service with the people about noon. I preached from Matthew VI, 9-10. In the evening we watched the cattle coming in from the grass

---
* Long pole attached to front of wagon, alongside which the oxen are harnessed or spanned
† Leather strap or thong

and water. They had fed well and I began to think that it was all for the best that we had been hindered on the road.

July 11th
We were roused at 3 o'clock in the morning by the post man from Kuruman. He brought the English mail - letters from our precious children in Birmingham and other dear relatives, and news of war in Europe. We started at 5 o'clock and as soon as it was light enjoyed the rich treat of reading our letters. It has been a day of constant and steady pulling through deep sand. We reached Motito early in the evening and found Mr and Mrs Frédoux and family well. They had looked for us on Saturday and baked bread accordingly. On Sunday morning, while in church, a thief broke into the house and stole two loaves.

July 12th
Mr Frédoux has kindly supplied Thabi with wood for a new disselboom, and has spent most of the day in the blacksmith's shop strengthening mine, which is much shattered. I have strung a piece of strong wood under the waggon to be ready for future accidents. We inspanned at dusk - crossed the rocky bed of the Lithakong River and are spending the night in a beautiful spot covered with large camelthorn trees, but no water.

July 13th
The cattle are away and we find a part of Thabi's waggon broken. It has been a troublesome job to mend it, as we have not got all our tools at hand. In the meantime the cattle have come and though one of Mr Price's is still missing we are forced to go on from want of water. The ox will probably be found at Lithakong and be sent into Motito. We have now reached Little Choai[*Cwaie*] and our old waggon marvellously escaped damage from one of the front oxen taking fright after the rest were loosed. He scampered hither and thither as far as the trek-tow would let him, scattering scheis* and rattling yokes till at length he fell and was released.

* Yoke-pin

July 14th
Hearing that we should find no water for some days, we filled every available vessel and proceeded on our journey. We outspanned for the night about 9 o'clock, gave the people a dish of mealies which were prepared for the purpose last night and have sent them with the oxen to seek water at Makang. We expect them back tomorrow morning.

July 15th
The oxen returned about 3 o'clock this morning and by four we were all off again on our journey. We passed Loharong and after a long day's journey have found water. I have pitched my tent by moonlight and we have determined to remain here till Monday to rest the oxen.

July 16th
Thabi came to our party at breakfast-time and said: "Do not suppose that you will drink water here, there is nothing but mud." On going to the pool we found that the oxen had trodden its contents into a substance similar in appearance to the material I have seen about London when ground for bricks. We carried some to the waggon in pails but after standing for half a day no division was discernible. The people laughed at our trying to make coffee with it.

Sunday July 17th
This morning we filled our vessels before the oxen went in and found it a little better. Two pots of coffee poured into cloths to filter during the day gave us 3 cups of clear coffee at night. Fortunately we boiled a large plum pudding yesterday in water which we brought with us, and ground a quantity of beef in Lyon's sausage machine, we were therefore at no loss for a dinner. At our morning service I expounded part of the 4th chapter of John.

July 18th
We left our muddy pool at sunrise, found the morning very cold. Ostriches and springboks passed near our waggons. After riding two hours came to a pool of water. We unyoked the oxen to drink, filled

our vessels and went on to Great Cuai[*Cwaie*]. As we approached the road descended amidst bushes and the salt beyond presented the appearance of a frozen lake covered with snow. There was fine grass for the oxen but the water was brack. I took out my rifle for the first time, made bullets and prepared for the game which was now beginning to appear. We are spending the night in rather an open country nearly half way between Great Chuai[*Cwaie*] and Setlagole.

July 19th
Rode from half past 8 till nearly 5 without stopping. Saw many springboks during the day but could not succeed in shooting any. On reaching Setlagole we found only a small hole in the bed of the river containing water, but by digging in the sand we found sufficient for all the cattle. It was a tedious job and tiring business but it was pleasing to see the poor creatures, two at a time, drinking freely the clean cool water. At midnight a lion's voice was heard; the guns were loaded and the oxen brought closer to the waggons. We have as yet had no encounter with His Majesty.

July 20th
We have spent the day here, but the cattle only have rested. Baking, washing, sewing, with the necessary accompaniments of carrying water, sawing and bringing on the shoulders heavy fire-wood, unpacking and re-packing the waggons, etc., etc., have wearied us all. Dear Lizzy was poorly yesterday but is better today. Soon after the children went to bed, a noise was heard and the cry of "a lion" was raised. All was bustle and clamour. Out the young men rushed with their guns, thinking that the lion had seized one of the oxen, or at least a calf. Soon two came rushing back for more powder and lead, away again they went; all was dark and nothing was to be heard but the noise of shouting of the people and barking of the dogs. At length the turmoil ceased and they brought in a springbok which had been wounded with a bullet of one of our men in the morning and had been chased to our encampment by a jackall [*sic*]. All rejoiced at the mistake.

July 21st

We slept but little during the night. The oxen were restless and towards the morning the voice of a lion again excited our men. After breakfast we rode nearly five hours - saw several troops of hartebeest and wild horses [zebra]. I succeeded in wounding one of the latter, but he escaped as I was obliged to return to the waggons. This evening we have outspanned without water. We have made our first kraal for the oxen. It was hard work cutting down and drawing the trees and bushes, but all worked cheerfully and it was soon accomplished.

July 22nd

This day was rather uninteresting. The road generally heavy sand. Mr Price's waggon was delayed an hour and a half trying to ascend a steep bank in the Maritsang[*Maritsane*] River. After dark one of our kind oxen suddenly threw himself down, we feared from fatigue; but on going up to him I slipped into a large hole just in front of him which excited my admiration at the sagacity of the animal, for had he not thus thrown himself down he would have been dragged into the hole by the other oxen, and both he and the waggon injured. When the oxen were turned out of the way he quietly got up and went on as though nothing had happened.

July 23rd

We inspanned at sunrise. Stopped for an hour and a half in the middle of the day - then went on till dark. We have had supper and our evening worship and now the people are tying up the oxen in the light of three glorious fires, which I and Setloki are doing our best to feed. This morning we saw four Bakalagari, two men and two women running like horses to escape from our waggons. They are a curious people. They sometimes hide in the grass and put up their legs in such a manner that they are mistaken for stumps of wood.

July 24th

At 2 o'clock we moved on. As the morning star sank lower and lower our driver expressed his fears that we should be forced to travel on the Sabbath; but to our delight we reached water just as the sun began to peep above the horizon. We soon forgot our fatigue amid the pleasing prospect around us. Water, grass, and trees in abundance. More like an English forest than what many suppose Africa to be. After breakfast we had a short service with the people as they are very tired. I have not had my clothes off for three nights and on lying down after dinner in the children's waggon I slept till tea-time. The people have spent the evening in singing hymns very softly.

July 25th
The cattle are enjoying the pasturage of this beautiful spot - we are all forgetting our fatigues. Yesterday our companions dined with us on venison, preserved potatoes and plum pudding. Today we dined with them - their bill of fare was roast beef and potatoes, rice and quince marmalade made by Mrs Price at Kuruman.

July 26th
We have had a short and pleasant journey today through a beautiful country with abundance of water. We are spending the night near to Molopo-oa-malare. We have met two parties of travellers who report that Sekomi the chief of the Bamangwato has killed three petty chiefs for their supposed attachment to Macheng, the rightful chief of those people.

July 27th
The country is still very beautiful and today we have had great variety of scenery. Several trees that we have not seen before now attract our attention. The Mahatla bush here grows into an elegant tree, and some aloes growing on the brow of a hill were quite majestic. One of a group of four that I examined must be twenty five feet high. Its stem resembles the trunk of a timber tree. One of our people remarked yesterday that some of the trees resembled those which white people plant in front of their houses.

July 28th
Reached Kanye, the town of the Bangwaketse. It is situated on the top of a rocky hill, to be safe from sudden attacks of the Boers. The country is good for cattle, the scenery beautiful in the extreme. We have

evidently entered upon a new and better country. We passed during the day hills covered with trees, the rich colours of which surpass in variety of beauty the plantations in England, the most delicate green mixed with bright yellow and deep red.

July 29th
Sekhutsane, the uncle of the chief Gasiitsive came down from his fortress to pay his respects in the absence of his nephew. He brought a bowl of sweet milk and another of sour and on leaving gave a hint that he expected a present in return. I gave him what I had previously intended - a shirt.

July 30th
The axle tree of my old waggon has been gradually giving way, we shall have to remain therefore a few days while the smith Adrian living here makes a new one. We are buying some young oxen today to increase our spans. I went up into the town, found the open space occupied by the chief clean and spacious with some good buildings, but the huts of the people generally are inferior, though there is an abundance of good wood for building and long grass for thatch.

July 31st
Went up and preached to the heathen on the hill from Acts X v.11-18. Paul and Sebabe the native teachers were both there - our own people, a party of Batluaco from Kuruman and another from Taungs. Paul starts tomorrow for Kuruman to take charge of the station during the absence of Mr Moffat.

August 1st
The waggon is not yet mended, we are therefore staying another day here. Some of the young women of the Bangwaketse came to see us. They seem willing to be instructed. One was brought up at Kuruman, she is now the wife of a heathen though her mother was a Christian. She laments her position and would gladly go with us as a servant if her husband would let her.

August 2nd

The waggon was finished and repacked about midday. We started at 4 o'clock and passed through an African glen that can be surpassed by few spots in beauty. Rocks and hills on either side covered with trees to the very top with openings here and there tempting an extra examination of their wild recesses or exhibiting in the distance high, blue mountains. At every turn we met women returning from their gardens which they are now picking. The variety of trees is interesting. Here we leave the road to examine a tree that appears much like a laurel. There we see others like oaks. Suddenly I came upon a tree with blossoms somewhat resembling the honeysuckle, springing out from the stem far away from the leaves. I plucked a branch and went along examining it when to my surprise I came upon the same blossom on quite a different tree and on examination found that it was a parasite, but unlike the mistletoe, branches containing these flowers and leaves peculiar to them are found on a variety of trees. Another tree like a miniature palm was pointed out to me. I took a branch and had it been summer used it as an umbrella. The leaves are curious and cluster in a bunch at the extremity of the stem. We outspanned for the night (after riding two or three hours) and made a kraal for the oxen. While chopping and sawing the sheep and oxen went off and were with some difficulty recovered. The search after the sheep was given up, Setloki declaring that it was impossible to find sheep at night. I therefore went out myself, but when amongst the rocks and trees I regretted having left my gun and began to feel for my knife and finding that safe went on and after some search found the poor sheep all huddled together under a rock. I returned whistling and when they heard me at the fires one of the drivers came out to meet me and remarked that now they should sleep in comfort as the sheep were found. While writing this I hear the jackalls, who will not thank me for bringing in the sheep. While at Kanye they ran away at night and our three lambs were all taken by the jackalls and one of the sheep was bitten.

August 3rd

Every traveller in Africa should know at least the rudiments of geology. When we rose in the morning a magnificent scene presented itself to our untiring eyes. Rocks and trees, glens and plains blended most romantically. It required very little imagination to conjure up the saurians and ichneumons and other monsters of bygone ages. The larger tree too under which we had encamped presented beauties which the darkness of last night concealed. The parasite was shooting out with its peculiar blossoms, just over our waggon and a little palm-like tree was shooting up under the branches promising soon to rear its head above its protection.

Mr Price endeavoured to train a young ox yesterday and when let loose it ran away and when we started this morning he was waiting for the return of his men who followed it. The country is still rocky. Sometimes we pass stones resembling Coranna huts, one rock was covered with boulders like the domes of a Turkish mosque. Ascending the sandy bank of a dry river the disselboom gave way and the oxen went off, leaving the waggon in the sand. We outspanned, mended and replaced the disselboom, dug water in the sand for the cattle, fried sausage meat for ourselves and went on to Moshopa. Here the Bakhatla resided after the attack of the Boers on their former town.

August 4th
Here is abundance of clear, sweet water and good grass, and as we promised to wait here for Mr Price we are enjoying a holiday. After breakfast I went up to the town. It was built amidst rocks and on ascending I came suddenly upon about 30 apes. It is a custom with the Bechuana to burn their towns when deserted. Only a few huts therefore remained which had escaped the flames. In the afternoon Mr Price came up after meeting with a series of disasters. His lost ox was nowhere to be found. His kettle fell from the waggon and was broken. The chain broke while descending a steep hill and they were forced to remain the whole night in an awkward position with the waggon resting against the stump of a tree. This morning they found that two of their oxen had gone back to Kanye. When he overtook us he was unwilling to stay and went on but his waggon sticking fast in the sand before us, we had time to pack up and precede him. At sunset we found the grass on fire in front of us and though we quickened our pace the fire crossed the road before us. Cutting down a green bough I ran on and beat out the fire along the path and by making the poor oxen run we got safely through. Soon after we came to an awkward bank which we had to descend, in doing which the disselboom

of the large waggon again broke and we narrowly escaped a capsize. We mended it by moonlight sufficiently to enable us to draw out the waggon to the other side of the river. I brought my other waggon safely through, but the other two waggons were very wisely kept on the other side. I have just been and cut down by the light of the moon a piece of wood for another disselboom.

August 5th
Rose before the sun and repaired my waggon. The piece of wood, however, did not please me. When we stopped in the middle of the day I therefore cut down a tree with Thabi's help and have made a strong disselboom which will, I hope, last till the end of the journey.

August 6th
After a long ride we reached Lithubaruba [*Dithubaruba*], the residence of Sechele. There in his fortresses on the top of a rugged mountain dwells the chief of the Bakwena with his people. Round the foot and in various nooks of the mountain are collected a large number of people of various tribes. Steep hills surround the whole on three sides and there is plenty of water in the spaces between. We drew up our waggons under a hill close to one of the places where the women and girls came to draw water. The house of the Hanovarian missionary stands a mile off and having put things in order I went to see them. They have built a neat house and are now busy with a kitchen. I have engaged to meet them tomorrow on the hill when morning and afternoon services are to be held.

August 7th (Sunday)
At the appointed hour we ascended the hills (no easy task) and passing the town came to the church, a neat little building, raised by Sechele. The plastered pulpit was substantial and novel, being covered with vandykes[*sic*] in brown and white. A narrow strip of brown ran along one side of the church, containing the names of Sechele's ancestors. The missionary, Mr Schroeder, a sharp featured German, occupied the pulpit in gown and bands. The congregation was small. After the service we were introduced to Sechele who, hearing of our arrival, came in from his cattle post late last night. We went to his

house, a comfortable building, the work of his missionaries. The table was laid out by a man servant in an inner room and we all sat down with Sechele and his wife. We partook of bread and coffee. Sechele offered thanks before and after eating. We sat conversing for about two hours and then returned to the church. The people were summoned by a trumpet. I preached from Psalm xxxiii.12. We then descended the hill and returned to the waggon. Mrs Helmore had during my absence collected the women and children who came about the waggons and endeavoured to instruct them, but they were a very unruly set.

August 8th
Khosilintsi, the chief's brother came this morning with an ox, a present from Sechele. About midday he came himself, dressed in a complete suit of tiger skins. Yesterday he wore a suit of black. He brought a poker with him, but whether it was intended as a sceptre or to break the head of some unruly dog did not appear. It was too short for a walking stick. I am sorry that I did not speak to him about it for he is a sensible and superior man. He has, I fear, been imposed on by some artful white man. Finding that Mr Price's waggon was distinct from ours, he sent for a goat and presented it to him. We then packed up and proceeded on our journey. Soon after starting a cry was raised that our loose cattle were getting amongst the pits, and on looking in front I saw the head of one of our calves peeping above the ground. It had fallen into one of the pits dug to entrap the Boers. They were dug in double rows with only a foot of earth between them and so completely covered with grass that they prove very dangerous. The calf was happily drawn out free from injury, but the horse of an English traveller was killed a few days ago by falling upon a pointed stake at the bottom of one of them. It was an interesting sight to see the long lines of women returning from their gardens as we left Lithubaruba the sun was setting and we went rather briskly on. After three hours riding Mr Price's waggon stuck fast in the deep sand and we were all therefore brought to a halt for the night. We have made a kraal for the new oxen, the rest must take their chance.

August 9th

This morning we inspanned several new oxen that had never before felt the yoke. The mode of proceeding is this. All the oxen to be used are brought up and made to stand in a line fronting the yokes. Leather throngs (rheims) are then thrown over their horns and the new one is made fast to a steady one. They are then drawn out one by one and arranged as they are to stand in the yokes. The new one is placed about the middle and with a quiet one before and behind and another by his side, he soon learns what is expected of him and in a day or two goes well.

About midday our guide overtook us, kindly sent by Sechele to point out the water on the road and to secure for us from Sekhomi what further assistance we may require. We reached Kopong early this evening and have been busy repairing an old kraal, and as we have now 60 miles in front without water we have determined to rest the oxen tomorrow.

August 10th

Our provisions are going very fast. I have now 17 mouths dependent upon me for food. We see no game now. The country is too woody and a large party of Griquas have been hunting before and driven away the game. My first work today was to examine what provisions are left in the waggons and take out fresh supplies. We hope to lay in a fresh stock of grain at the Bamangwato. As we have now deep sand to go through I have made a new disselboom for the children's waggon. I am well satisfied with my day's work, though my arms ache severely.

August 11th

Our cattle have had a good feed and a good drink of water. Every available vessel is filled with the needful fluid and at half past ten we start with some anxiety. At half past three we stop, let the oxen feed, cook our dinner and at six are off again. We ride till ten then let the oxen out to rest and start again soon after midnight.

August 12th

At half past three we again halt and sleep for a couple of hours - get breakfast and start again at half past nine. The deep sand tries the oxen sadly. It gets heavier and heavier. On we go till about three. The poor oxen then rest till five. Mr Price has much trouble with his oxen and the sun goes down before we have fairly started. Thabi's waggon is gone on ahead, but after a few hours we find it fast in the sand and it requires our united efforts to extricate it. At half past ten o'clock we again make a halt. I lay down upon the seat of my waggon and slept till two. We then inspanned and soon after sunrise reached Boatlanama.

August 13th
There we found two deep pits requiring six men to hand up the water and pour out for the cattle, but as there was but little left in the pits, we drew a little for ourselves and went on till 10 o'clock. We then had breakfast and at 12 started for Lophepe, which we reached safely about 6 o'clock. Here is abundance of pure water and the cattle shall enjoy it for a day or two after their fatiguing journey.

August 14th
"Welcome sweet day of rest." The people were early to rest last night. We have all had a good wash and feel much refreshed. A number of Bakwena travellers attended our morning service. I expounded the 23rd Psalm.

August 15th
The cattle have fed well and are better than might have been expected. Two of mine are, however, very lame. The country here is good for cattle. The soil is limy and covered with thorn bushes. It was here that Mr Oswell was caught by a bush of "wait-a-bit" thorns, thrown from his horse and protected by his dogs from a lion while he lay immobile. Dr Livingstone found no water here on his last journey through this country. This day has been spent as most of our halting days, in cooking, baking, washing, packing, repairing and sundries. The consequence is that we go to bed very tired, regretting that we have not had time to read, or write to our friends.

August 16th
The weather has become much warmer and we shall not be able to travel much longer in the middle of the day. We started again at 2 o'clock this afternoon. The cattle have recovered from their fatigue and travel

well. We have come about 11 miles. Mr Price whose waggon was some distance behind ours, saw a family of giraffes walking near the road.

August 17th
Rode this morning to Mashuwe, found Dr Holden's waggons and learned that the Griqua hunters had killed five elephants in the woods through which we passed. Dr Livingstone speaks of the never failing supply of clear water there. We however found the quantity small and the quality bad. Thus it is in this country. The waters are constantly changing. We left in the afternoon, travelled through heavy sand and at night found that we have got out of the road.

August 18th
We crossed the country and soon got into the right road and after an hour and a half reached a pit of water where the oxen drank, two or three at a time. We then continued our journey till sunset and stopped in a romantic spot surrounded by hills. As we bought some milk on the road we enjoyed a supply of porridge made with oatmeal kindly given to us by Mrs Moffat when leaving Kuruman.

August 19th
Six hours of good riding brought us to the gorge of the Bamangwato mountains. Here we found Mr Thompson's party and had the pleasure of delivering a packet of letters and papers which we received for them after leaving Kuruman. There are two villages of Bakalagari occupying this spot. The water comes down from the mountains and we hear Sekhomi's people singing on the top where most of them reside. Our guide is gone to report our arrival, and to deliver a message which Sechele has kindly sent requesting Sekhomi to treat us as his friends and provide us with guides and render us all the assistance which we may require.

August 20th
After breakfast the Hanovarian missionary, Mr Schulenberg who has been only a month here, came to see us and soon after Sekhomi made his appearance, sending before him a pot of beer as a present. He was very friendly and promised every needful assistance. After he left, the people

began to crowd round our waggons bringing corn, sheep and oxen for sale, which we wanted, and ivory, feathers, carosses* and skins which we did not want. It was amusing to see the trafficking going on. Some crowded around Mr Price's waggon, some round Thabi's who also bought, and the rest round our tent. Men, women and children brought little bowls of grain and having sold their contents filled them up again from bags and skins fastened about their bodies. They would take nothing but beads; corn, beans, sheep, goats and oxen were all offered for beads, some of which will be used by the women in purchasing garden tools from other tribes.

August 21st
This morning we ascended the ravine leading to Sekhomi's town. It was a noble sight to look up at the huge perpendicular basaltic rocks on either side. After ascending for half an hour over smooth and slippery stones, and between large blocks we reached two huts standing in a large enclosure with the water passing along on one side and a village on the opposite bank. This is the missionary's residence, built by the chief. Ascending still higher we reached an extensive flat covered with thousands of huts, and rocks rising all round like a high rampart. We found upwards of two thousand people assembled in the open space appropriated to public meetings and Mr Schulenberg addressing them in their own language. At the close of his address he kindly asked me to come forward and say a few words to them. It was an animating sight and the people listened attentively. In the afternoon I preached to about a thousand people, half of them children and young people. Should anything oblige me to turn back from the Zambesi I would gladly stop here to aid in instructing these masses.

August 22nd
This has been a very fatiguing day. I rose early and searched in both waggons for articles suitable for barter. The Bawanketse and Bakwena would have nothing but guns, powder and lead. Here the Bamangwato and Bakalagari care for nothing but beads. We have purchased three muids† of corn and one of beans, all in small quantities. The noise of the

* Kaross - Jacket or coat made of animal skins
† An old dry measure for corn, etc., equivalent of approx. 24 gallons

people and the heat of the tent are almost unbearable. It was a relief to see the sun set and the people return to their homes. We then quietly measured the grain and stowed it away.

Mr and Mrs Thompson and Dr. Palgrave came to our tent in the evening and made us forget our fatigue with agreeable conversation.

August 23rd
The bartering today has been confined to oxen and sheep and half a muid of corn. The waggons are packed and preparations made for starting tomorrow. Dr Holden arrived about sunset. He came out in the *Athens* with Mr Price and his companions, and hoped to join Dr Livingstone's expedition at the Cape. He is now travelling towards the Lake.

August 24th
The guides came early this morning. An ox which I purchased from Sekhomi gave indications of lung sickness. I mentioned it to him and he at once took it back and sent me another. Early this afternoon we left without regret the towns of the Bamangwato. The wind coming down from the mountains has rendered our stay very disagreeable and the people are the least interesting of any Bechuanas that I have yet met with. Three hours' ride brought us to the Unicorn Pass. Here we have drawn up for the night, and found a lad who has joined our party, being sent by his father to the Zouga to buy tobacco from a friend there.

August 25th
After breakfast we travelled about two and a half hours and found water for the oxen in the yoke but not for the others. There we met some people who left Sekhomi's this morning, having taken a short cut. They told us that news had come of the arrival of Mr Moffat and his son at Sechele's. We outspanned for the night about sunset - made a kraal for the cattle as our guides say it is a lion country and Letloche is still far. Five of our cattle were lost at the water and the men who went back to seek them have not returned.

August 26th

The cattle got out at a weak part of the kraal during the night and were not brought back till nearly ten o'clock. It took us only two and a half hours to reach the water, which has shaken our confidence in our guides, as we could very well have come in last night. We intend to remain here a few days, and our work is already marked out for us. The axle trees of two waggons, (my own and Thabi's) are broken and we have this afternoon cut down two trees, cut them into suitable lengths and brought them to our encampment with the aid of four oxen. Trusting to the waggon menders of this country is in too many instances like trusting to a broken reed. My broken axle tree is the one that Adrian made for me at the Bawanketse.

August 27th

The adzes are busy at the blocks. The wood is so hard that my old adze is rendered useless and I have had to get out a new one. We shall not regret our delay here as there is good grass and plenty of water and the cattle are doing well. Our people have returned without finding the lost oxen, we have therefore sent others to Sekhomi to request him to make enquiry for them amongst his people. They are a sad set, much addicted to stealing, but if the chief speaks the oxen will be recovered.

August 28th

Spent another quiet Sabbath in the open country. A few stragglers attended our midday service. In the evening we sat with the children under a rock by the water and sang some of Curwin's hymns.

August 29th

The country seems bare of game. The hunters who have preceded us have probably driven them away. We are in consequence kept upon beef and mutton and as the weather is now warm we have commenced cutting and drying the meat. The large tree in the midst of our encampment looks exceedingly picturesque with joints and festoons of flesh hanging from its boughs.

The men have returned with the oxen. Information was given to Sekhomi and the cattle were soon discovered at a neighbouring kraal. A young man had walked twenty miles in order to obtain payment for taking the oxen from the kraal to Sekhomi's, a distance of two or three miles.

August 30th

Mr Thompson's party arrived this evening and brought a letter from Mr Moffat written at Lophepe. The whole Matabele party were resting their cattle, as we did, and hope to reach Sekhomi's tomorrow night.

Mr and Mrs Thompson are an interesting and intelligent young couple. Mr, or Captain Thompson was in the Crimea. He then had a sun-stroke, returned to England, married and was advised to travel for his health. Mrs Thompson, daughter of a late admiral stationed at the Cape, felt a predilection for the Colony and on their arrival they were advised to follow on Dr Livingstone's route. Mr Palgrave, a medical gentleman, is accompanying them.

August 31st

We have sent off a messenger to meet Mr Moffat and request him to ride over to see us. Towards sunset a party of men brought a sheep for sale, but as they wanted what I could not well spare, I sent them to Mr Price who bought their sheep. At night, feeling chilly after work, I went for my warm jacket which I had placed in the morning at the back of the waggon. It was gone and our suspicion immediately fell upon the stranger. As they were supposed to be sleeping in the neighbourhood, I was determined to follow them and seize their gun till the stolen property was restored. On being charged with the theft they stoutly and indignantly denied it, but no sooner was the gun seized then the jacket was turned out of a bag and restored. Sekhomi's people are the worst specimens of Bechuanas that I have yet met with.

September 1st

We completed the repairs of our waggons and prepared to receive Mr Moffat. To our great disappointment the messengers returned in the evening with letters stating that Mr Moffat and his party were going on immediately. We have therefore determined to start tomorrow.

September 2nd

The morning was cloudy and cool, we therefore started about midday. Mr Price passed us, leaving Mrs Price in our waggon. He unfortunately took a wrong road, got behind and did not overtake us till midnight. We outspanned before reaching Kanne as the sand is heavy.

September 3rd
We reached Kanne after a short ride, found a number of pits hedged round by the inhabitants of the neighbourhood, each containing a little water. By taking the oxen two and two to the pits all had a drink, but the pits were so entirely emptied that when the Bakalagari came they had to wait for some hours before sufficient water collected again for them to draw. This scarcity obliged us to proceed. Starting at noon we travelled till near sun-set through deep sands. Mr Price and Thabi preceded us and when we overtook them they were ready to proceed again. We find it desirable to travel in this way to prevent the waggons from hindering one another. After travelling two hours by moonlight we came to a stand-still. We rested the oxen for a short time and then got on for half an hour when our waggons again stuck fast. We therefore stopped for the night, having travelled only six and a half hours instead of ten, as we had proposed.

September 4th
Started about sunrise, rode for three and a half hours, rested till 5 o'clock in the afternoon and rode slowly through the deep sand till 6 o'clock in the morning. Enjoyed a cup of coffee and lay down to sleep at 2 o'clock.

September 5th
Rose at 5 o'clock, found the cattle that we left sleeping near the waggons gone. Roused the people and two immediately followed on their track. The whole day has passed and the men have not returned. We sent off the sheep and two oxen that remained with two men in search of water and help to take on at least one of the waggons with the poor children. We gave them each a cup of water and sent them early to bed. About midnight our oxen were brought back without having tasted water. The men, after finding them, wandered and when at last they found their way back to the waggon, both men and oxen were completely exhausted. We soon inspanned, but after proceeding a little distance one of our oxen fell. Soon after the other waggon came to a stand and after an hour's useless effort to urge on the oxen, the anticipated course was resorted to. The children were dressed and sent to the large waggon, the water was

divided and my family was sent on with all the oxen. I remained with Lingkomi and the other waggon till help shall come.

September 6th
The sun is just rising. Here we are, in the midst of a sandy forest, far from water and uncertain of help. A little water is boiled and we enjoy a cup of coffee and some biscuits. A little cheerful conversation followed and as the heat of the day increased we lay down to sleep. About sunset we take more biscuits, a few pieces of dried quince and a little sugar candy. All is still. A single scream of a jackall has alone disturbed the silence that reigns around.

September 7th
Slept comfortably, having had little rest for some nights past. At sunrise put on half a pint of water, another half only remaining in our canteen. Coffee was soon made, the water being removed the moment of boiling to avoid loss by evaporation. It is said that bread is the staff of life but though we have meal and corn sufficient to last us for months, they are useless without water.

Eleven o'clock. Moriegi has just arrived with nearly two quarts of water. How welcome! Our little saucepan is on the fire and boiling before I have time to get out the tea and biscuits. The news he brings is discouraging enough but under the circumstances we may be hopeful. Proceeding in search of water he passed Mr Price's waggon in the same predicament as ourselves, then Mr Thompson's and then Thabi's, which had just reached Logaganeng. Mr Thompson's party were able to send for water with their horses and have [already assisted]* Mr Price......* As the waggons reach the water one by one we shall, I hope, obtain assistance.

(2 o'clock). The sound of horses' hoofs. A man has arrived from Mr Thompson with two horses, one heavily laden with water. We can now cook and prepare for departing as we hear that cattle are on the way.

(3 o'clock) The oxen have arrived, six of Mr Price's, five of Thabi's and three of my own. We started at sunset, rode till midnight when we were met by a man with a calabash of water sent by my kind wife. After resting the oxen awhile, we rode on till sunrise.

*paper torn in original, words obliterated.

[*Since this journal was written for his daughters, Holloway made light of their sufferings on this stretch of road. Anne wrote a more detailed letter to Emily Stuart, which is quoted in full in Appendix A. In a further letter to her sister she mentions that the guides they had engaged led them astray and confessed later they were ignorant of the road and had no idea where the water holes were. "This was the first time that we had been forced to travel during the blessed hours of the Sabbath."[2]*]

September 8th
The cattle were sent on and in a short time our own oxen arrived and we proceeded to within four miles of the water. The sun being hot and the sand heavy we sent the poor beasts to the water till the cool of the evening when we joined the rest of the party and were grieved to hear of the sufferings of my dear wife and children after our separation.

September 9th
The water of Logaganeng is insufficient for our party. It is procured from a small well and has to be hauled up in buckets and poured out for the oxen, which is a tedious process. We have therefore determined to go on two miles further to Nkanane where there are two wells and the difficulty of drawing is much less.

September 10th
Nkanane. We came here last night and find it in every respect preferable to Logaganeng. We have slaughtered an ox and our waggons are decorated with festoons of meat. Mr Price is gone on to the next place, Banenkunu which he purposes leaving on Monday afternoon.

September 11th
Last Sunday we were forced to travel morning and evening. Now we are enjoying a day of rest, thinking of beloved friends in England and longing to reach the interesting times we hope to find on the banks of the Zambesi. Surely all our toil and expenditure of time in travelling will be compensated for by the abundance of missionary labour.

September 12th

We left Nkanane a little before sunset and rode to Banenkunu (a distance of ten miles). An uninteresting spot with one well, which has been exhausted by Mr Price's oxen before leaving. The water is, however, collecting and tomorrow ours will have a sufficient quantity.

September 13th

We watered the oxen this morning and finding some pits filled with stones and rubbish we cleaned two of them out, and had the pleasure of seeing the water gradually collect. Future travellers will reap the benefit of our labour, though we shall not. We left in the evening and rode for three hours to Malocuai where we found water for cooking with. Soon after midnight we proceeded on our way. While inspanning fourteen of Mr Price's oxen made their appearance, having wandered in search of water.

September 14th

Outspanned about sunrise and met Mr Price's men in search of the rest of his oxen which had likewise wandered during the night. We came up to Mr Price's waggon about midday. Some Bakalagari had brought him some water in eggshells and as our presence could do no good we went on in the evening, promising to send him help, if needful, on coming to the next water.

September 15th

The moon enabled us to travel during the night. It is fatiguing, but with 60 miles without water, travelling at the rate of two miles an hour and the heat during the day so great that the cattle are glad to crowd together under the trees, we can well dispense with sleep for a few nights. When we stopped this morning the people proposed to send the cattle on to the water. This, however, I forbade as the distance to Lotlakane is considerable. They were therefore driven under the shade of some large trees and have spent the day with little suffering. Tomorrow we hope to reach the water early.

September 16th
We travelled well during the night and reached Lotlakane sooner than we expected. The waggon which had caused me much anxiety from the time we left Nkanane broke down within sight of the Palmyra trees. I was taking a sip of water, thinking the difficulties of another stage were at an end, when down came the waggon to the ground, but so gently that no one was hurt. Our other waggon was in front, we therefore walked to the halting place. But alas! The first news we heard was that there was no water. The poor oxen were running about from one pool to another, covered with mud. Our first effort was to clean out the mud from one of the pools, but no sooner had we made a little progress than the cattle came rushing in and made it worse than it was before. To add to our troubles Mr Price's oxen came in, seeking water and then Mr Thompson's horses. It was midday before we could get sufficient drinking water to send back to Mr and Mrs Price and now, late at night, our cattle are driven into the kraal without having slaked their thirst.

September 17th
Roused soon after midnight by the sound of Mr Thompson's waggons. Got up and informed him of the unpromising state of things, and he considerately tied up his oxen. In the morning we all set to work and as our numbers now were more than doubled we managed, after a hard day's work, to clear out all the mud, and the water accumulating rapidly, all the cattle drank freely before dark. A pack ox was sent early in the afternoon laden with water for Mr Price and in the morning his trek oxen were able to follow.

September 18th
Mr and Mrs Price arrived this morning in good health. They had not suffered from want of water as Mr Thompson kindly left them some as he passed. It was not used when our first supply reached them. We are thankful that we are all together again and that a good supply of water is now ensured to us during our stay here. This may be fore some weeks as our cattle require rest and other circumstances combine to render it desirable.

September 19th

As the muddy pool occupied all our attention last week, my poor waggon has been left to lie where it fell. I have slept in it each night to keep away the wolves. One was driven away the first night and another last night. This morning I was roused by one pulling at the yokes. I fired the only bullet left, which I was sorry for afterwards, as a troop of zebras came at daylight within gun-shot of the waggon.

September 20th

Today has been spent in splitting dry Palmyra trunks and cutting them into suitable lengths for a hartebeest house. The trees stand 60 feet high and upwards. The trunk is composed of fibres resembling those of the cocoanut and may for aught I know be used for the same purpose. Being closely bound together by the bark, the whole must possess considerable strength. The fruit is the size of a small orange but is almost entirely stone, covered with a thin coat of pulp resembling in flavour a stale bun. The stone, or shell, contains the vegetable ivory.

September 21st

Put up the frame of my hut using two slender trees growing $2^1/_2$ feet apart for the door posts. The branches spreading over the top of the hut cast a shade over it.

September 22nd

In the absence of the usual thatching material I have used Palmyra leaves. There are numerous bushes that have sprung up from the seeds, but appear unable to shoot up into trees. These have supplied me with my thatch. A hartebeest house resembles a thatched roof placed on the ground. It is easily constructed, will stand any weather and is very convenient for a short sojourn. The dimensions of this one are 15 feet by 12 feet with a window covered with calico at each end and the door-way in front. Collecting material and building have occupied only three days.

September 23rd

There are now five encampments. Thabi and Mr Price on our left and Mr Thompson and Dr Holden on our right. Dr Philip used to say that a missionary on coming to Africa should blot the word "comfort" from his vocabulary. I have not done so yet, and have endeavoured to make our present position comfortable. Our two waggons look to the west and the tent is pitched between them. Near the door of the tent stands a fine mimosa tree, under which we have shade the whole day. Here are lying tools of various descriptions for repairing the waggon. On the right of the waggons stands a pretty tree, under the shade of which is fixed the coffee mill. Then comes the sheep kraal at the extremity of which are two spreading trees, under which are the kitchen, dormitory and working place of the men. Opposite and forming the third side of the square is the house which we designate Palmyra Lodge and a little back is another tree to which is fastened the corn mill. The fourth side opposite the tent and waggons is open, giving us a view of the pits where the oxen are watered.

September 24th
As Mr Thompson's party intend to leave on Monday and we shall in all probability not meet again, we invited all the friends to dine together in our little hut. Nine persons sat down about sunset. The first course was soup made with Crimean vegetables and curry with rice. Second, cold roast beef and compressed potatoes and sausage meat pie. Third arrowroot pudding and stewed dried fruits. Tea followed immediately.

October 13th
We remained at Lotlakane till this afternoon, fully engaged in mending and painting the waggons and other needful occupations.

On the 30th of last month a baby was added to our party, obliging me to give up handicraft for a time and act as the doctor. Everything was favourable and Mrs Price and the child are doing well. At the close of the month Thabi went on to the Zouga to purchase grain from the Baharutse. Soon after starting this afternoon my unfortunate waggon ran into a hole, damaged the new axle tree, the wood of which was admired by everyone who saw it. It was cut from the centre of a fine camelthorn tree. We travelled till late very briskly.

October 14th

We rode this morning for four hours. Passed several Palmyra trees but saw no game. Indeed we find less now than we did during the early part of our journey. The scarcity of water is probably one cause of this. We have had another good ride this evening which will enable us to reach Nchokotsa early tomorrow.

October 15th

Started soon after midnight. The waggon gave signs of failing and at last came down as at Lotlakane. However, knowing that we could not be far from Nchokotsa we left it and all went on in the other. It was still dusk when we caught sight of the salt pan, and it is not to be wondered at that Messrs Oswell and Livingstone on first seeing it mistook it for Lake Ngami, which they were then in search of. We outspanned before the sun rose. The spot looked dreary enough, the water was brack, and had a peculiar disagreeable taste besides which was, however, removed by keeping it in a vessel for some time. One tree alone seemed suitable for a new axle, but after cutting it down and working at it for some hours in a burning sun, we found it so eaten by the ants as to be useless. Happily a waggon belonging to Sechele came up in the afternoon and as it was empty I borrowed it to bring the goods from the broken waggon. This enabled me to bring the crippled *Experience Tower* to our encampment. In the meantime Mr Price proceeded towards the Zouga, Nchokotsa water having no charms for either man or beast.

October 16th

We have enjoyed a quiet Sabbath. Our afternoon service was interrupted by a thunder storm which entirely changed the aspect of things. The atmosphere was cooled, our vessels were filled with pure water, the cattle no longer drank at the brack pools.

October 17th

We took an early breakfast and Sechele's people kindly continuing the loan of their waggon, we proceeded towards the Zouga.[*] Preferring Dr Livingstone's route, we reached the river early in the afternoon, having

[*] Now known as the Boteti

travelled only eleven miles. When Dr Livingstone passed, the river I am told was dry. Now there is a broad though shallow stream with the banks covered with reeds, but no trees. There are plenty of wild fowl and I shot two for supper.

October 18th
Sent Moriegi to Mr Price, who is higher up the river, to request him to purchase some mealies [*corn-on-the-cob*] for me from the Baharutse. After much walking selected a tree for a new axle. Wading in the river after wild fowl finished the day's work.

October 19th
Squared and brought home the axle wood. Willie, who showed symptoms of fever while at Lotlakane, has been very ill and still causes us much anxiety. We get very little sleep at night from his restlessness.

October 20th
Worked for some time at the axle and then rejected it, finding it unsound in the centre. I have cut down and brought to the waggon with a team of oxen a curious tree which seems very tough. The bark is covered with excrescences, each one tipped with a thorn. They look like large bird's claws.

October 21st
Busy with my strange piece of wood. It promises to answer well. Willie is still very ill. He has evidently got the country fever. Drs Holden and Belgrave pronounced Lotlakane a very unhealthy spot. Lizzie there first complained of heat and weariness.

October 22nd
Mr Price and Thabi arrived this morning, having gone a round of some fifty miles after leaving us at Nchokotsa. They have suffered much from mosquitoes. Mr Price is covered with sores from them. They had to make fires every night round the cattle kraal while the poor oxen stood in the smoke as a refuge from mosquitoes and their attacks.

October 23rd

It was pleasant meeting again and spending a Sabbath together after the scattering of our party. Willie continues ill and Mrs Price is suffering from pain in the side.

October 24th

We have got everything ready for starting, but I am so completely worn out with work and sleepless nights, that I have determined to stay tomorrow and rest a little.

October 25th

The wild fowl are now very wary and it is difficult to shoot them. We have had them during our stay here for breakfast, dinner and supper. We have not succeeded in killing any game besides. A fine giraffe came one day towards our waggons, but turned off before he got within gun shot. It was a curious sight at night to see the Makharikari fishing with lighted bundles of reeds on their shoulders and spears in their hands.

October 26th

Crossed the Zouga and went on to the Kobe [*Koobe*], a distance of nine miles.

Found it better than we expected from Dr Livingstone's description. There were two pools, one of which we cleaned out for the cattle. We dug another for our own use, which soon filled with very good water. Shot a dove, prepared and cooked it immediately in Eastern style, which Willie enjoyed exceedingly. Lizzie is poorly and I fear has the fever.

October 27th

Started after breakfast but the jolting of the waggon increasing Mrs Price's pain in the side, we returned. Thabi and the sheep were far ahead of us, and it was thought best for them to proceed. Thabi's waggon was to have followed them but Rasalina having killed a zebra it is detained till tomorrow.

October 28th

Mrs Price is better today. We started early in the afternoon and have reached the neighbourhood of Ntwetwe. There is good grass here, and the country is well covered with trees. The cattle feeding near the three waggons at sunset would make an interesting picture.

October 29th

Six hours were taken up this morning in crossing the saltpan Ntwetwe. Not a tree was to be seen. It looked like an arm of the great desert. As we approached the other side we found the ground softened with rain which had recently fallen, and at length we discerned in the distance Thabi's waggon first in a quagmire. We turned to the right to what appeared firmer ground. Going to Thabi's waggon I found that they had got into the mire last night, and being unable to extricate themselves, they had remained there the whole night. In the morning they unloaded the waggon, dug away some of the mud from the wheels and drew it out, but no sooner had they reloaded and inspanned than it sank again on one side. It seemed a hopeless affair and I had just thrown off my coat and taken a spade when the shouts of the people attracted my attention and I saw our large waggon sinking in a similar manner. Running back I directed the other two waggons to turn more to the right. Mr Price's, which was last, got out on that side but the other passing over treacherous ground sank deep on one side and became fast. The powerful oxen of the large waggon pulled nobly through and went on with Mr Price's waggon to a clump of trees in the distance. Rain coming on softened the mud and enabled Thabi's oxen to pull his waggon out, but on returning to the other one we found it sunk so deep on one side as to threaten to upset should it get in motion. We were therefore forced to dig away on the other side. The rain increased our difficulties, and after breaking the disselboom and the trektow we were forced to unload the waggon. It was dark before we mastered our difficulties, and drew our crippled waggon to the encampment.

October 30th

Although rain has fallen during the night no pools are formed except on the salt pan, which are too brack to be used. Mr Price and Thabi, fearing to be in difficulties from want of water, went on. As rain continued to fall during the day the oxen have not suffered from thirst.

October 31st

Having worked for several hours during the night we had a new disselboom ready by nine o'clock and after a little hindrance following a wounded zebra we started and soon came in sight of the first baobab tree under which Dr Livingstone outspanned [*Chapman's Baobab*]. It is indeed a noble and wonderful looking tree, but so unlike ordinary trees in its general appearance, in the colouring of its boughs and the manner in which they shoot out from the main trunks, that it looked more like a monster tree planted with the roots upwards. The leaves were only just forming and I really think that a bunch of carrots cut in halves, and the root nicely trimmed, would if exhibited with the powerful microscope of the Polytechnic give a good idea of this baobab. We found some of the fruit on the ground. It is like a gourd, full of seeds the size and shape of tamarind stones. The white pulp covering the seeds is the part eaten. It has a pleasant acid flavour. We reached the water early in the afternoon and found Mr Price and Thabi encamped under another baobab [*Green's Baobab*].

Proceeding in the evening we came to another water, but as there is no grass and it is reported to be a lion country we have tied up the oxen and propose travelling early tomorrow. As it is cloudy and no one saw when the moon set, there has been a great dispute as to where the sun will rise tomorrow. Some of the men seem quite bewildered.

November 1st

Travelled without any track over heavy ground, fatiguing to the cattle. Came to good water about sunset. There are several baobabs all with single stems. They look very strange [*Baine's Baobabs*].

November 2nd

Rain falling during the night has made the ground wet and heavy. In the afternoon we passed a village of Masaroa, whom Dr Livingstone calls Bushmen, and outspanned near the water under a baobab in blossom. It had a large, white flower. The Masaroa very much resemble the bushmen in appearance, but their language is quite distinct. Mr Price has had great difficulty in getting through the heavy sand. At last his front ox fell down from exhaustion and his waggon breaking, he was brought to a standstill for the night.

November 3rd
This morning was spent in mending and re-packing Mr Price's waggon and as some of the oxen are missing we are reluctantly detained another night.

November 4th
The Masaroa having found our lost cattle, we travelled for about an hour when, coming to a pool in the middle of a wood, we outspanned during the heat of the day, but the oxen becoming scattered in the forest, we were detained for the rest of the day.

November 5th
After a short ride we came to the village of Horaye, of whom Dr Livingstone speaks in his book. His son Mokantse is a fine looking man, but for some reason or other he is unwilling to give me a guide. We saw Dr Livingstone's old guide Shobo and gave him some tobacco in remembrance of his deeds. I, however, felt no inclination to seek him as a guide. The people all insist upon it that there is no water beyond and that the fountain at Maila is dry. The appearance of the country however belies them and starting a little before sunset, two guides soon followed us, although they still persisted that we should find no water. We travelled by moonlight through heavy sand, and at length entered a wood which greatly increased our labour, as we had to cut down many trees and frequently to take the waggons one by one through damp and heavy ground. Our large waggon having to wait frequently for the others, did not reach Maila till day break. The rest came in one by one. There is water enough both for ourselves and the oxen.

November 6th
A Sabbath day's rest was much needed after the work of last night. There is good grass for the cattle and the men are much cheered with our prospects.

November 7th
Kaisa and his people left this spot some time ago. Their garden land is very extensive and, finding two *lekika*, we have stamped a quantity of mealies. This is quite a treat and providential for there is nothing that

Lizzie during her illness has desired more than boiled mealies. We intended proceeding this afternoon but the oxen did not come in till late.

November 8th
We left Maila this afternoon. Travelled for some hours over heavy sand and through rather dense wood. We outspanned for a short time and then leaving Mr Price and Thabi, went on to the water.

November 9th
The other waggons came up to us this morning and we prepared to proceed together in the afternoon, but as our cattle have not made their appearance they have got the start of us. Their cattle drank up most of the water and there is only about a pail full of dirty water remaining. We fear that Moriege, who went after the oxen, has lost himself.

November 10th
This morning two men went out in search of Moriege and the oxen. He was found and brought in by one of the men while the other drove the cattle to drink at the last water. It appeared that the cattle had fed not very far from the waggons, but that when it was time to bring them in the man drove them off in a different direction, wandered about till he was bewildered, then wisely kept the oxen together till he was found this morning. In the meantime we dug out the pool and got water enough for the sheep and by digging through a rock Setloki procured clean and cool water for ourselves. This was the last of a series of pools where, by digging, water may be found at any time of the year.

Holloway Helmore's diary stops here.

Communication was naturally becoming increasingly difficult and we must assume that he continued to record their experiences and movements, though the remaining pages were never received by his daughters. Perhaps they were destroyed by the Makololo when they ransacked his wagon and pilfered his belongings. Two letters, however, written by Anne to Olive and Annie after leaving KhamaKhama, but before entering the Mababe Depression have survived, which gives us more information about this stretch of their journey. We take up their story from the letter to Olive, quoted here in full:

"North of KamaKama
November 24th 1859

My darling Olive

It is now your turn to get a letter from me but I fear it will be a long, long time before you receive it for there are few opportunities of sending or receiving letters now. We have had none from you since the May ones, which overtook us at the Matlaring, just beyond Kuruman. I am afraid the next has been forwarded by way of the Matabele. If so, I do not know when we shall see it, for it is likely to be long before we have any communication with that mission. However, we must be patient and the letters will perhaps be doubly sweet when they do come. Although I long to hear of you I do not feel anxious about you my dear girls, we daily commit you to the care of your Heavenly Father and He never disappoints those who trust in Him. I hope that you, dear Olive, are setting the Lord always before you and endeavouring to act as in His constant presence. Now is your time to prepare yourself for future usefulness - and your character as well as usefulness will depend very much on the use you make of present advantages. As the eldest of the family you will have a strong influence over the rest, and seek especially to guide dear Anne and Emily in the way of life. Make it your business to seek their conversion, amongst your daily prayers with your mother's. Let them ascend together to the throne of grace. I look forward with delight to the time when we shall be all united again, but still I think it is your duty to remain in England as long as you can, you may never be there again.

You see we have not yet got to our journey's end, it is a long journey indeed, but we have had so many hindrances, sometimes from the waggons breaking, sometimes from cattle wandering, sometimes from fatigue, drought and other causes. We have already been 20 weeks on the road and shall be three or four weeks yet. Six weeks ago dear little Willie was taken ill with fever and for several days we scarcely thought that he would recover, the fever was very high with delirium. It was a full month before it eventually left him. At times he seemed to be getting over it, then it would return. He was reduced to extreme weakness and mere skin and bone, it made me sad to look at him, but he is getting well again. His appetite is good and today he is playing on the bed with Selina and Henry for the first time.

A fortnight after Willie had been taken ill dear Lizzie was seized with fever and erysipelas in the back but she too is getting well now, so you see dearest Olive you have much to be thankful for. Selina and Charlie (as we call him) are well and all send their love to you all.

I need not tell you much about our journey as you have Papa's journal. The country, almost ever since we left the Bamangwato has been quite flat and mostly covered with forests of Mopane and other trees. The Mopane is a very elegant tree. The leaves, of a light delicate green, fold together and hang down, shaking about with the slightest breeze, giving an idea of coolness which is very pleasant on a hot day. I will enclose a few Mopane leaves. We meet with some beautiful flowers. I often wish it were possible to transport them to you, white and lilac are the prevailing colours but sometimes yellow and scarlet are to be seen. Few of them have much scent alone, but about sunset their united fragrance is delicious.

Monday November 28th:
Lizzie is getting well rapidly but Willie is still so weak on his legs that he has to be carried about as an infant, however, as his appetite is good and he is becoming quite lively I hope he will soon be as strong as before.

Yesterday dear little Eliza Price was baptized by your Papa. We had a pleasant English service, it was quite a treat in the wilderness. The Bechuanas were present as spectators and seemed interested. Papa has service in Sechuana regularly every Sunday. Mr Price is learning the language but cannot preach in it yet. Our cattle, at least some of them, have been lost ever since last Monday. Four men were absent seeking them three days and nights and returned with some of them, without having tasted food all that time. They lost their way, which is very easy to do as the country is covered with forests and thick bush. Now another party is out after the rest of them, this is their third day. We have had no road for many weeks, some of the party have to go before sawing down trees and chopping bushes to make room for the waggons to pass and after all we frequently become entangled, so it is very slow work. There are no wild beasts here but elephants and occasionally troops of wild horses [*zebra*]. These latter we sometimes manage to shoot, they are excellent eating and so is the gnu.

December 26th:
A happy Christmas to you my children! It is now nearly a month since I laid down my letter to you, dear Olive, yet strange to say, we are only five miles nearer to our journey's end than we were then. I told you that a party of our men had gone out in search of some of our oxen which had been stolen by the Masaroa (or Bechuana Bushmen). They returned on the fourth day with all but three, one had been left sick on the road, the other two, fine large hind oxen the Masaroa had killed and eaten. It was a great loss but there was no redress for it and as our pools were almost dried up we were glad to go forward. As we proceeded we found the country more and more dry, and at last we were brought to a complete standstill for want of water. One waggon was unloaded and sent back with all the casks, Mackintosh bags and vessels we could find to bring water; all the oxen, sheep and all the men excepting two were sent back likewise and what little water still remained divided amongst us who stayed. This was only enough for drink, there was none to cook with and before the waggons arrived, which was two days and nights, we were so weak from want of food that the children and I could scarcely walk. The weather was at the same time extremely hot, the thermometer at 8 o'clock in the morning stood at 96° [*F*] and in the middle of the day at more than 105°. Papa and the two men who remained went out in the evening in search of water and travelled all night but they could find none. I forgot to say that Thabi stayed with one of his men and they too searched for water, for we were unwilling to go back if there was a possibility of getting on. However, all the pools were empty, so we were most reluctantly obliged to retrace our steps, but by this time the ponds we had left were dried up too, so after travelling a day and a night and until 9 the next morning the poor cattle were so exhausted with thirst they could go no further and we were compelled to unyoke them and send them on with the sheep and most of the men to the nearest water. We hoped that they

would return that night and take us on but day after day, night after night passed and neither man nor oxen came and our sufferings were again very great. I was most anxious about Lizzie who was still weak from her recent illness. I thought she would have fainted when I had not a draught of water to give her. One afternoon about 4 o'clock Papa set out with two men taking our Mackintosh bags and returned about half past 9 next morning with a supply of water. When they arrived they were so exhausted that they dropped on the ground unable to speak. Papa looked so ill that I was quite alarmed. They had walked 38 miles and carried the water 15 miles. Having found water parties were sent in succession each night to return the following one. Fancy every drop of water we had for drinking, cooking or washing ourselves brought a distance of 30 miles going and coming. At length on Sunday December 11th we were aroused very early by a heavy rain. We spread out a sail and caught enough to replenish our water vessels. This was indeed a shower from heaven, it revived our languid spirits and filled us with thankfulness to Him who had remembered His promise to His servants (Isaiah XLI verse 17). We now hoped to go on but the clouds passed away, the pools remained empty and the oxen having come, we rode back 15 miles to the pool from which we had been obtaining water. It appeared that on leaving us with the oxen and sheep the men had set off for KamaKama but losing their way did not get there till the following night and our two poor little calves, unable to walk so far in such hot weather, were left behind to perish and also our entire flock of 24 sheep and lambs were lost through the carelessness and indolence of the man who was driving them and have not been heard of since. This is a very heavy loss indeed.

    I must now say a few words about your coming out, for there are so few opportunities of sending letters to you now that I do not like to delay writing on that subject. We are not sure if the Directors will allow a grant for your schooling for two or three years. If only two you will have to leave school next midsummer, for we cannot afford to pay for you and you will have to come out by any suitable opportunity that Dr Tidman may find. We should like you to come by the missionary ship but I think that will not be till 1861 so I hope you will be able to stay at school another year. You will find it pass quickly enough. But as we do not know how it may be I shall give you a few directions in Anne's letter, they will be useful to you whenever you come. Both Papa and I have written on the subject to Aunt Emily and she will correspond with Dr Tidman and let us know the result. When you come out Aunt must please write to Mr Thompson to meet you at Cape Town and likewise to the Berry's [*relatives in Cape Town*]. I dare say they can spare you a room in their house, if not they will arrange with Mr and Mrs Thompson. You must remain at Cape Town till you hear from us, there are some very nice people there. If you should have any money to lay out before leaving England you will like to purchase books. I send you the titles of a few which I think would be very valuable: "Life and Times of Countess of Huntington", "Life of Mrs Fry", "Memoirs of Charlotte Elizabeth Adelaide Newton"…… Lizzie says I am to tell you to bring some comfits; little baskets that we may have a Christmas tree the first Christmas you are all at home.

Your sisters and brothers send warmest love, so does Papa. The God of love be your friend…… my dear child. Your affectionate Mama, Anne Helmore."[3]

This is the last communication which has survived from the Helmores. Anne was eagerly looking ahead to their three daughters joining them in their new home; by the time Olive and her sisters received this letter, their parents were already dead.

We have to rely upon Roger and Isabella Price to tell of those fateful ensuing weeks. Isabella also kept a journal on their journey.[4] She wrote daily until Letlhakane. After this she did not write anything until Friday January 13th, when she covered events since the birth of their baby daughter Eliza. Therefore, though the first part is repetitive, it portrays this part of their journey from her viewpoint.

"Friday January 13th, 1860

Well, how many weeks have passed since I closed my journal last. Little did I then think it would be so long before I continued it. What shall I say of the past?

We went on to Lotlakanne, ourselves starting first, though we arrived last, in consequence of the wandering of our oxen, and some of them were actually five days without water.

When we arrived at Lotlokanne, [*sic*] we found that our oxen must have several days' rest before we could proceed. Moreover, Mr Helmore's axle-tree had broken again and required to be mended. This was a pretty place, full of Palmyra trees, and we pitched our tent under the shade of a large tree, determining to halt here. Mr Helmore built a pretty little hut, and as it was thatched with Palmyra leaves, it bore the name of *Palmyra Lodge*.

I could linger long at this spot, sacred now to me, for after we had been there eleven days, my precious child was born (September 30th). I was ill about twenty-four hours, but was graciously sustained, and was surrounded by the greatest attention and kindness. Mrs Helmore spent the night with me in the waggon and her generous attentions afterwards were of a kind I hope I shall never forget. The people have given Baby the name *Mosari ia tsela*, the Woman of the Way.

We went on pretty comfortably, only that Mr Helmore's axle broke again, and he had great difficulty in getting wood for another.

We now began to have some thunder storms which made the air damp; this gave me cold, first inflammation in the side and cough, and then I had a gathering [*abscess on the breast*], from which I suffered most intensely. I tried many things to disperse the swelling and inflammation but at length when it became very bad, I used cold water and gutta-percha; this brought it to a head. The morning it broke was a high day with me, though I was obliged to send for Mrs Helmore to assist me.

During all this time we were graciously dealt with, for wonder of wonders, Roger had been so successful as to be able to purchase a cow, yielding a good supply of milk, so that my darling baby did not suffer at all from my indisposition; on the contrary she seemed as healthy as was possible. Her papa used to feed her, indeed, Roger is most fond of her and she of him.

Well, after a time I got strong again and was able to nurse Baby without any artificial assistance.

We went on from the Zouga, when two of Mr Helmore's children were taken ill with fever; they suffered long and gave great anxiety to their parents; however, after a time they recovered, and are now stronger than they were before.

We came to KamaKama, where we got rains, and proceeded from there, getting water almost every few hours. We went on, getting water every day, till we came to a pool, where we were sadly detained by the straying of our oxen; several men went off in search of them, and they were away so long (I think four days and nights) that we became very anxious about them. When they returned, we found they had suffered much from hunger and they had not found all the oxen; three of Mr Helmore's had been stolen.

While at this pool (which now bears the name of "Baby Pool"), we dedicated our little one to God in the ordinance of baptism. The service was performed by Mr Helmore (in English) in our tent. After the service we gave all the men cake and coffee. Many friends were thought of then. Baby wore the robe Miss Mackness gave me, and the cap Mrs Hughs gave me and the shawl Mrs Livingstone gave me, and the petticoat Mamma gave me, things she has never worn since.

After having been detained at this place very long, we at length set off again. We went on to another pool, where we took in water, and again to another, where we filled all our water vessels. Mr Helmore was before us. We were on our way to the fever ponds, though with no road and no guide, when we came up to Mr Helmore. We found they had neglected to fill their water vessels and had not a drop of water. They had been suffering very much. We gave them some, when they refreshed themselves. But what was to be done, how could they proceed. They knew not the way, and as to water, where should we find any?

The masters and men all held a consultation and after commending the matter in prayer to our Heavenly Guide, they determined that Thabi's wagon should be unloaded and go back with all the oxen for water, taking all our water vessels. Meantime, 2 of the men should be sent forward to seek water. This was done. I cannot tell you how glad we were to get the water when it came, for as we had shared ours with the Helmores, it ran out and we could scarcely keep up our spirits. However, Roger and I are never low-spirited at the same time

Well! No water could be found. Mr Helmore traversed the country night after night, and the men went in various directions but no water. What was worst of all, Konati found the fever ponds also without water. There was no alternative, we must either perish or turn back.

A gloomy Sunday morning was that when we set out on our return, since we could not suffer ourselves to perish. We travelled night and day, as long as the oxen could bear it, passing empty pools on our way, for they had by this time dried up, till we came to Baby Pool, where the water had also dried up. Here we halted and sent the oxen on to water at the next pool - alas for this, we hoped they would return in the evening, instead of which we did not see them again for a fortnight. The men were tired and slept, the oxen took their own course right away to Kama Kama. The sheep wandered likewise. Of the oxen, 3 perished, with Mrs Helmore's calves. Mr Helmore's sheep have never been found, a nice little flock, principally ewes. This was sad indeed. The men returned all safe and well, this was cause for thankfulness and they had not fared badly, as they had met with plenty of game.

During our stay at Baby Pool we suffered much from want of water. We husbanded what we had as much as possible. Oh, I shall never forget going one afternoon to Mrs Helmore's wagon. The dear children were crying piteously and they had no water. Poor Mrs Helmore was so weak from privation she could scarcely be kept from fainting. Mr Helmore had determined to walk a distance of 40 miles that night to obtain water. We spared them a little of ours, though we knew not when we should get more. Mr Helmore performed his journey and to see the joy of the children when they got plenty of water, it was truly overcoming. Little Henry said: 'how happy we are now Papa has brought us water.'

Mr Helmore found water nearer, so that now we were able to send for it, though it seemed rather precious to hear a poor man had to walk 30 miles for every drop of water we had. Oh, none can tell what a precious thing is water to those who have been deprived of it. The day the Helmores suffered so much the temperature stood at 107° in the shade.

At length the men and oxen returned and we went back to the next water, well placed at being near that element once more, muddy as it was. This was a small piece of water and we sent our oxen still further back so that the water might hold us out, and very providentially the very morning that we filled our vessels with the last of the water, there was a heavy rain which refilled the pool.

As soon as the rain came, we determined on retracing our steps back again to Baby Pool, where now the pools were filled of delicious water.

Here we spent Christmas Day and now we made a fair start for the 'Fever Ponds.' When we came to them we found no water in them, but we found water soon after.

Then we came into a forest as dense as could well be imagined. Roger and his men had to spend three quarters of their time in chopping down the trees. After three days hard work they determined to send the oxen to water. The men said 'to go back for water we know is far and to go forward cannot be much further and if we perish we will not turn back.' So off they went, all of them, leaving Roger and me quite alone, feeling not a little anxious both for them and ourselves. They took a small quantity of provisions with them and a little water and set off in excellent spirits.

Well! We proceeded to measure out our water for so many days as we thought it ought to last and tried to keep up our spirits, remembering that the very hairs of our head were numbered - when to our joy on the morning of the third day we saw the oxen with Konati, but the other two men were not there. The oxen had wandered back to water and Konati had followed them. The others had gone on.

We were now obliged to go back to water. Here we joined the Helmores again, and were detained some long time for want of water. We now proceeded upon the plan of not venturing on till we had someone to spy the country.

While we were sitting waiting for rain, I was taken ill with fever and diarrhoea, which have weakened me very much."

There is a further break in Isabella Price's journal, and she did not take up her pen again until a week after their arrival at Linyanti.

1 Personal collection (Original in L.M.S. Archives)
2 Personal collection Anne Helmore to Elizabeth Garden, 22.10.1859 (Original in Transvaal Archives, A551)
3 Personal collection, Anne Helmore to Olive Helmore, 24.11 to 26.12.1859 (Original in L.M.S. Archives)
4 Original in the L.M.S. Archives, also published in *Isabella Price, Pioneer* by her niece Maud Slater,

CHAPTER SEVEN

Linyanti, 1860

Oh Providence, how mysteriously art thou dealing with us

The missionaries and their party plodded on, across the Mababe Plain, chopping trees as they went to clear a path for the wagons. At one stage they were eight days in a forest with no water and two of their men endured ten days without food or water, seeking oxen that had wandered away in desperate search of that precious liquid. "In the same forest for four days we had to be entirely dependent upon water that the Bushmen could suck out of hollow trees, where it had been standing I do not know how long. It was more like water from a dunghill than anything else; still we were glad to get it and only wished there were more of it,"[1] Roger Price afterwards said.

Eventually, at the end of January they arrived on the borders of Sekeletu's domain. It was customary practice, and a mark of courtesy, to await the chief's permission before entering his territory. In this instance, Chief Sekeletu kept the party waiting for several days before he sent word that they should proceed to his capital, Linyanti.

Faced with a large area of tsetse-infected country, they travelled through the night, driving the oxen as hard as they could; this fly, deadly to animal and man, is less active at night. They managed to get through just as the sun came up. When they arrived on the banks of the Chobe River they were assisted by Sekeletu's men, who took their goods across in canoes. On 14th February 1860 they reached Linyanti; they had at last come to the end of their long, perilous journey.

We shall return to Isabella Price's journal for the next part of their story:

"Linyanti, February 21st (1860).

We were travelling more than a fortnight, getting from our last resting place to this town, where we arrived on the 14th. Nothing of any particular interest occurred on our way till we came near to Linyanti, when we were met by a large body of men, sent by Sekeletu, who helped us through the rivers.

We came through the tsetse country unhurt. We rode as fast as we possibly could during the whole of one night and then came to the Chobe, where our wagons were taken to pieces and towed to the opposite side. We then had two days' journey to this town, across another river on our way.

An ox was slaughtered for the people who assisted us, and noisy indeed were they about it. For my own part I was poorly during all that last journey. Dear Mrs Helmore took Baby quite away from me and nursed her at night as well. This was a great relief to me.

This is a most unhealthy place. Never shall I forget the miseries of last week. As I lay in the hut, almost suffocated with the heat and crowds of people surrounding our every way. We were literally mobbed by the people and the noise that they make is truly deafening.

The king has paid us several visits, each time bringing with him a host. The Makololo do nothing. They have a tribe serving them, the Makalaka. These do all their work. The chief has seven wives. They do not live with him but each lady has her own house. Their houses are very neatly built around a large court and all enclosed with a fence. The Makololo are much cleaner in their person than the Bakwenas. The more respectable parts of the community wear a piece of drapery tied gracefully over one shoulder. The king's wives and many other ladies wear at their legs heavy brass rings. Poor creatures, they give them severe pain. They like beads - earrings, bracelets, etc. in profusion.

We find it very difficult to deal with the people. Our supplies having run low, we wished to purchase of the people native corn, goats, etc., but no, none of them will sell. We have made Sekeletu and his wives presents and in return have received oxen for slaughter and a little corn, but we should much prefer to barter fairly with the people.

Nothing has been heard here of Livingstone and the people have formed no plans for removing to a healthy country, so that our course is rather obscure. Sekeletu wishes us to remain here till Livingstone comes. Mr Helmore is quite desperate. I am quite put out about it, because every day one or other of the men is being taken ill and the place, I am sure, will not agree long with any of us.

Sekeletu seems quite jealous of me. He saw Roger the other day getting something for me and he said: "You were sent by your wife, you are the servant of a woman." Then he wishes Roger would not always eat with me, but let them eat together. We do not find it as Livingstone described it - the women ruling the men - far otherwise.

March 3rd

All are now down with this nasty slow fever, with the exception of Roger and myself and Konati [*Bechuana oxen driver*]. Everyone of the Helmores, poor things, so that one cannot help the other. Molatsi [*Price's Bechuana driver*] and Monatse [*Price's Bechuana leader*] we found when we arrived here quite safe, which much rejoiced our hearts. They have both, however, been ill all the time they have been here and last evening, after severe struggling, Molatsi breathed his last. Oh, we are very grieved. When the other men return home and carry to his friends the sad tidings of his death alas, how will their hearts bleed. He had been so faithful to us of late and of dear Baby he was so fond which made me like him none the less. Roger and Konati attended his funeral, which took place a few hours after his death.

"No useless coffin enclosed his breast, nor in sheet nor in shroud they laid him.

But he lay like a Mohican, taking his rest With just a kaross around him."

Sekeletu has sent me a girl for a nurse maid and a comfort it is indeed to me, as my hands are not so tied. Baby seems very fond of her and now I can devote my time to the poor invalids.

March 7th

As Roger went to look round at the invalids this evening, he found dear little Henry cold in death. He communicated the sad news to his father, who bore the trials with marked calmness - his mother has not been told. Oh, how fond she was of him - and a sweeter child there certainly could not be. Roger had the dear little fellow removed at once and sewn up in a piece of carpeting. He was hastily buried by the side of

Molatsi. Oh, how I wish we could get away from here, especially for our Baby's sake. She looks pale and does not seem so well as she did. Roger too is feeling low.

March 8th
Today I have been ill myself and dear Baby too - and have not been able to help the others at all.

March 9th
Oh, providence, how mysteriously art though dealing with us. My own sweet little one has today taken her flight from us. I saw a change in her countenance this morning and determined to keep her in my arms altogether. She took no food yesterday and this morning refused the breast. Wine, however, she took well.

Roger suffered much this morning from oppression of the chest and just before mid-day wished for a cold sheet. I refused help at first, as I saw my precious one was dying, but on finding it really needed I laid her on the mattress for a few minutes while I tended Roger. She turned her head and gave me a look, then to the other side and gave her Papa a look. I seized her to my bosom and gave her a press. Then, laying her on my lap I found her eyes were fixed and she ceased to breath.

I immediately washed her and dressed her in that dear little night gown which Mama gave me, and in which we always liked to see her. Then I wrapped her in two pretty karosses given her, the one by Mrs Hughes, the other by Mrs Thomas, sheepskin, beautifully draped, and the precious little bundle was laid in the grave by the side of little Henry. [*She was little more than 5 months old*].

Oh, I do feel lonely tonight. My little one was pretty, very pretty and her disposition very sweet. She was much beloved and noticed by all the people. When I think of her sweet little face beaming with smiles upon me - I feel it is hard to part with one so precious, and yet she is now a little angel, spared from all the evils of life. I did not murmur - I feel I can say "Thy will be done", but my heart bleeds at the parting. My heart's desire is that I may become more holy and devoted to the service of my Master.

March 10th

Today have busied myself with the invalids. The Helmores lie in a wretched condition. The servant maid they had will do as little as she possibly can. Mrs Helmore is almost unconscious, so weak that I have been obliged to feed her with a spoon. Selina is evidently near death. Some of the men are dangerously ill. Ah, these are scenes which make me almost rejoice that my precious one passed away so soon and so sweetly. Hers was a happy little life and I love to think of her peaceful death, though little did I expect such an event so soon.

March 11th

Again waited upon the invalids. Mrs Helmore very ill through the night. I have some hope of her recovery. This afternoon dear little Selina died. One of the men went into the tent and found her lying close to her father, quite dead. She too was hastily buried. Roger, though very weak, sewed her up in a quilt and she was laid by the side of our darling. So, dear Baby lies between the brother and sister.

Thabi too, the native [*teacher*] who has accompanied us, died this evening, a few hours after Selina and was buried by her side. His death when known at home will produce quite a shock, as he was a most estimable man and highly respected by all who knew him. His son had been dangerously ill, and to see his devotion to him, it was truly pleasing. Now five of our number have been called away. Who will be the next? That passage of Scripture 'Be still and know that I am God' has much calmed me today.

March 12th

This morning when I went to the tent I found Mrs Helmore dying. Her husband, who seemed almost indifferent when the children died, was sitting up by her side and asked her if she still breathed. Ah, she breathed not much longer and half an hour after, her spirit had fled. She was wrapped in a long strip of calico (after a Moracain fashion) and she too was borne to the tomb. Poor Mr Helmore seems wonderfully calm, but there is a certain sort of indifference to everything manifested by most in this fever. They just lie like sheep and sleep except when extreme restlessness prevents them - then they seem too wretched to think of anything but their own suffering.

March 14th

Ah! How my heart sinks within me - Roger is seriously ill, delirious, [*barely conscious*] and when I came from the Helmore tent and then later at witnessing [*the suffering of the men*] I [*try to*] open my heart to Roger. He notices nothing and seems indifferent to everything, thus I am quite alone and have no one to whom I can unburden my feelings but my heavenly Father is very gracious and left upon me the light of his countenance.

May 26th

I think I am just now recovering from a long and severe illness. Poor Mr Helmore is no more, so his two poor orphans are now in our charge. He had recovered from his fever and was getting quite strong but on visiting Sekeletu, who was down with fever, the return walk was too much for him and threw him into a fever again. Oh, it was sad indeed to see him borne to the tomb. He was the truest and sincerest Christian. He slept for many hours and it proved to be the sleep of death. He too was bound in calico and buried by the rest of our little company. The old man who drove Mr Helmore's sheep [*Setloke*] has also breathed his last several weeks before Mr Helmore so that now there lies in the grave 8 of our small company. Mr Helmore's two dear children Lizzie and Willie of course live with us. We intend to take them to Cape Town and there see them safely, we hope, to board a ship for England. This was promised their father just before he died. It has been quite a charge for Roger to pack so many wagons and to have all the responsibility of attending to Mr Helmore's goods as well as his own and the poor fellow has suffered so much all the time. Ever since [*the beginning of*] May he has been unable to touch a mouthful of food and has suffered from violent sickness.

As we had to wait for a guide before we could proceed on our journey and we thought as we were all so ill, we should not do amiss to come with our wagon and spend a few days out of town. The chief [*of the village*] here is very kind and he presented Roger with an ox and one of his wives has given us corn and milk. Our guides, we hear, have arrived at Linyanti so we leave here tomorrow and have 2 days' journey before us.

We have been robbed most fearfully of late whilst the packing of the wagons was going on so that now we have only just enough things to use and scarcely that. As we require the help of the Makololo at the rivers, we of course feel so much at their mercy indeed. They could detain us here altogether if they wished. The consequence has been that Roger has had to part with almost everything in his possession to Sekeletu, even to our tent. Sekeletu is a most inveterate beggar. Still we shall be glad to have done anything if we can but get away from this unhealthy place.

Nothing has been heard from Livingstone. The Makololo have formed no plans for removal to a more healthy country; there is no healthy district anywhere in this part of the country. Roger and I do not know what it is to have a day's health. Eight of our number have already died. These facts have made our duty seem [?clear] to us, that we ought to remove south as quickly as possible. We do hope to start this week. I think none of our friends would know us, we are so reduced. Roger is so thin and pale and he looks more like a dead? than a living one, and I am so thin that I am obliged to plaster my poor bones and have lost the use of my legs."

These are the last words that Isabella wrote, in a small neat hand, her words closely packed onto thin sheets of blue writing paper. The rest of their story is obtained from the letters and reports of her husband, Roger Price.

Firstly, to supplement the details given by his wife Isabella, when they arrived at Linyanti they were told that Sekeletu was away hunting. An ox was sent to them for slaughter and on the third day the chief himself appeared. Sekeletu, still a young man of about 22, was suffering from leprosy. No word, he said, had been received from Livingstone. Livingstone had left Linyanti in November 1855, promising to be back with his wife and the 110 men he had sent to help him. Now, more than four years later he had not returned, nor had he sent word of his whereabouts. Sekeletu was angry. He refused to move, Price said, or even point out a healthy spot where the missionaries could settle and wait for Livingstone.

"You are the doctor," he told Holloway, "and we must not be separated. You must settle here with us." Reluctantly they set about building temporary houses, in the hope that Livingstone would soon arrive.[2]

The following Sunday Holloway went the short distance to the chief's k*gotla* (meeting house and, in practice, the local community hall) and preached. Another week went by and on the Sunday Holloway again held a service for the Makololo people. During the ensuing week, with the exception of Roger and Isabella Price and one of their servants, all were laid low. The first death, that of Molatsi, occurred little more than two weeks after their arrival. On the third Sunday, Price went up to the town and conducted a service, but returned feeling ill. During this time, although quite ill themselves, Roger and Isabella managed to tend to the sick.

"On the evening of 7th March," Roger afterwards told Olive, "I went round to see if I could do anything for my all but helpless friends before retiring. The poor dear children were sleeping together on a mattress just behind my hut; and your dear Mamma was lying beside them on a cushion, also asleep. Your Papa also was lying a few yards off and the men all scattered over the place like so many logs of wood, unable to help themselves or each other and I was but very little better. I went to see the dear children; I put my hand on each forehead, when I came to dear little Henry I found him cold, he had slept the sleep of death. I immediately went and told your Papa who took very little notice of it, but requested me not to tell your Mamma that night that her 'darling pet' was no longer. I took him out and laid him in the tent and wrapped him up for the grave."[3]

He recalls little of Selina's death, though he buried her. As Isabella said, he was very ill at the time. Anne Helmore, Price said, accepted her end stoically. Holloway had recovered sufficiently to sit with her a while. She told her husband that she had no desire to live, she was tired of this world of sorrow and pain and wished to be with Christ her Saviour.[4]

After Anne's death Holloway, Lizzie and Willie improved considerably. A few weeks later, about the middle of April, some messengers arrived from Matabeleland with post. They were ordered by Sekeletu to leave their bag of post on the ground at the border and return immediately, having been told that the missionaries had not yet arrived.[5] Holloway's and Price's anger and distress can well be imagined when they discovered that the messengers had been sent away without their having been given a chance to give them letters to take to their loved ones. Holloway immediately went up to the town to see Sekeletu, who was said to be ill.

He returned feeling very tired and unwell. Over the next few days his condition steadily worsened. Realising his end was near, Roger helped Isabella, who was desperately ill herself, into Holloway's tent.

"We entreated him to tell us what his wishes were with regard to his children and property. He listened attentively to what we said, and after a while he seemed to become willing to speak. But alas it was too late, he had lost the power of speech....... It was impossible to understand what he said."[6]

By asking him questions they were able to ascertain that he wished them to take Willie and Lizzie to the Cape Colony and put them on board a ship, to be united with their sisters in England. The following day he lapsed into unconsciousness and thirty five hours later he died.

"All these I wrapped up and consigned coffinless to the silent tomb with my own hands, with the exception of my own child, which died in the arms of its mother whilst she sat by my bedside as I lay in a wet sheet. Never have I seen so much Christian courage, patience and zeal for the Christian cause displayed as in Mr and Mrs Helmore amidst all that they suffered, both on the journey and at the Makololo. But oh! what a morning the 22nd of April was to me when I followed Mr Helmore's remains to the grave. What a responsibility then fell upon me and I myself was at the gate of death."[7]

There were strong allegations that the missionary party had been poisoned by Sekeletu. He had not been out hunting when they arrived, Price was told by one of the chief's own attendants, but had been in his hut. The ox which had been slaughtered for them the day after their arrival was poisoned by the chief himself, as was the beer with which they had been supplied. The debate as to whether those who died did so of fever or poison was kept alive by Price long after he left Linyanti, despite the acceptance by the London Missionary Society, upon Livingstone's advice, that it was fever. This question has never been resolved. To this day there is no doubt in the minds of the African people of whatever tribe, the Makololo included, that they were poisoned. The question is fully dealt with in Chapter Ten.

The events of those last unhappy weeks at Linyanti are best told in Roger Price's own words, in his subsequent report to the directors in London:

"...... After Mr Helmore's death I forthwith began to make preparations for returning to the south, although I was so weak that I was obliged to be carried or led about from box to box and packing for a couple of hours in the morning would lay me up completely for the two following days. However, I managed to get all ready by the end of May. Up to the time of Mr Helmore's death the Makololo were pretty quiet, whether we lived or died they did not trouble us much one way or the other. But when he died and I began to prepare for going away, then began our real troubles. By day things were taken before our eyes, by force if they were not delivered up willingly, and by night stealing by wholesale; my clothes that I had been wearing during the day were stolen at night from the foot of my bed. When I was ready to go away, Sekeletu came and without any ceremony took possession of Mr Helmore's new wagon and a host of goods of his and mine. That being taken he demanded two front and two hind oxen, wherewith to train others; then he compelled me to remain and let my men train oxen for him. All my guns and ammunition, both tents and a host of other things were taken whilst I was still at the town. One day I was lying on the ground hardly able to move, when messengers came from Sekeletu demanding some more goods before I could go away. I said if they did not let me go soon they have to bury me beside the others. I was simply told that I might as well die there as anywhere else.

At length on 19th of June we left the town accompanied by His Majesty in his new wagon. In the evening we reached the river of Linyanti, and on the following day all the remaining goods were taken over in canoes. That being done a message came to me from Sekeletu to this effect: that now the goods were on one side of the river and the wagons on the other and that they would remain so until I went over and delivered up all Mr Helmore's goods. I remonstrated but in vain, I was like a lamb in the lion's mouth. A great many of my own things also I had to deliver up. Three cows also and several oxen were taken at that river. Having thus got a good draining there, I proceeded to the Chobe. I took out all my goods ready for crossing and then a message came to me, that Sekeletu had hitherto only got Mr Helmore's goods and that now he must have mine. After a good deal of pleading, I was allowed a few things for the journey, such as a couple of shirts, a vest or two, two or three pairs of trousers, an old coat that I had worn in England about two years, an old pair of shoes which I had on, etc. Then my wagons were crossed. Already they had taken all my bed-clothing with the exception of what was just sufficient for one bed, for the other we had a karross. But before my oxen could cross the Chobe I must needs deliver up one blanket.

Every grain of corn which I had for food for the men they had taken, and for all these things I did not get even a goat for slaughter for the road. These were my prospects for a journey of upwards of a thousand miles to Kuruman.

Having at last succeeded in getting my oxen through and secured some Makololo to be guides through the tsetse, on the 26th June I set out after sunset and travelled through the night to get out of the tsetse district.

Having found that the road we had taken in going to the Makololo was impracticable on account of drought, I struck across the country to southwest, to the River Mababe and there to the Tamalakane, intending to follow that river down to Lake Ngami. Before I arrived at the Mababe, however, Mr Helmore's old wagon broke down completely and I could do nothing but take the few things that were in it and put them into my own and the native wagon.

Alas, when will this dark chapter end? On the plain of the Mababe on the evening of the 4th July, Mr Helmore's two children, my own dear wife and I met together for our evening meal, when we entered into conversation about what we had seen and suffered; and feeling that we were beginning to breathe again the free air of the desert, we admonished one another to forget the past and think of our mercies; for we felt that we had still what might through the mercy of God bring us within reach of help.

My dear wife had been for a long time utterly helpless, but we all thought she was getting better. She went to sleep that night, alas! To wake no more! In the morning early I found her breathing very hard. I spoke to her and tried to wake her; but it was too late. I watched her all the morning, she became worse and worse and a little after midday, her spirit took its flight to God who gave it. I buried her the same evening under a tree, the only tree on the whole of the immense plain of the Mababe. This was to me a heavy stroke but God was my refuge and strength, a very present help in trouble. Such things are hard for flesh and blood to bear, but God knoweth our frame, and as our day is so is our strength. With a heavy heart I left that place on the following day and crossed the Mababe, still having some Makololo who had engaged to guide us until we could get Bushmen. These we found on the southern side of the Mababe. The Makololo then turned back, having, as we learnt afterwards, given full instructions to the Bushmen to take us into the midst of the tsetse and then run away - this they faithfully did on the following day. However, having fixed my position as nearly as I could under the circumstances I guided myself by means of the compass to the Tamalakane which I followed down to the Zouga.

Whilst travelling on that river the spokes of one of the wheels of my wagon broke and I had to borrow a wheel from Lechulatebe, the Chief of the Lake, to take my wagon up to his town, where I made new spokes, which I am happy to say have brought me safely this far. Whilst doing that, however, my oxen began to die one after the other, and when the wagon was ready, my oxen were done for. Out of 44 head of cattle with which I entered the tsetse, I have today three. Thus I was fixed at the lake, having nothing wherewith to buy an ox or even food for myself and the two dear children - to say nothing of all the men. We had to be entirely dependent on the tender mercies of Lechulatebe, and we had no hope of getting away unless some trader happened to come from whom we could get help.

At length, after I had been there a little more than a month, I heard of my dear friend and brother Mr Mackenzie, who was then on the Zouga, intending to follow us to the Makololo, little knowing what had taken place.

I immediately got a canoe and went down the Zouga to meet him. He returned with me to the town, taking his own wagon up. He had also a quantity of goods for Mr Helmore and myself and with these we were able to purchase as many oxen as sufficed to take my wagon. Meeting with my dear friends Mr and Mrs Mackenzie was to me like a resurrection from the dead. I can never feel sufficiently thankful for their kindness to me and the two dear children.

Of course there was no alternative but to retrace our steps to Kuruman. As I was coming down the Zouga I met a man who had just come from the Mababe where I had buried my wife. I thought, when I had put her poor body in the ground it would be allowed to mingle with the dust; but no! The horrid cruelty of the Makololo had not yet been satiated. When they left me they went and disinterred the body of my dear wife, cut off her face and took it home with them to be exhibited in the town. These, my dear Sir, are some of the doings of the Makololo; and the agony of soul I have suffered, you can more easily imagine than I can express...."[8]

Why did Sekeletu behave so appallingly towards the departing remnants of the party? One reason may have been the evil influence of one of their party, Mahuse. Mahuse was from Kuruman and a friend of Thabi, who expressed a wish to accompany the party. He was well known as a man of bad character and Moffat had recommended that he should not go. Holloway, however, thought Thabi's influence would be of benefit to the man. Mahuse abandoned the party soon after their arrival and went to the Makololo village, where he was treated as a celebrity. Price was convinced that it was he who persuaded the weak and gullible Sekeletu that when someone died it was customary in Bechuanaland for the chief in whose country the death took place to take possession of all his goods. Sekeletu must have known that this was not true, but the idea appealed to him and, goaded by Mahuse, he acted accordingly. Another important factor was the influence of the slave traders or *Mambari*, with whom Sekeletu was dealing. As they constantly reminded him, the missionaries would insist that he abandon this mutually lucrative trade. Sekeletu was a hard, cruel tyrant, hated even by his own people. True, he was expecting Livingstone and his wife to come and settle with him, which he would have welcomed since Mary would have acted as a shield from any likely Matabele attack. Furthermore, he was anxiously awaiting the doctor's return to cure his leprosy. He therefore had reason to find the presence of these missionaries unwelcome. However, this is no excuse for his hostile treatment of them, nor his abominable behaviour as the remnants of the party prepared to depart Linyanti for their return to Kuruman. His actions defied all the basic laws of hospitality and courtesy in Africa. Strangers always awaited permission on a chief's borders to enter his realm. This the missionaries did and he accepted them. He was therefore honour-bound to ensure their safety, welfare and comfort whilst they were his guests. That he failed in his obligation has been held against him to this day.

Price, Willie and Lizzie and the remaining Bechuana survivors were given food, shelter and protection by Chief Lechulatebe of the Batawana on the banks of Lake Ngami. There is no doubt that without his help they would have perished. Here Lizzie and Willie, who was quite ill with fever, were put under the personal care of the chief's head wife. Price lost track of time but they must have been there for about six weeks.

The incredible story of how John Mackenzie came to the rescue is one of strange coincidences; surely providence played a part. He has left us a detailed description in his autobiography, *Ten Years North of the Orange River*, from which the following is drawn.

Unaware of these grievous events, he and his wife, three months into her second pregnancy, left Kuruman on 25th May 1860 to join the other missionaries at Linyanti, taking in a separate wagon the rest of the Helmore goods, tools and additional supplies. They journeyed well along the same route, through Kanye and Shoshong, and found the remnants of the Helmore camp at Letlhakane. Still in the dry season, they crossed the Zouga [Boteti], then the Ntwetwe Salt Pans. Again here they found evidence of the previous missionaries' journey; broken wagon parts and, on a baobab, Price's initials. For many months, however, there had been no news either from or of the Helmore/Price party. On 16th August they arrived at Masarwa, Mokantse's village where his brethren had stopped on November 5th the previous year and where they were refused guides. The next day they reached Maila, just south of Khamakhama, a village of Makalaka refugees who had fled from Matabeleland. Here an old Bushman, who had just been to the Mababe, was brought to Mackenzie.

"This old man knows something about the country to which you are travelling," he was told by the chief Putse. "Perhaps what he tells is lies, perhaps it is the truth; I shall have discharged my duty when you hear his story."[9]

The old man proceeded to relate to Mackenzie what he had heard; that the Makololo at Linyanti had killed the headman of the missionary party and his wife; that several little children and others had died; that the other missionary and his wife had left Linyanti and were now on their way south. The chief Sekeletu, they said, had poisoned an ox and some beer and sent it to the missionaries and after their deaths he had seized their goods. "This is the news from Mababe," the old man concluded, while Mackenzie smiled benignly at him; the story was too incredible, it could not be true.

He discussed this rumour with his men and they agreed to ignore it and carry on with their journey and in a few days it was forgotten. He had difficulty, however, in obtaining guides to take them through to Mababe.

"There is no water beyond KamaKama," he was told, "if you wish to go, you go alone." No one would accompany him; they had, they said, seen what happened to the white men who had travelled through that region the previous year; they had nearly perished from thirst.

"Which road do you propose?" Mackenzie asked. They suggested a route to the north-east, in the opposite direction, thus approaching Linyanti in a roundabout way from the Zambezi, "because there is water on that road." The party agreed and guides from the Makalaka were appointed. As they were preparing to go on, Mokantse, the chief of the Bushmen at Masarwa arrived. He had come to greet the missionary before he left, he said.

"There is another road to Linyanti," he added. He pointed to the north-west, just south of the route the Helmore/Price party had taken. "It goes this way and it is quicker than the road you are taking and there is plenty of water." Frustrated and confused, Mackenzie responded by calling together the Bushmen and the Makalaka and explaining his mission and how urgent it was for him to reach his destination as quickly as possible.

"Decide between yourselves which is the best route to take," he told them. A long discussion ensued between the two tribes, in a language Mackenzie could not understand. He retired to his wagon and prayed. Mokantse finally came and announced that it would be best to take the road to the north-west. Mackenzie's men agreed to this route and on the 20th August, with two Bushmen guides, they continued on their long journey.

Following the tracks of the previous missionary party they proceeded for some while and then turned in a more westerly direction, along an undefined track. They travelled thus until late in the afternoon, when Mackenzie realised that they were travelling due west, then turning south, away from their destination. He checked his compass and then questioned his guides.

"Why does not that *selo* [thing] of which you inquire inform you of the direction of the next pool of water as well as tell you where Linyanti is?" they retorted. Toiling through deep sand under a burning hot sun, they travelled for about ten days, then came to a large river.

"Is that the Chobe?" asked Mackenzie eagerly.

"No, it is the Zouga," his guides replied. MacKenzie was angry. He had already crossed the Zouga some weeks previously. His guides assured him that they were on the right road, they would soon be turning north. At a village called *More oa Maotu* they rested for more than a week, then with fresh Batawana guides they proceeded, following the Zouga to its junction with the Tamalakane. The story of the tragedy at Linyanti persisted. His new guides continuously alluded to it. They tried to persuade Mackenzie to go to their chief Lechulatebe at Lake Ngami. Mackenzie was still sceptical; he suspected this was a trick by Lechulatebe to prevent him from going to the Makololo. He cross-questioned the men and found their statements contradictory. Eventually, in exasperation they would say: "If you can't believe what you hear, go to Linyanti and see for yourself."

After leaving *More oa Maotu* they travelled inland for a distance, where the river took a bend to the south. Two days later, on 8th September, they were approached by a couple of men coming up from the direction of the river.

"I come from Lechulatebe," the leader said," he greets you and sends you boats by which you are to cross the river."

"I do not intend to cross the river," Mackenzie replied. "I'm on my way to the Makololo. Present my compliments to your chief and tell him I hope to soon visit him." The men stared in disbelief.

"What can we make of this man," the leader exclaimed, "what shall I say to make him believe?"

"Tell him about the white man in the boat," suggested the other man.

The leader pointed towards the river. "You refuse to believe what everybody tells you. In that boat there sits a white man who says you are his dear friend,"

"And why did you not bring him with you that I might see him?"

asked Mackenzie.

"Because he is sick and tired, and wished to remain," was the response.

Still Mackenzie was reluctant to accept their story. "I am going on to the ford in the river where I shall sleep tonight and rest tomorrow because it is Sunday," he told the men. "If you do indeed have a white man in your boat bring him to the ford and then I shall believe what you say." He presented them with a gift and they returned to the river. Mackenzie proceeded on his journey. Towards evening as he neared the river, he seated himself next to the driver in the front wagon. This was the testing time; he would soon know whether the stories he had heard were true. Suddenly the driver pointed, exclaiming "*ki ena!*" [It is he!] Mackenzie sprang down and walked quickly towards the river. Coming towards him was a European, thin, haggard, dishevelled and shabby. He soon realised that it was indeed his friend and fellow-missionary, Roger Price.

"But can all this that I hear be true?" he exclaimed, grasping Price's hand. The answer was obvious, even before Price whispered: "All is true."[10]

Had the Bushmen and the Makalaka at Maila contrived to lead Mackenzie to Price, despite the former's stubborn refusal to accept what they told him?

One can imagine the deep sense of grief and sorrow that hung over the camp that evening. Ellen Mackenzie wept openly for her two dear friends Anne Helmore and Isabella Price. All the men were subdued, sensing the distress of the three white people. In his weakness and feverish state Price had lost track of time. He had also, Mackenzie noticed, lost his memory and kept repeating himself. Leaving the two large wagons by the river in the charge of their trusted servant Mebalwe, the Mackenzies with Price proceeded immediately to Lechulatebe's village in the small wagon, where Willie and Lizzie Helmore and the rest of the party were waiting. On the way Price related his full, grievous tale.

"But how did you know that I was near at hand?" Mackenzie asked.

He was sitting in Lechulatebe's courtyard one day, when some men who had been to the Bamangwato country returned, Price related. He had listened without interest while they reported on their spying mission and the political state of the country. His attention was suddenly aroused when he heard the men state that at *More oa Maotu* they had seen a white man from Kuruman, a teacher, with a red beard and a span of red oxen and a wife and small child. He was on his way to Makololo country. Price immediately jumped up.

"But that is my friend and brother! I must go to him," he exclaimed. Lechulatebe promptly put a canoe and some men at his disposal and he set off to meet Mackenzie.

Lizzie and Willie gave Roger Price a warm welcome when he returned. They all agreed there was no alternative but to retrace their steps to Kuruman. Purchasing sufficient oxen and repairing the wagons, with heavy hearts they prepared for departure. The men they had brought travelled separately in Thabi's old wagon. We assume nine survived, though we cannot be sure. We know that Carl, Thabi's son, who had been desperately ill with fever did recover and return to Kuruman. Mahuse stayed with the Makololo. The others mentioned in the journals are Moriegi, Lingkomi, Saboknena, Kuisang, the young woman Kionecoe, Monatse and Conate. Molatsi and Setloki died at Linyanti.

On 26th September John Mackenzie and his party left Lechulatebe, expressing with words and gifts their gratitude for his hospitality and shelter. They rejoined Mackenzie's men and the other two wagons at the ford and journeyed along the same route to Shoshong, capital of the Bamangwato, which they reached on 1st December. Here they remained for some time to await the birth of a baby son to Ellen Mackenzie. Resuming their journey in early January, they soon met Robert Moffat on his way up to render assistance. They all arrived at Kuruman on 14th February, 1861, exactly one year after their arrival at Linyanti.[11]

The tragic news had preceded the party to Kuruman. Starved of news from the missionary party itself, they anxiously questioned anyone who had been north. As the Mackenzies had been preparing for departure, Mary Moffat wrote a long letter to her dear friend Anne Helmore, unaware that she had died, with which she sent clothes, shoes and provisions.[12] In June, Jeannie Moffat wrote to Olive, comforting her and assuring her that they shared their anxiety over the lack of news from their parents. A man from Lekhatlong, Khobare had been north and had heard of the terrible sufferings from thirst the party had endured north of Shoshong.[13] In October reports reached them that the party had arrived at Linyanti and that Livingstone was also there and all was well. This joyful news was immediately conveyed to England. The three sisters, starved of news from their parents for almost a year, were reassured.

Soon afterwards, a hunter and trader, Joseph Aarons arrived from the Victoria Falls where he had seen Livingstone and some men from Makololo country and heard of the tragedy. Although many details were inaccurate and incomplete the grievous facts were clearly true. "Would that we could tell you which of your precious brothers or sisters it is, but we cannot hear," Jeannie Moffat again wrote to Olive on 11th November.[14]

News of the death of their parents and siblings would only have reached England almost a year after it had happened. Crushed so heavily, so soon after the previous comforting news, the orphaned Olive, Annie and young Emily were comforted by their Aunt Emily, herself in shock over the loss of her beloved brother and his wife. In their grief they all drew comfort from their deep religious belief, which had taught them to accept whatever had been pre-destined.

The atmosphere at Kuruman when the survivors returned was heavy, everyone was in mourning, stunned by what had happened. Whilst Robert Moffat immediately set about writing a full report to the directors in London, Mary and her two daughters Jeannie and Bessie bustled about, trying to comfort Lizzie and Willie and rebuild the health and strength of the survivors. Many years after, Willie, who was just six years old at the time, was to tell his wife he recalled those days clearly.

"I remember crying into my pillow at night, and either Jeannie or Bessie coming in and holding me in their arms. I remember the dreadful thirst on the journey and also the Makololo beating on our wagon and shouting as we left Linyanti. I remember the wolves [*hyenas*] howling around our battered wagon when we were waiting to be rescued at Lake Ngami and I remember sleeping in the hut of Lechulatebe's head wife when Roger Price went to meet Mr Mackenzie." A reticent man, these memories were too painful for him to be able to talk freely to others.

Roger Price was soon restored to his former robust health and in April he set out for Algoa Bay [now Port Elizabeth] with Willie and Lizzie to fulfil the promise he had made to their father to send them back to England, to be re-united with their sisters.

On 21st August 1860 the two children sailed from Cape Town, "in the care of Mr de Jongh," on board *The Dane*;[15] the same missionary ship that had brought them with their parents and Selina and Henry to Cape Town in August, 1858.

1 L.M.S. Archives, Price to Tidman, 20.2.1861
2 Ibid
3 Personal collection, Price to Olive Helmore, 1.12.1861 (Original in L.M.S. Archives)
4 L.M.S. Archives, Price to Tidman, 20.2.1861
5 Personal collection, Price to J.S. Moffat, 23.4.1861 (Original in L.M.S. Archives)
6 Personal collection, Price to Olive Helmore, 1.12.1861 (Original in L.M.S. Archives)
7 Personal collection, Price to Mrs Stuart, 4.12.1860 (Original in L.M.S. Archives)
8 L.M.S. Archives, Price to Tidman, 20.2.1861
9 Mackenzie, p.158ff
10 Mackenzie p.179ff
11 Smith, p.115
12 Personal collection, Mary Moffat to Anne Helmore, 22.5.1860 (Original in L.M.S. Archives)
13 Personal collection, Jeannie Moffat to Olive Helmore, 11.6.1860 (Original in L.M.S. Archives)
14 Personal collection, Jeannie Moffat to Olive Helmore, 11.11.1860 (Original in L.M.S. Archives)
15 S.A. Archives, Cape Town, South African Advertiser and Mail, 21 August 1861

Chapter Eight
The Zambezi, 1858 to 1863
Where was Livingstone?

Holloway Helmore's first question after he had reached the Linyanti was: "Has Livingstone arrived?" The answer was no, no word had been received from him, or of him. All had expected that he would long since have made his way up the river to the Makololo, as planned.

Where was Livingstone? He had arrived at Kongone at the mouth of the Zambezi on 14th May 1858.[1] His party had assembled the specially designed iron steamer *MaRobert* (so named after Mary; this was the name given to her by the Makololo, as the mother of Robert, their eldest son) and, using it as a pilot to the larger *Pearl*, sailed up the Zambezi to Shupunga.

The next few months were spent sailing back and forth from the mouth of the river, bringing up supplies. His plan was to then proceed to Tette, collect the Makololo whom he had left there in early March 1856, and continue up the river as far as the Victoria Falls. On 14th February 1860, however, the day the Helmore/Price party arrived at Linyanti, he was still at Tette; nineteen months after arriving at the Zambezi.

The biggest of the many problems which beset the expedition, and the main reason for his delay, was that he had discovered the Kebrabasa Rapids were far more formidable than the minor ones he had declared them to be and that the Zambezi was, after all, not navigable at this point. Having declared to the outside world that he had found a way up the river into the dark interior and that these regions were open to commerce and Christianity,[2] Livingstone's consternation and humiliation can be imagined.

Where did he go wrong? As we have discussed in Chapter Four, on his journey to the east coast in 1856, about fifty miles from Tette he diverted from the river, having been told by the local chief that the terrain on the north bank was too rough and hilly and infested with tsetse. He therefore missed this impassable barrier, which was to shatter his dreams and hopes of access to the coast from the Batoka highlands.

When he had made enquiries at Tette he was told that there were a series of strong rapids at Kebrabasa (known locally as Kaora-basa). However, based on the information he was able to obtain and after taking his habitual scientific soundings and calculations, he had decided that they would be navigable for about three months of the year when the river was high.

On 8th September 1858, Livingstone reached Tette and was warmly welcomed by the Makololo men. Although always referred to as Makololo by Livingstone, he conceded in his *Narrative* that there was only one man of that tribe in the party. The rest had been drawn from the other subservient tribes in the area.[3]

Of the 110 men he had left two and a half years previously, thirty had died of smallpox and six had been killed by a neighbouring tribe. "We shall sleep tonight," they told him. "We have been laughed at. People have said that you abandoned us, that you would never come back."

Livingstone began preparations to proceed up the Zambezi to return the men to their chief. Before doing so, however, his nagging misgivings about the rapids prompted him to take a party to go and inspect them. He set out in the *MaRobert* in November 1858; at this time of year the river was low. He was dismayed at the sight that greeted him.

"The lofty range of Kebrabasa, consisting chiefly of conical hills, covered with scraggy trees, crosses the Zambesi and confines it within a narrow, rough and rocky dell of about a quarter of a mile in breadth; over this, which may be called the flood-bed of the river, large masses of rock are huddled in indescribable confusion……. Blocks of granite also abound, of a pinkish tinge; and these with metamorphic rocks, contorted, twisted, and thrown into every conceivable position, afford a picture of dislocation or unconformability, which would gladden a geological lecturer's heart; but at high flood this rough channel is all smoothed over, and it then conforms well with the river below it, which is half a mile wide. In the dry season the stream runs at the bottom of a narrow and deep groove, whose sides are polished and fluted by the boiling action of the water in flood, like the rims of ancient Eastern wells by the draw-ropes. The breadth of the groove is often not more than from forty to sixty yards, and it has some sharp turnings, double

Livingstone's Zambezi journey, 1853 to 1855.

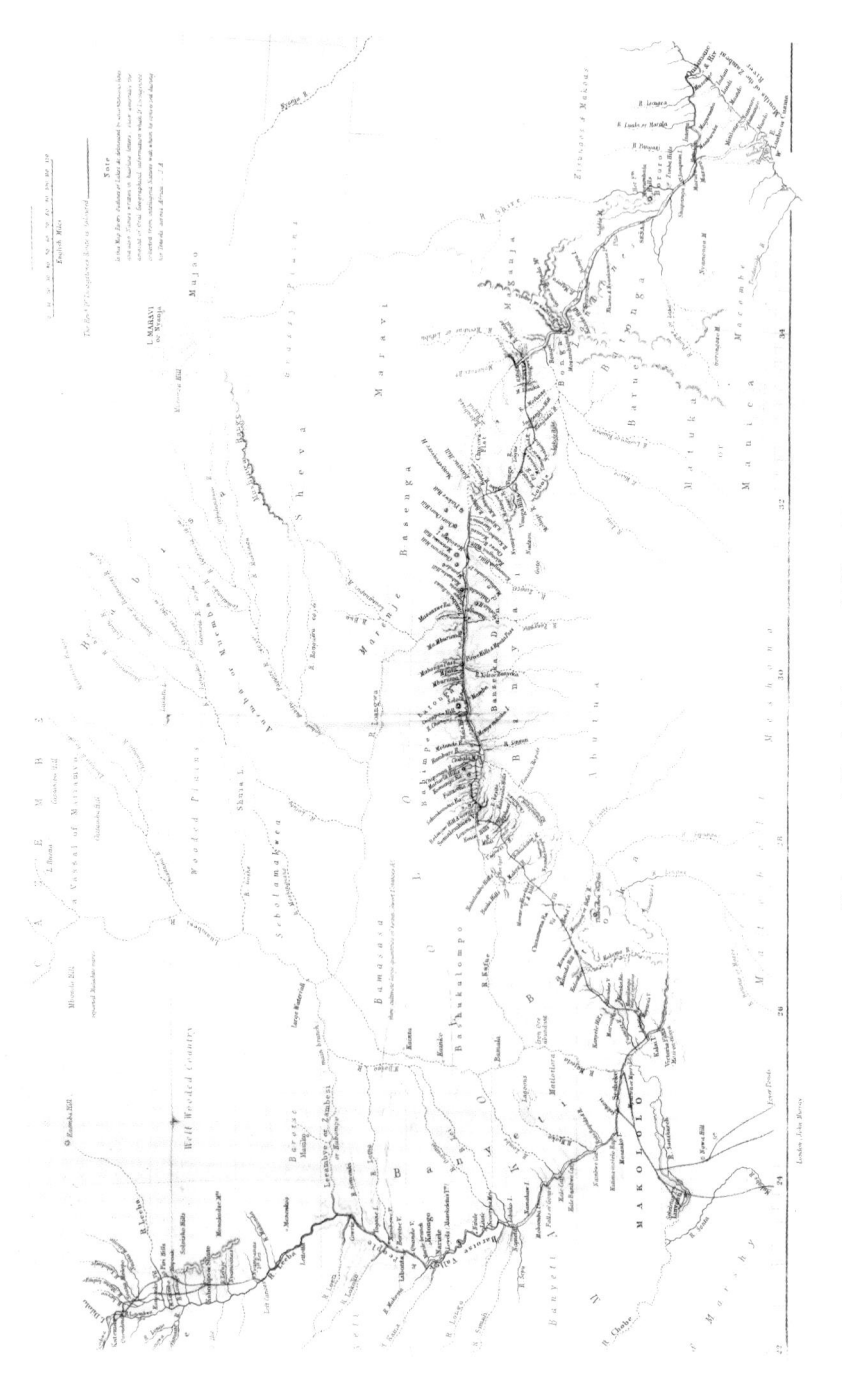

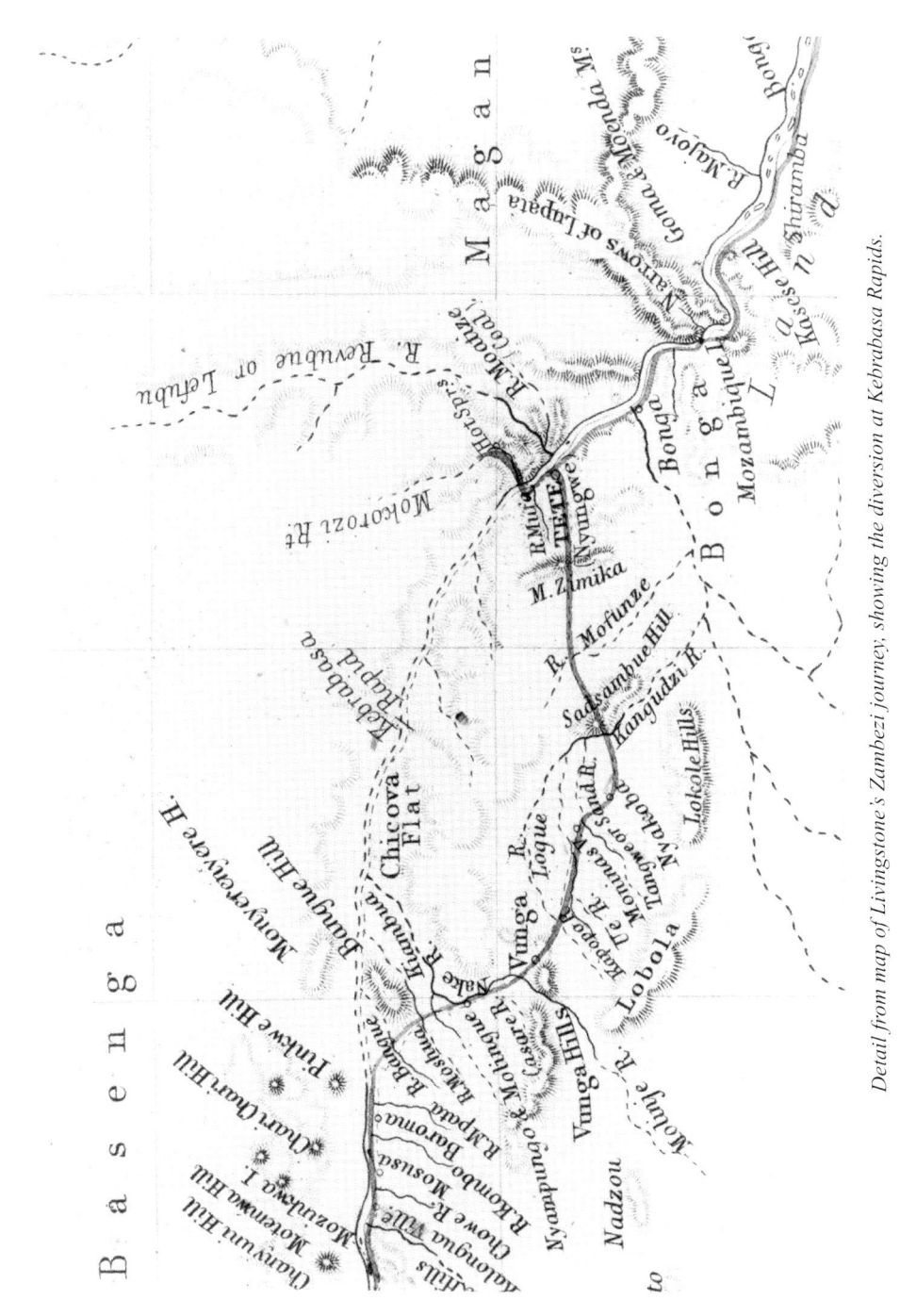

Detail from map of Livingstone's Zambezi journey, showing the diversion at Kebrabasa Rapids.

channels, and little cataracts in it. As we steamed up, the masts of the *MaRobert*, though some thirty feet high, did not reach the level of the flood-channel above, and the man in the chains sung out, 'No bottom at ten fathoms.' Huge pot-holes, as large as draw-wells, had been worn in the sides …"[4]

This was only the first seven miles of the gorge. It was all too clear to Livingstone, as he acknowledged, that he had grossly under-estimated the power of the rapids and that he had been deceived by the opinion ventured by a local man that the rocks could be blasted with gunpowder. He realised that further exploration of the rapids would be necessary and, returning to Tette, he made preparations for a deeper survey of the rapids beyond.

Later that month he set out again with Kirk, the botanist and Rae, the ship's engineer. Ten Makololo men accompanied them, also a Portuguese hunter with his party of men. The latter had hunted in the region and claimed to know it well. Leaving the steamer at a safe spot near where they had already explored, the party made their way on foot through rough, hilly country. They came across some strong rapids, worse than those lower down the river, but Livingstone decided that when the river rose the water here would be smooth. Their guide assured him that no further barriers existed and they commenced on their return journey. After marching for a few hours, however, one of his Makololo men came to him, saying that he had been told that a further cataract, worse than any of those they had seen, existed higher up the river.[5] Exhausted, angry and frustrated as he was, Livingstone would not concede defeat. Accompanied by Kirk and four Makololo men he retraced his steps, whilst the rest of the party continued back to the steamer. Even before he came to this new obstacle he must surely have realised that it was impassable.

> "The slopes of the mountains on each side of the river, now not 300 yards wide, and without the flattish flood-channel and groove, were more than 3000 feet from the sky-line down, and were covered either with dense thorn bush, or huge black boulders; this deep trough-like shape caused the sun's rays to converge as into a focus, making the surface so hot that the soles of the feet of the Makololo became blistered……."[6]

Upon Livingstone's own admission, the Makololo, exhausted and with bleeding feet, told him that they 'always thought he had a heart, but now they believed he had none,' and begged Kirk to intervene, as they thought he had gone mad.[7] Livingstone would not even consider turning back until he had satisfied himself about this last obstacle. The cataract of Morumbua, when they finally reached it, stood between two mountain peaks. Even at 100 feet above low water, the rocks were smooth and worn with huge pot-holes. Livingstone, however, calculated that at full flood the river would rise at least 80 feet. It was as if he was willing the violent forces of nature to modify to his wishes. Unable to admit the true state of affairs to anyone, he wrote to Lord Malmesbury who, with a change of government, had succeeded the Earl of Clarendon as Foreign Secretary in London, and requested him to arrange for another vessel to be sent out to him:

"We are all of the opinion that a steamer of light draught of water, capable of going twelve or fourteen knots an hour, would pass up the rapids without difficulty when the river is in full flood, in January or February," he said.[8]

This is not true. Kirk knew immediately that the rapids were impassable, in fact, none of the men in the party shared his opinion.[9] Perhaps Livingstone, in continuously asserting that the rapids were navigable, was attempting to strengthen his case for a new vessel. In his heart he must have known that this was an insurmountable barrier to the Batoka plateau of the Zambezi. In his journal, on his return to Tette, he poured his despair:

"Things look dark for our enterprise. This Kebrabasa is what I never expected. No hint of its nature ever reached my ears. The only person who ever saw the river above where we did was José St. Anna (Colonel Nunes' nephew) and he describes it as fearful when in flood. This I can well believe... What we shall do if this is to be the end of the navigation I cannot divine, but here I am, and I am trusting Him who never made ashamed those who did so. I look back on all that has happened to me. The honours heaped on me were not of my seeking. They came unbidden. I could not even answer the letters I got from the great and noble, and I never expected the fame which followed me. It was Thy hand that gave it all, O Thou blessed and Holy One, and it was given for Thy dear Son's sake......."[10]

In refusing to admit the true state of affairs to anyone, Livingstone was deceitful. His thoughts now turned to means of saving face and overcoming his embarrassment.

In the months that followed, there is no evidence that he gave Holloway Helmore and his missionary party a thought. Although unaware that they too had postponed their departure for Linyanti till the following year, he had clearly no thought of getting there himself in time to introduce them to Sekeletu.

In all fairness, communication was difficult. As we know, right up to the time that the party left Kuruman ten months later, in July 1859, no word had been received from Livingstone. Apart from the slave trade, there was no link between Tette and Linyanti and it would have been extremely difficult to have sent a message by this route. Despatches to and from the expedition party were conveyed around the coast to Cape Town, for onward transmission either inland or to England. However, even Mary Livingstone, up to the time she returned to Cape Town, had only a vague idea as to her husband's movements.[11] Moffat and Helmore clearly expected that Livingstone would have left the east coast fairly promptly and headed inland, therefore it would have been futile to have sent letters to him by steamer. Their letters were sent overland to Linyanti. In point of fact, between then and May 1860, Livingstone and his party would be spending a lot of time going back and forth between Kongone at the mouth of the Zambezi and Shupunga or Tette.

At this stage, the Makololo men, on learning that it could be another year before they would be able to return to their homelands, suggested that Charles Livingstone should escort them overland. This Livingstone's brother agreed to do. According to Livingstone, however, the men then had a change of heart. Since they had been instructed by their chief to return with Livingstone himself, they feared his wrath if they disobeyed. "I mention this to shew that in all their conduct since they have been associated with me, they have been actuated by intelligent motives,"[12] he wrote to Lord Malmesbury. As we shall see, when Livingstone eventually did set out to take them home, most of these men had a further change of heart and very few did actually return.

Refusing to face defeat over the Kebrabasa rapids, in December 1858 Livingstone left his brother and Baines to carry out further surveys at full flood, whilst he and Kirk explored the Shire. This river ran north from the Zambezi near Shupunga, and Livingstone hoped to find a further passage to the Central Plateau. He found no connection between the two waterways, but despite being subject to attack with poisoned arrows from hostile natives, his thoughts from then on concentrated on exploring this region. He found the soil fertile, with cotton growing prolifically and the climate of the highlands suitable for human habitation.

In March 1859 he made a second excursion up the Shire River and this time reached Lake Shirwa. Returning in May, he found he had other problems.

Livingstone's relations with Africans were always cordial; he seemed able to relate to them easier than to his fellow Europeans. In July 1858, just a few months after the start of the expedition, he had had a serious quarrel with Commander Bedingfield and dispensed with his services, with strong letters of condemnation of the man being sent to London.[13] He took on the task of navigation himself. Now, after his return from Lake Shirwa, he dismissed Thornton for alleged laziness. Thornton, who was engaged to carry out geological surveys, suffered frequent attacks of fever and must inevitably have felt lethargic and sleepy. Whether dismissal was justified or not is an open question.[14] Then, a few weeks later, he dismissed Baines the artist, who had been appointed storekeeper, for alleged theft of goods. These allegations came mainly from Livingstone's brother Charles, and again it is questionable as to whether they were justified. In the December Baines was put on board a steamer at Kongone, having been obliged to leave most of his possessions, including his paintings at Tette.[15] Livingstone used Baines's paintings in his *Narrative,* though in the Preface he merely states:

> "I have to acknowledge the obliging readiness of Lord Russell in lending me the drawings taken by the artist who was in the first instance attached to the expedition."[16]

Nowhere does he mention Baines by name. Thomas Baines was stung by these allegations of theft. After leaving the Zambezi, he returned to Cape Town. From there, in 1860, he joined James Chapman on an expedition to the Interior. The two men sailed up the west coast to Walvis

Bay and from there travelled overland to the Chobe, where Baines hoped to meet Livingstone, but they waited there in vain. Baines subsequently spent the next seven years attempting to have his name cleared. Fortunately, his memorial is not this alleged slur on his character but the many beautiful paintings which he executed on his travels around Southern Africa; including those of the Victoria Falls and of Baines's Baobabs, which he executed on this journey.

Another problem Livingstone and his companions had continually to deal with was fever in the swamps around Tette and the mouth of the Zambezi. Invariably one or more of them was laid low and the cure which he advocated did not always work effectively. Although they seemed to spend much time in this region merely going back and forth between Kongone and Tette, it must be remembered that on occasions the men would be laid up for weeks at a time with fever.

At the beginning of July, 1859, when the Helmore/Price party was setting out from Kuruman for the Linyanti, Livingstone was still on the Zambezi at Tette. Since the vessel he had requested had not yet arrived, he had again put off returning the Makololo to their home. It is doubtful that he knew of the delays and he must have assumed that they were already at Linyanti. At this stage too it is unlikely that he knew that his wife would not be with the party going to Linyanti. It was only on 4th November 1859 that he received a letter from Mary advising of the birth of their baby daughter, Anna, a year previously.[17] By the end of February 1860 we know that he had had no further news from Mary.

Livingstone was making preparations for his third trip up the Shire, upon which he set out in August, 1859. On this trip he reached Lake Nyasa; he claimed afterwards to have been the first European to discover this vast lake, though this was disputed.[18] Livingstone's thoughts were now turning towards colonisation of this region.[19] He found these highlands ideal for European habitation, healthy, with fertile soil ideal for the growth of cotton and easy access to the mouth of the Zambezi and the Indian Ocean.

> "By purchasing cotton from the people on the banks of the Lake and ivory from the traders who annually come past in great numbers from their tribes far in the West, there is a high degree of probability that we could cut [off] the slave trade of a large district at its source."[20]

Despite the unease and jealousy with which the Portuguese were closely watching his movements within and on the borders of their territory, his ambitions for Barotseland were receding; through these newly explored regions he had found a means of overcoming his embarrassment over Kebrabasa.

By the end of October he was back on the Zambezi. The *MaRobert* was by now leaking so badly as to be in constant need of repair and he was still awaiting the lighter launch he had requested. However, his plans had altered for this vessel's use; its first service, he had decided, would now be "the accurate survey examination of the river Rovuma…"[21]

Early in February 1860 Livingstone finally turned his thoughts to fulfilling his promise to the Makololo to return them to their homeland. It was about this time, unbeknown to him, that the Helmore/Price party were nearing the end of their arduous seven-month trek. Due to a bad harvest, however, he found that it would be difficult to obtain food on the long march before the new crop was ready, therefore he delayed his departure yet again.

On 15th May 1860 he set out from Tette; by this time Holloway was dead and Price was preparing to leave Linyanti. He was accompanied by Kirk and his brother Charles, and the remnants of the party who had brought him to the east coast more than four years before. As we know, of the 110 men he had brought, thirty had died of smallpox, six had been hacked to death by a neighbouring tribe and the headman Sekwebu had drowned himself off Mauritius. Of the 70-odd left, relatively few were willing to go back

> "A number of men did not leave with the goodwill which their talk for months before had led us to anticipate; but some proceeded upon being told that they were not compelled to go unless they liked, though others altogether declined moving. Many had taken up with slave-women,…… Some fourteen children had been born to them; and in consequence of now having no Chief to order them, or to claim their services, they thought that they were about as well off as they had been in their own country,"

Livingstone explained.[22] Thereafter, even from those who did set out with him, every night some slipped away and returned to Tette. Before they had passed the Kebrabasa rapids, thirty had turned back and Livingstone was anxious that there would be insufficient left to carry back the many presents he was taking to Sekeletu.[23]

Perhaps, just as he refused a passage back to England from Loanda on the west coast in 1854 in order to return his men to Linyanti, he now felt obliged to do the same. There was no other reason in his mind for undertaking this journey and in fact his companions considered it a waste of time. The trip was notable for the violent quarrels that erupted between the two brothers, leaving a bitterness that remained for the rest of the expedition.[24] Fever, isolation hardship and frustration over delays must inevitably have resulted in frayed tempers.

They travelled six hundred miles and within three months, on 4th August, had reached the borders of Makololo country. From here they could see, in the valley below them, the vapours rising from the Victoria Falls, though this was still more than 20 miles distant from them. Here too, Livingstone learned for the first time of the tragedy that had occurred at Linyanti.[25] They waited here whilst word was sent to Sekeletu, who was at that time residing in the higher, healthier region of Sesheke, in Holloway's old wagon.[26] Sekeletu gave immediate orders to let them proceed without delay. He was overjoyed to see his old friend again; his leprosy was in an advanced stage and he was living the life of a recluse, not allowing anyone to see him but his immediate family. Believing himself to have been bewitched, many people had been put to death and no doctor would come near him apart from one old woman. Over the next few days Livingstone and Kirk dressed his sores, which covered his whole body, and left him in far better condition than they had found him.

Livingstone questioned Sekeletu and his Makololo about the circumstances surrounding the tragedy that befell Holloway Helmore and his party. Naturally he heard a one-sided version of events and never afterwards made any attempt to communicate with the one adult European survivor, who gave an entirely different story. He based his judgement then and afterwards on Sekeletu's story. Writing at length in his *Narrative* about the honesty and integrity of the Makololo, he cited how he made the three-day journey to Linyanti on horseback to collect some mail which had been left for him from Kuruman. There, he said, he found his old wagon intact, just as he had left it in 1853.[27] Nothing had been taken and some of his goods had been removed to the huts of Sekeletu's wives for safe-keeping. How could the Makololo have been accused of theft? He was shown the unmarked graves of Holloway and the other victims. A bitter twist to the tale is that he admits taking from his wagon a supply of the medicine, "which had been lying only a hundred yards from the spot where the Missionaries helplessly perished …"[28] If he was convinced that these medicines would cure the African fever, why had he not advised Holloway beforehand of this fact?

Fulfilling his role as Consul, Livingstone delivered his credentials and a letter from Lord Clarendon addressed to Sekeletu, requesting him to accept Europeans into his territory and hoping for a mutually advantageous trading relationship. Sekeletu's reply was sent by Livingstone to Lord John Russell, who was now Foreign Secretary, with a covering letter dated 6 September 1860, written from Sesheke. The Sechuana original is quoted in Appendix C. Its translation reads:

"Sekeletu rejoices at the words of the letter that has arrived, but the country has disabled him while fleeing from Mosilikatse. He finds great affliction where he is. People perish, cattle perish. Is that not a great affliction! The country (called) Phori and Mpakane (Highlands near the river Kafue) is beautiful, and people might dwell there properly, but how can I live alone? If I lived alone I should not even sleep in it. Had (Mrs L.) MaRobert come, then I should have rejoiced, because Mosilikatse would let her alone, and us, she being a child of his friend Moshete (Moffat). And Sekeletu says to the Lord of the English, Give me of your people to dwell with me, and I shall cut off a country for them to dwell in.

A path towards the sunsetting has already been burst open by Monare (Dr.L.) and a path towards the rising sun he is now bursting open, and the Lord (Queen) assisted Sekeletu by sending the iron ship. Will she not single out some of her people to live with him and hold intercourse? Thus the path would be burst open permanently. Then would there be sleep (or prosperity) to man.

The country of which we think is one of cottons and the Batoka tribes weave it. Subject tribes and the Banajoa also sow cotton and use it.

Let there be friendship with him (Sekeletu) for ever so that we may

mutually feel pleasure.
So speaks Sekeletu"
His finger mark.
Sesheke 9th Septr. 1860.
In presence of Mamire, his finger ( ) mark. [*Sekeletu's stepfather*]
Witnesses: D.Livingstone
J.Kirk." [29]

In the letter enclosing this request from Sekeletu, which had been read out to his council and received their hearty approval, Livingstone makes a strange comment:
"… The Revd. R. Moffat having long been the friend of Mosilikatse, it is universally believed that the presence of any member of his family would secure the Makololo from war. Had his daughter Mrs L. come, they would at once have removed to a country where both cotton and sugar grow luxuriantly. She travelled overland a thousand miles from the Cape to join me here but, hearing that it was impossible for us to ascend in the small and weak steamer at our command, she returned at great expense to Cape Town.…"[30]

Livingstone may not have known where his wife was, but he must have known, as we know, that Mary Livingstone did not travel to Linyanti with the Helmore/Price party after all. Had she done so, they would clearly have been made more welcome and the story may have had a different ending. The importance of her part in this sad story cannot be denied.

Sekeletu was anxious for Livingstone to return with Mary, but Livingstone's thoughts had turned elsewhere. This did not, however, prevent him from leaving Sekeletu with the impression that he and others would be back, via the east coast; also from assuring the British government that the Highlands of the Batoka were suitable for European habitation.[31]

On his return journey, on 10th November 1860, when at Chicova just west of the Kebrabasa he wrote to Tidman:
"On reaching the country of the Makololo in August last, I learned to my very great sorrow that our much esteemed and worthy friends, the

Helmores, had been cut off by fever after a very short residence at Linyanti.

Having been unexpectedly detained in the lower parts of this river until May last, my much longed for opportunity of visiting the upper portion was effected only by performing a march on foot of more than 600 miles, and then I was too late to render the aid which I had fondly hoped to afford ……

From all I could learn the Makololo took most cordially to Mr Helmore. They wished to become acquainted with him - a very natural desire - before removing to the Highlands, and hence the delay which ended so fatally … He told the people subsequently to the death of his wife that nothing would prevent him from going and doing his duty whither he had been sent …

The Makololo are quite ready to move, they are perishing themselves, and should they not depart from these Lowlands soon they will break up as a tribe …"[32]

As the party entered the region of Kebrabasa, Livingstone, fearless and defiant even against the forces of nature, decided to challenge the rapids in their small, light canoes which they had purchased from the Makololo. This frightening experience is best described in his own words:

"A fifteen feet fall of the water in our absence had developed many cataracts. Two of our canoes passed safely down a narrow channel, which, bifurcating, had an ugly whirlpool at the rocky partition between the two branches, the deep hole in the whirls at times opening and then shutting. The Doctor's canoe came next, and seemed to be drifting broadside into the open vortex, in spite of the utmost exertions of the paddlers. The rest were expecting to have to pull to the rescue; the men saying, 'Look where these people are going! - look! look!' - when a loud crash burst on our ears. Dr Kirk's canoe was dashed on a projection of the perpendicular rocks, by a sudden and mysterious boiling up of the river, which occurs at irregular intervals. Dr Kirk was seen resisting the sucking-down action of the water, which must have been fifteen fathoms deep, and raising himself by his arms on to the ledge, while his steersman, holding on to the same rocks, saved the canoe; but nearly all its contents were swept away down the stream.

Dr Livingstone's canoe meanwhile, which had distracted the men's attention, was saved by the cavity in the whirlpool filling up as the frightful eddy was reached. ..."[33]

Though badly shaken and thoroughly drenched, miraculously they all survived. Kirk managed to rescue his canoe and bale it out but he had lost pretty well everything; his clothes, surgical instruments, chronometer, barometer and his irreplaceable volumes of notes and drawings. Was it worth it? Only to Livingstone, perhaps, who could say that he had managed to negotiate the Kebrabasa rapids.

They arrived back at Tette a few days later. The enigmatic Livingstone was now intent upon distancing himself from the Makololo mission.

"… You may have heard, ere this reaches you, of the sad fate of the London missionaries at Linyanti. They were spoken of as in connection with the Zambesi Expedition, though I only knew of their movements so far that they had yielded to my dissuasion as to attempting to enter this river by the sea till it had been explored. I was ready to render whatever aid I could, as indeed I am to every mission intended to spread our common Christianity. …, "[34]

he wrote to the Universities Mission. In this same lengthy letter, written from Tette and dated 29th November 1860, he imparted detailed information and advice for the missionaries about to depart from England, headed by Bishop Mackenzie. There was much scope for missionary fields, not only along the Shire but also amongst the Makololo, he declared, though he casually added that "in some years the flood of the Zambesi is not sufficient to smooth over the rapids of Kebrabasa."[35]

After this he concentrated his thoughts on the new regions of the Shire. Despite his declaration to various people, including the Makololo chief, no further attempts were made to negotiate the Kebrabasa rapids, in full flood or otherwise and the Makololo were left to languish.

Early in 1862 he received a reply from Tidman to his letter of 10 November 1860 with regard to the fate of the Makololo mission. Tidman was clearly angry with Livingstone:

"… The disastrous events which followed the journey of our friends to the Makololo country will for ever form a sad page in the history of our Society, and from the fact of the mission having been undertaken at your instance and upon the strength of your encouragement and also from the fact of your having been connected with dear Helmore by the ties of personal friendship we well know that, in common with ourselves, you would deeply deplore the mournful issue of the expedition. It is indeed a painful aggravation of the case and as you observe, a source of unavailing regret that, at the very time when our friends were dying one after the other from the effects of the fever, you were in possession of an antidote of known efficacy and which might have been applied with success by your presence had aid been available....

There are some statements in your letter which we have been quite unable to reconcile with the ascertained facts of the case. It seems that on reaching Linyanti you were taught to believe that the Makololo entertained very friendly feelings towards Mr Helmore, and that their reason for detaining him at that place was that they might cultivate his acquaintance, whereas, according to the statement of the survivors of the party, Sekeletu positively refused to allow them to leave his place, or to point out any healthy locality where they might await your arrival. Their settling down, therefore, in this scene of death was a necessity forced upon them by the will of a despot against which there was no appeal....... The only way in which we can reconcile the statement of your informants with these facts, is by supposing that Sekeletu and his people... apprehensive of your resentment, should the truth become known to you, purposely misrepresented the case.

We can at present form no definite plans in regard to any new attempt to open a mission among the Makololo and in the meantime our efforts will be rather directed to strengthening the mission in the Matebele country....

Mrs Livingstone is leaving by the mail which conveys this letter and I hope she may be permitted to join you in good health."[36]

Always resentful of criticism, Livingstone was stung to retaliating with equally strong language. Marking the letter 'Private' he responded from the *Pioneer*:

.... "I confess that the statements respecting the treatment endured by the Makololo missionaries are perfectly astounding, yet far from supposing myself proof against misrepresentation I cannot conceive how I could have been so grievously misled as you imagine. If you allow me to state a few particulars connected with our visit I may possibly appear not altogether unreasonable in withholding my assent to the statement so generally received, even should the opinion that the mission ought to be abandoned not be modified.

Sekeletu was labouring under a skin disease when we arrived, which we do not even know but now believe to be leprosy. He was shut up apart from his people and with the exception of his mother and a near relative, no-one was admitted to his presence save Dr Kirk and myself. He had been spirited enough in the belief that the disease had been inflicted by witchcraft for which some influential headmen had been executed, but he treated us with exactly the same cordiality as he did in former years when I was alone.

He was by no means popular and was believed by many to be more deformed by the disease than we found him to be. Some had talked openly of deposing him, which was equivalent to killing him, but from both well and ill affected we received the unvarying testimony that Mr and Mrs Helmore had been highly valued by chief and people. The subject tribes are by no means so tongue-tied there as they are under Mosilikatze, yet not at Shesheke and Linyanti alone did they speak well of our departed friend but on the east coast utterance was given occasionally to expressions respecting Helmore which were particularly gratifying. Dr Kirk who alone of our company understands Sechuana, received the very same impressions that I did.

Molaka, the son of a man who escaped execution in the witchcraft affair by flight to Lechulathebe, had certainly no great love for Sekeletu, yet he spoke of Mr Helmore receiving supplies of meat whenever he asked and when nearly insensible the chief asked him if he needed meat and Mr Helmore shook his head and smiled. The difference of social position to which you refer was not viewed by the Makololo as the missionaries may have looked upon it. Upon speaking kindly of Helmore they often remarked 'he was just like you, a man with a heart', i.e. a kind man.

… Helmore was said to have declared after the death of his wife 'that Price being a child might return, but he (Helmore) never would go back, but proceed onward as soon as I came whither his elders had sent him'…

Only two influential men objected to the whole tribe removing hither [*to the Highlands*] and the general belief was that had he lived a little longer Mr Helmore would have led them to the south east....

It was also very painfully apparent that no feelings of respect were entertained towards Mr Price. I have refrained from saying a word to anyone on this point but yourself. Thus, while Helmore was represented as receiving supplies of meat, 'Price might ask long enough before he got any'.

We never heard a syllable to his (Helmore's) disadvantage, but we overheard one man tell another who had come from Tete [*sic*] that, having gone to Mr Price's wagon while the latter was at a meal he was kicked away and he added that had Sekeletu not been there 'I would have fought with him.'

Some remarks made at a public meeting at Cape Town about binding a man to his wagon, etc. and fortunately unreported in the papers, and a statement about using his revolver with the Makololo at the Royal Observatory before going into the country at all lead me to make some abatement as to the colouring without questioning Mr Price's veracity. It was abundantly clear that he had failed to secure the respect of the chief or his people. This is no justification of any wrong the Makololo may have committed, but it is improbable, if they received no provocation, that they should show so much rapacity towards Mr Price and leave my goods safely in my wagon and in their huts, though the boxes are unlocked....

... there, with his wife, lies at Linyanti and of the whole he [*Helmore*] alone had an object worth risking his life for. There, without a tree within a hundred yards to mark the spot, he rests from his labours, as good and as devoted a missionary as ever left England. I collected a few bones and placed them over his head - there is not a stone in the country but these will soon vanish and his memory will remain only in man's hearts.

I still feel convinced that a flourishing mission might be established..."[37]

About Helmore, despite his comments, he wrote to John Smith Moffat: "Mr Farebrother[*] goes about the country telling at public meetings

---
[*] One of the London Missionary Society's agents

that I am morally responsible for the loss of the missionaries at Linyanti……. Helmore did not write to me even. I think they wanted to do it all themselves and have it to say that they did not require any aid from me. A precious mull they made of it."[38]

In attempting to whitewash his beloved Makololo and vindicate his own part in the affair, he was prepared to blacken others; even those who could not answer from their remote and silent graves. As the foregoing evidence has revealed, nothing could be further from the truth. Holloway Helmore appealed in vain for advice. His big mistake was to place too much reliance and faith in Livingstone.

Livingstone's scathing remarks about his brother-in-law (Price was by now married to Elizabeth Lees Moffat) were equally unjustified and there was no foundation for any except one of the allegations. The incident about firing a revolver was explained by Price in a letter to Tidman dated 4th November, 1861:

"When I went to the Makololo I had two double-barrelled guns which were supplied to me by the Directors and in addition another double-barrelled gun…… I may here state that with one of these pistols, I had to defend myself at Linyanti after having first given public notice to Sekeletu that I should do so. My notice was of no avail and I had to resort to my pistol. Afterwards it was taken from under my pillow when I was too ill and weak to think of anything but the grave. This is one of the many incidents in connection with the Makololo mission which I have not mentioned in public. Some may find fault with my having resort to such means; let such try and put themselves in my position, alone among thousands of barbarians…….[39]"

Despite all the difficulties they had encountered, a year after saying farewell to Sekeletu in 1860, Livingstone wrote to Tidman asking if the London Missionary Society intended to make another attempt to establish a mission amongst the Makololo. If so, he said, "I may possibly be able to render some assistance - My friend Helmore unfortunately neglected to give me any information, and it is to avoid the pain I suffered in consequence of being left in the dark till aid was unavailing that I now beg leave to trouble you."[40]

In the same way as Livingstone was prepared to overlook Sekeletu's ill treatment of the Makololo mission, the latter seemed prepared to overlook the contemptible way in which Livingstone had treated him. Although clearly angered by Livingstone's long absence with his men, he welcomed him back gladly in August 1860. He had brought only a handful of the men he had taken away but this seemed irrelevant. He was anxious for Livingstone's medical skills to treat his leprosy and, more importantly, he was still desperately anxious that Livingstone should return with his wife to settle amongst them. His tribe was dying out in the marshes. There were few true Makololo left by then. It is doubtful whether Livingstone had any genuine intention of doing this. What is clear is that he still led the chief to believe that he was opening his country to the east coast and that Europeans would be coming to settle on the Highlands. Sekeletu had cut his tribe off from all trade links from the south, declaring that the Doctor would soon be opening more lucrative routes to the coast. When these did not materialise the Makololo were left stranded. He had promised to return with his wife Mary, but did not do so. He betrayed them. With the death of Sekeletu three years later, the once mighty tribe that his father Sebituane had led north, looking for paradise, disintegrated in the fever-ridden marshes. This episode is dealt with later in this book.

Mary Livingstone was finally re-united with her husband in January 1862, having left her children in England under the guardianship of Livingstone's parents. She travelled in company with the ladies voyaging to join their men folk of the Universities Mission; the sister of Bishop MacKenzie and Mrs Burrup. Charles Mackenzie and his party of missionaries had arrived a year previously and had chosen Magomero, on higher ground on the shores of the River Shire as a site from which to operate their missionary labours. The next few months were full of tragedy. The Bishop had travelled down to the Zambezi to greet his sister. Constant delays as the *Gorgon* tried to negotiate the sandbanks and then in allowing the passengers to disembark, plus unloading supplies and the new vessel which had at last arrived, forced a prolonged stay by all in the fever-ridden areas. On 31st January, the day that the ladies finally reached dry land, Bishop

Mackenzie, stricken with fever, died a few miles upstream. Two missions to spread Christianity emanated from Livingstone's Central African venture and both ended in disaster.

Livingstone's anxiety about Mary's prolonged stay in the marshes was justified. She was with her husband just three months before she too died of fever, on 27th April 1862. A sad and bitter woman at the end, she openly criticised missionaries, had become cynical about her own faith and had resorted to drowning her sorrows and loneliness with alcohol. To her husband she was a mixed blessing. That he was genuinely fond of her there is no doubt, but he was prepared to abandon her and leave her to fend for herself and their children, for long stretches at a time, whilst he went about what, to him, were more important undertakings.

Mary was buried under a baobab tree at Shupunga. Her husband was stricken with grief, but there were more than enough problems to be dealt with and he busied himself assembling his new vessel, the *Lady Nyasa*. Using this vessel he made further exploratory ventures to Lake Nyasa and the River Rovuma until he received a despatch from Lord Russell in July 1863 recalling the Expedition.

Who was to blame for the tragedy that overtook the Makololo Mission? We cannot point a finger at any one person. Holloway Helmore himself must take some of the blame for not waiting for word from Livingstone to proceed; and for taking his wife and children, even though he did this in good faith. Tidman pointed a finger at Livingstone, but he and his fellow directors are to blame for arrogance, bad and hasty planning and lack of judgement in allowing the expedition to go ahead with insufficient funding and resources. Anxious to be first in the field, they allowed themselves to be carried on the tide of adulation for Livingstone. It is a pity that they did not await the veteran Robert Moffat's sound advice before the new missionaries set sail. There was clearly conflict between Tidman and Livingstone, which added to the problems. Sekeletu must take much of the responsibility. Although there is no firm evidence that he poisoned the missionary party, there is sufficient evidence for strong suspicions. Further, had he allowed them to move to healthier territory until Livingstone arrived, the outcome may have been different. His treatment of Price as he departed was inexcusable. Livingstone, however, despite his protestations, must take the largest share of the blame. True, he was unavoidably delayed in getting to Linyanti but he failed to support a venture that he had instigated. He was well aware of the fact that the Makololo would not have moved out of the marshes without Mary Livingstone as a safeguard. His callous indifference and his subsequent behaviour and comments are unjustifiable.

Livingstone's influence on Central Africa is a lasting memorial. He opened up the area and brought it to the attention of the world and he was instrumental in bringing the abhorrent slave trade finally to an end. His courage, endurance and determination have rightly put him amongst the greatest men of the nineteenth century. However, like all great men and all great deeds, they are achieved at a cost and many paid the price through Livingstone's dogmatic attitude and untrustworthiness; not least the members of the Makololo mission and his own wife, Mary.

On his return to England in July 1864, Livingstone busied himself with further talks throughout the country and with writing another book about his travels. To the sorrow and regret of the Helmore family, he made no effort to call or communicate with them, although he knew Olive and Anne well.

How did the orphaned children of Holloway and Anne fare? They remained under the guardianship of Emily Stuart. Funds were set up by sympathisers and received generous public support, especially in Cape Town and they were further supported with a grant from the London Missionary Society until they had completed their education.

All four sisters then took jobs as teachers or governesses. In August 1877 Anne Sophia, the author's great grandmother, set sail for South Africa with her new husband, Dr Robert Palk. Willie soon followed her and over the next twenty five years the other three sisters joined them. They remained close throughout their lives. Olive never married; she died in May 1919. Anne died in March 1936, at the advanced age of 92. The two sisters, who shared so much in life, lie side by side in the cemetery at Potchefstroom.

Willie, who had survived the Linyanti tragedy, married Elizabeth Aldridge of Birmingham in 1889. The couple settled in Kimberley, the rapidly growing town where diamonds had recently been discovered; just a few miles from where Lekhatlong had stood. Here Willie was the town's leading pharmacist until his death in 1941, at 88 years of age. They left no children.

The other Linyanti survivor, Lizzie, married John Henry at Kroonstad in 1888, not far from Potchefstroom. Alas, she died in childbirth a year later. Her widower then married Emily. Soon after they were married, in 1895, John and Emily were co-leaders of the Henry-Steyn trek, a party of pioneering farmers who finally settled at Chipinga, on the eastern border what of was then Southern Rhodesia, now Zimbabwe. Emily died in 1929, leaving one surviving son. Most of the descendants of Holloway and Anne still live in South Africa and Zimbabwe and keep in touch.

The Makololo mission failed, but Holloway Helmore had not failed. Although Livingstone, not he, was the first to take Christianity to the Makololo, his brief stay amongst them is affectionately remembered to this day and has left its mark. Others followed and took up where he left off. We must also not forget his eighteen years amongst the Batlapin at Lekhatlong, where his mission thrived and prospered. Willie's wife, Lizzie Helmore, on a visit to Cape Town in the early part of last century, recognised a very old bushman from the Lekhatlong area. "Did you know Monare Helmore?" she asked him.

Yes," he replied. "He taught me all that ever I knew."[41]

1 Zambezi Expedition, (2),p.266
2 Livingstone to Tidman, 2.3.1856, quoted in Chamberlin, p.257
3 Narrative.p.156
4 Narrative, pp.53/54
5 Zambezi Expedition, (2),p.294
6 Narrative, pp.59/60
7 Ibid
8 Zambezi Expedition, (2),p.297
9 Seaver, pp.337/8
10 Zambezi Expedition (1), p.63
11 L.M.S. Archives, Isabella Price to her parents, 1.2.1859
12 Zambezi Expedition (2), p.301
13 Zambezi Expedition(2), p.272
14 Seaver, p.346
15 Jeal, p.228ff
16 Narrative, Preface
17 Seaver, p.352
18 Zambezi Expedition (2), pp.338/9
19 Ibid, p.344
20 Livingstone to Lord Malmesbury, 15.10.1859, quoted in Zambezi Expedition (2), p.334
21 Zambezi Expedition (2), p.343
22 Narrative, p.157
23 Ibid, p.159
24 Ibid, p.231
25 Narrative, p.247
26 Seaver, p.375
27 Narrative, p.295
28 Narrative, p.297
29 Zambezi Expedition (2), p.395
30 Ibid, p.391
31 Ibid, p.391
32 L.M.S. Archives, Livingstone to Tidman, 10.11.1860
33 Narrative, p.334
34 Zambezi Expedition (2), pp.359/60
35 Ibid, p.359
36 L.M.S. Archives, Tidman to Livingstone, 5.7.1861
37 L.M.S. Archives, Livingstone to Tidman, 25.2.1862
38 Seaver, pp.376/7
39 Smith, pp.107/8
40 Quoted in *The Dark Interior*, Ransford, p.174
41 Personal collection

Part Two

CHAPTER NINE
On the Missionaries' Trail, 1999
The past and present merge

1. Did they die of fever, or were they poisoned?
2. Where did the Helmore/Price party have their camp at Linyanti?
3. Where are their graves?

These are questions for which no answer has yet been found.

At the end of April 1999, one hundred and forty years after the Helmore/Price party undertook their long trek, four of us set out with a guide to try to obtain answers to these questions.

The idea of following the same course as that of the missionaries had first taken root about three years previously. We felt that to see and experience the conditions under which they had travelled on that long, difficult journey would help us to understand what they had suffered. When we were put into contact with an excellent guide, who not only knew the country well, but also the Helmore story, our objective started to become a reality.

We approached Pierre Craven of African Getaway Safaris with a sketch containing the names of the towns, rivers and water holes which were mentioned in the diaries of Holloway Helmore and Isabella Price. From this he worked out a route which was possible to cover with a four-wheel drive vehicle. This followed quite closely the original missionary trail as far as KhamaKhama. From here the missionaries themselves had to cut a path, yard by yard, through the bushes and forests of the Mababe Plain; it is no better now, therefore we readily accepted a detour. The party consisted of myself, my husband Cyril, our son Vincent and daughter-in-law Chantal, the wife of our other son.

When Pierre called for us, the white Landrover Defender was clean and sparkling; and the trailer was already packed to the brim with tents, camping equipment, cans for extra diesel and water, groceries and provisions, all in small, convenient, ready-to-cook packs; and even a small freezer containing fresh meat. Our baggage, one hold-all per person, was stored in a holder on the roof rack. How different our preparations were, in contrast to the missionary party. They had had to carry large sacks of corn, beans, flour, etc. and rely upon shooting game for meat. We, of course, had no livestock to herd, or draught oxen to inspan and outspan.

"Make sure you carry everything you'll need for the whole journey, especially plenty of sun bloc, batteries, camera film and insect repellent," Pierre had warned, "as we may be far from any shops for days at a time - and don't forget your malaria tablets." As if we would.

Friday 30th April, 1999

By 8.30 a.m we were on our way and soon left the leafy northern suburbs of Johannesburg for our first destination, Kimberley. We made a brief stop at Potchefstroom, to visit the site of the old home where my mother was born and where my sisters and I had spent many happy days in our childhood. Anne Sophia Palk, the daughter of Holloway and Anne Helmore, had built this house and it had been the family home for about sixty years until, in 1955 it was sold. In its place there now stands a large residence for elderly people; Anne would have approved.

We reached Kimberley early in the afternoon.

This town is of special interest to us. It sprang up out of the dry scrub near the Vaal River after the discovery of diamonds in the area in 1867. Holloway and Anne's only son, Willie, who survived the tragedy, came and settled here in Kimberley on his return to South Africa in about 1881, living in the town until his death in 1941. Amongst the early pioneers, he opened and ran a successful pharmacy in partnership with his brother-in-law, Helmore and Aldridge.

No-one visits Kimberley without seeing the Big Hole and that is what it is, its depths submerged in water, black and unfathomable, long since abandoned, having been emptied of its glittering stones. Those stones brought fame and fortune to such men as Cecil Rhodes, Barny Barnato and Alfred Beit. It also brought distress and disaster to many of the resident tribes, as greed and power over-rode ethics, and the British finally gained control of Griqualand.

We stayed overnight at a guest house in the Magersfontein range of hills. This area was the scene of considerable activity in December 1899.

The Boer forces entrenched themselves here during the siege of Kimberley and held out for about two months before Roberts relieved the beleaguered Rhodes and starving citizens.

Saturday 1st May

Our first objective was to locate the site of Holloway's old mission and the town of Lekhatlong or Dikgatlhong, 60 km north west of Kimberley. We were aware that the mission station had been razed to the ground in 1908 by the Cape Government.[1] We also knew that it had stood at the confluence of the Vaal and Harts Rivers, on the north-west bank of the Harts.

We enquired at nearby Delportshoop. The history of the old mission, with its ups and downs of hope and despair, joy and sorrow, is sadly forgotten by most.

"There is a farm called Dikathong on that site," said one helpful citizen, giving us directions. It sounded promising. We located the farm. The farmer himself came in from his fields, a young man, welcoming and friendly, but he knew nothing of an old mission station on the site. He had bought it about ten years ago, he said, as an established farm. However, by studying the surroundings and the river courses, we knew the location was right, it was where Holloway had moved with his people in 1841, soon after his arrival amongst them. The red soil was hard and dry, with sparse typical *Vaalbos* of acacia, or Karroo sweet thorn and buffalo, or *'wag-'n-bietjie'* thorn. A large plantation of cacti spread down to the banks of the river. Holloway and Anne had cultivated a vegetable garden in this soil and planted some fruit trees.

Kevin Shillington has written of the dam on the Harts River that Holloway built in the early 1850's, the remains of which, he claimed, were still visible in the 1970's.[2]

"Do you know anything about the old dam?" we asked our host.

"*Ja*, it's down there," said the farmer, pointing towards the river, "follow me, I will take you there," and hopping on his small scooter he set off in a cloud of dust.

Sure enough, about 4 km from the farm, we came across the weir which Holloway had built on the west side of the dam. Over the years the walls of the main dam have been breached, creating a new watercourse, but there is no doubt that this is what remains of Holloway's dam, just a few kilometres upstream from where the Lekhatlong mission station was sited. Holloway had constructed it to enable his beloved BaTlhaping people to settle and remain well fed, even in years of drought. After his departure from Lekhatlong in 1856, the dam had not been properly maintained but its sturdy mud walls had withstood the ravages of the fast-flowing river for well over a hundred years.

Ironic, isn't it, we mused, the local farmers are descendants of those Boers against whom Holloway and his colleagues had set up such strong resistance when they tried to settle in this region. They are farming the land that once belonged to Chief Jantjie Mothibi and his tribe. What happened to the BaTlhaping and to Jantjie and his descendants?

After the discovery of diamonds in 1867 there was much wrangling over land between the Griquas, the Bechuana tribes, and the British, with additional rival claims by the Transvaal and Orange Free State Boers. Jantjie Mothibi still held the land at Lekhatlong, but diggers were moving into the area and it was difficult to maintain control and preserve digging rights. A dispute as to whether the land at Lekhatlong belonged to Jantjie or Waterboer was settled in Waterboer's favour in 1871.[3] In the same year, as more and more immigrants [*Uitlanders*] flocked to the area in search of diamonds, Nicolaas Waterboer, who had succeeded his father Andries as leader of the Griquas in Griqualand, was persuaded by an unscrupulous agent to appeal to the British government for protection. Griqualand was proclaimed British territory and in 1873 the whole area, with inestimable wealth in its soil, became a British Crown Colony.

Jantjie died in 1881, having spent his last years in exile north of the British colony in Bechuanaland. He was succeeded by his eldest son, Luka Mothibi, born about 1835 and thus well known to Holloway and Anne. On numerous occasions Luka and his men were involved in skirmishes with British Colonial troops and in 1897, at Langeberg, he was killed by British troops.[4] The remnants of the BaTlhaping tribe are now settled mainly at Taung, some miles north of Delportshoop.

We were at Kuruman by mid-day and enjoyed lunch overlooking the Eye of Kuruman. This natural eternal fountain of crystal clear water, bubbling up out of the sands of the Kalahari at the rate of about twenty to thirty million litres daily, was the reason for Robert Moffat's decision to move his mission from nearby Lattakoo in 1824.

The Kuruman mission station was the focal point for the London Missionary Society's activities in this area until well into the twentieth century. It is now run by a trust formed by the United Congregational Church and, under the leadership of its resident director, the Reverend Dr Steve de Gruchy, it has become a thriving educational institution and conference centre, with a newly built, comprehensive library.

The old mission buildings still stand, a memorial to the Moffats. The home that Robert and Mary built of mud bricks with thatched roof is little altered since they lived and worked there a hundred and sixty years ago. The roof has been raised, a new floor put in and the walls re-plastered and white-washed, but we were able to see the living rooms, the bedrooms, and Mary's kitchen just as it was. We were also able to see Robert's old study, with the shelves which he made himself and in which he spent many a long hour on his mammoth task of translating the Bible into the Sechuana language. Mary, becoming increasingly anxious over the effect on his health, once locked him out of his study, a sore point between them for years afterwards.

Holloway and Anne would have spent many happy hours in this home on their frequent visits to Kuruman. One could conjure up a picture of Mary and Anne in the kitchen, exchanging news, discussing their children and lamenting on the hard life of a missionary's wife in Africa.

"The heat is unbearable," Anne would have complained, "I have no energy and my eyes ache constantly. I can't bear the strong sunlight."

"And I'm never free of my head aches," Mary would have responded. "You should wean little Emily now. I had to wean my Helen at eight months because of my weak state of health. It seems to be the lot of us missionary wives to suffer much from debility in this country."[5]

Hamilton's house, built in 1826, is also still there. Robert Hamilton was Moffat's fellow missionary. He was working in Griqualand before the Moffats first arrived in 1817.

The brick thatch-roofed church which Robert Moffat built in 1838 is still used regularly for worship. It has seating capacity for 800 people, with two wings either side of the pulpit. On the wall is a plaque commemorating those brethren of the London Missionary Society who lived at Kuruman and were part of the church and mission, from Robert Hamilton (1816) to Sias Arends (1966); one hundred and fifty years of mission work at Kuruman, and the giant among them was and always will be Robert Moffat, who was there from 1820 to 1870. He was then pensioned by the Society and he and Mary, after more than fifty years in Africa, were obliged to return to England. Mary left her heart in Africa. She lived just five months after landing in England, breathing her last on 10th January 1871, aged seventy five. Robert Moffat survived for a further twelve years, being cared for by his youngest daughter, Jeannie Moffat, at Tunbridge Wells in Kent.

Outside the Moffat homestead a long, broad, tree-lined avenue runs parallel to the channel from the Kuruman fountain. On this path the wagons would have lined up when any missionaries were arriving or departing. It would have been here, on this piece of ground, that the Helmore/Price party lined up their four wagons on the morning of Friday the 8th July 1859 and waved farewell as they set out for Linyanti. Mr Sykes, who was to go on the Matebele mission, led the prayers. There would have been no eager anticipation of their new mission, they all knew the dangers that lay ahead. Tears would have flowed, for Mary Moffat and Anne Helmore were good friends and both knew that the chances of ever meeting again were slim indeed.

This too is where our journey really started, following as near as possible the route that they took. It took them seven months to their arrival at Linyanti, on 14th February 1860. We planned to do the same journey in twelve days. "Is life really moving that much faster now," Vincent wondered.

"Well, we don't need to inspan and outspan and cope with rounding up stray oxen and ploughing through the thick sand with the wagons, constantly repairing broken axles and *disselbooms*," Cyril responded. "We have a diesel engine, an air-conditioned vehicle and we trust we'll not have to dig water holes and dry river beds for our water."

"And we won't be stopping in the middle of the journey to await the arrival of a baby," Chantal added. "Remember also, things being what they are, we shall not rest on the Sabbath and in the morning we shall start heading north."

Sunday 2nd May
We slept overnight at a nearby holiday village and were up early. Those early missionaries could hardly have envisaged people wanting to spend a holiday in this region. After a quick, early breakfast we were on the road towards Gaberone. Ours was a tarred road, long and straight with hardly a car in sight, heading in a north-easterly direction towards the Botswana border. We followed pretty closely the route that the Helmore/Price party took, though for them there was no road there, only a track criss-crossing the veldt. There was hardly a tree in sight; just a flat, open plain of red sand and *vaalbos*; sparse, dry grass with camelthorn. Water was already scarce for the missionaries on these plains and it was only by digging in the dry river beds that they were able to obtain sufficient for themselves and their oxen. One such river was Setlagole near Vryburg, quite dry now, even at the end of the rainy season. We crossed the river within hours of leaving Kuruman; they took eleven days to reach this spot. Half an hour later we crossed the Maretsane River, which had just a trickle of water; it took our earlier travellers three days to cover the same distance. It was here that the Price wagon had difficulty ascending the steep bank on 22nd July. The banks were certainly steep and sandy, covered with thick bush.

Habitation is scarce on these plains, mostly concentrated around the small towns. We passed fields of maize and sorghum with the odd herd of cattle, but for the most part it was miles of emptiness, as it would have been for our missionaries.

We had a lunch stop at Mafikeng-Mmabatha. Mafeking was the capital of the former Bechuanaland Protectorate, made famous during the Boer War for being under siege for seven months, as Baden-Powell held out with his small garrison against the Boers. Mmabatha was purpose-built by President Maputo as his capital of the former South African homeland of Boputhuswana. Now the two towns have merged, creating a large, sprawling town of old colonial homes and offices and new concrete blocks.

We crossed the Molopo River at the border post of Ramatlabama and entered Botswana, continuing to Kanye, which we reached at about

3 pm. The Helmore/Price party arrived here on July 28th, twenty days after leaving Kuruman. It was then the town of the BaNgwaketse. They spent five days here, whilst Holloway's old wagon was being repaired. Kanye is a picturesque town, set on the edge of the spectacular Kanye Gorge, in amongst the hills; the first hills we had seen since leaving Kuruman.

Soon afterwards we made a stop at Kolobeng, where David and Mary Livingstone founded a mission station amongst the BaKwena people and their chief Sechele. Only the foundations of the house and church which Livingstone built remain now and in the small graveyard lies their baby daughter Elizabeth Pyne who, we recalled, was born in 1850, soon after the Livingstones returned from their journey to Lake Ngami. Mary herself was very ill at the time. In August 1852 Kolobeng was sacked by the Boers, who suspected Livingstone of supplying firearms to Sechele and his people. At the time Livingstone was in Kuruman, preparing for his memorable journey through Central Africa, having been to Cape Town to despatch Mary and their children to the care of his parents in Scotland.

We could well understand Holloway Helmore's exclamations of delight over the lovely countryside which they passed through in this area. Hills and valleys abound with rocky outcrops formed from huge, strange-shaped boulders, surrounded with silvery green camelthorn bushes and tall aloes. Set against the background of red Kalahari sand, with a deep blue sky above, it must have provided a welcome relief from the flat plains they had traversed for three weeks. They, of course, saw this same view in its fresh spring coat, with flowers and blossoms, which moved Holloway to write some lovely poetic phrases in his journal, such as:

"It requires very little imagination to conjure up the saurians and ichneumons and other monsters of bygone ages. The larger tree under which we had encamped presented beauties which the darkness of last night concealed. The parasite was shooting out with its peculiar blossoms, just over our waggon [*sic*] and a little palm-like tree was shooting up under the branches, promising soon to rear its head above its protection." [August 3rd]

These hills have not always been so peaceful. They have seen fighting and bloodshed and it is easy to imagine scenes of ambush and battle amongst the rocks. After Livingstone had left Kolobeng, Sechele took his people to Dimawe, a few miles away, and it was here, in 1852, that a commando of Boers attacked. The Boers killed 60 BaKwena and took two hundred women and children captive; but they also suffered the loss of 36 of their commando.

Seven years later, when the Helmore/Price party passed through, they found Sechele and his BaKwena people at Dithubaruba, "on top of a rugged mountain," [August 6th]. They were then under the care of a German missionary. Our earlier travellers had difficulty getting the wagons through the deep sand along this stretch.

"We go very slowly for our waggons [*sic*]are heavy. I often think how you and Anne would enjoy the journey," Anne Helmore wrote to her daughter Olive.[6] "… We continually see new trees and plants, sometimes we pass through forests of acacias where it is difficult to find a road for the waggons [*sic*] on account of the projecting of branches of large trees. Occasionally we come to a hilly country where the slopes on each side are covered with beautiful trees to their very summits. … Sechele was very glad to see Papa especially when he told him that Mr Stuart of Bloemfontein was his brother-in-law."

Our overnight stop was at an hotel in Gaberone, the capital of Botswana. This rapidly growing city is a conglomerate mixture of modern and traditional; of sky-scrapers and corrugated roofs; of sophisticated shops and pavement traders along the main street. It has paved sidewalks and sandy tracks, cars and horse-drawn carts; a large industrial and commercial centre of purpose-built office blocks and factories, and small home-industries.

The population of Botswana is about 1.6 million, living in an area approximately the size of France. There is but one telephone directory, about three inches thick, for the whole country.

Monday 3rd May

With Gaberone receding in the distance we looked forward, northwards, to the Botswana of bush, wild animals, small villages, and mile upon mile of flat, open, sandy plains. The Kalahari Desert is not just bare sand such as the Sahara; its thick, sandy soil hosts a variety of vegetation, mainly silver-leaf terminalia woodland, with straw-like, dry grass. Cattle and goats and a huge variety of wild animals graze and browse on this vegetation.

There was no sign of water along our route that day, the river beds were dry. However, the Botswana government has installed a network of water pipes underground so that the remote villages, as most of them are, do have a constant supply. Water or *pula* still is the most precious commodity in Botswana. Driving through this dry region one could imagine the horror these local people would feel at the waste in Britain through leaking pipes, or taps left running.

During the morning we passed our first Veterinary Cordon, or buffalo fence, still acting as a barrier between wild and domestic animals. About forty years ago these fences were erected across thousands of miles of Botswana, with the aim of keeping the buffalo from domestic stock to try to control foot and mouth disease. Millions of wild animals perished as their migratory routes were cut off. The wildebeest population was almost wiped out and the numbers of zebra and hartebeest have dropped drastically. It has been a tragedy for the wild life, and the effects are still evident.

The fences, however, still remain. Botswana's cattle-ranching industry is subsidised by the European Community and the World Bank and they lay down strict guidelines regarding the segregation of domestic livestock from wild animals, in an effort to control the spread of disease. It is, therefore, difficult to overcome this problem. One positive aspect, however, is that it keeps the cattle out of the Okavango Delta, thus preserving this area for the wild animals.

Shoshong was our next destination, about 200 km from Gaberone. We were still on tarred road; but not for much longer, Pierre warned us. Shoshong is a small, pretty, traditional Tswana town, set in the Shoshong Hills. At the centre is the *kgotla*, which serves as the traditional meeting place for the chief and his *indunas*, as well as the community hall. Next to it is the general store and around these are the homes. These are circular, the walls made from the red Kalahari sand, with a thatched roof supported by a ring of poles and each one surrounded with a picket fence.

When the Helmore/Price party came here, Shoshong was the town of the BaNgwato people (known then as the Bamangwato) under their chief Sekhomi. He was the grandfather of the great chief Khame, whose descendant, Sir Seretse Khama played such an important part in the development of modern Botswana until his death in 1980. Our earlier travellers found the town built out of sight in the mountain, as a protection against a surprise Boer attack. They spent five days here, stocking up on food supplies, bartering beads for beans and corn.

When John MacKenzie called at Shoshong in 1860, on his way to join Helmore and Price, he was told of the good impression Holloway had made on the people when he had preached to them.

"He knew how to speak," the people said.[7]

MacKenzie did not then know that he and his wife were shortly destined to return to Shoshong and settle for a few years amongst the BaNgwato as missionaries. So too was Roger Price. After the traumatic experiences of the Makololo tragedy, Price found happiness again in marriage with Elizabeth Lees Moffat, affectionately known as Bessie, daughter of Robert and Mary. The young couple's first assignment was at Shoshong, where they were soon joined by the MacKenzies. They lived here from May 1862 until February 1866. They were then moved to Logagen, or Molepolole, where they remained for a further eighteen years.[8]

This area is heavily over-grazed and grass is very sparse. We skirted the Shoshong Hills, following the road towards Serowe. The Helmore/Price party went more directly, through a pass which they called Unicorn Pass [August 24th]. We soon linked up with their route again and, heading in a north-westerly direction, drove the short distance to the Khama Rhino Sanctuary for our first night of bush-camp. Pierre headed for his favourite spot, under a large, beautiful Manketti tree.

Our tour was basic camping and self-participation; no relaxation with iced sundowners whilst others did the work.

"Now, let's see how quickly you can put up the tents," said our guide, bustling about, unpacking bags and rolls. "The quicker we can do it, the more time we'll have for a game drive."

Our first attempt was slow, clumsy and lengthy. Half an hour later, panting but victorious, we were ready and set off for a nearby water-hole. We were fortunate to get there in time to see a white rhino emerging, muddy and contented. Poachers have hunted these magnificent creatures almost to extinction, and sadly there are only sixteen of them left in the whole of Botswana; hence this rhino sanctuary. As we drove along we spotted a Whalberg's eagle and we also came across a large herd of gemsbok, with their long, straight horns and large, bushy tails.

Later Pierre cooked us a hearty and tasty dinner, which we sat and enjoyed around the camp fire. The sky above us was an inky black dome, smothered with myriads of tiny, twinkling pin-pricks of light, the Milky Way cutting its own opal pathway through the maze. The crickets set up their nightly chorus and in a nearby tree a pearlspotted owl uttered its high-pitched 'tee-tee-tee.' The moon rose at 9 o'clock, bathing the scene in a luminous silvery glow, casting sufficient light to see the ground.

Our earlier travellers often travelled through the night to avoid the heat of the day; on a night such as this they would have had no difficulty in seeing every obstacle on their path.

Tuesday 4th May

The sunrise this morning was beautiful, golden rays shooting across a deepening blue sky, heralding another action-packed day. Down came the tents and back into their canvas bags they went. By 8.30 we were on the road again, travelling due west along the tarred road which runs from Serowe to Maun. How much easier our journey was along this stretch of road, compared to that of those earlier travellers. This distance of approximately 200 km took us two and a half hours, compared to their fourteen days. It was here, between Shoshong and Letlhakane, that Anne and her four children suffered so severely from thirst, with no water, whilst Holloway was stranded some miles back in the deep sand with a broken axle on the old wagon. Holloway's journal, written to Olive, makes light of their plight, but Anne, in a letter to Holloway's sister Emily, gives a graphic description of their sufferings. She was faced with the distressing task of granting her crying, parched children a teaspoonful of water at a time. Her letter is quoted in full in Appendix A.

Letlhakane is to us of especial interest. It was here that the Helmore/Price party remained for about four weeks, creating a small settlement at a water-hole amidst the *palmyra*, or Real Fan palm trees, which grow up to 20m high and are indigenous to this region. They had already been considerably delayed and could ill afford a lengthy stop. However, the short sojourn must in many ways have been a welcome respite from the rigours of the journey. Here Isabella Price's baby was born on September 30th 1859, delivered by Holloway with Anne's assistance.

It is difficult to relate present-day Letlhakane to that water-hole in the midst of the desert, surrounded by *palmyra* trees. A small town has now sprung up, in the heart of a thriving diamond-mining area, with a general dealer store, a petrol station and a number of houses. Taps and pipes have replaced the water-hole. Alas, apart from one or two lone specimens, the *palmyra* trees are gone.

Aware that it would be some time before we reached another town, we filled the tank and all spare drums with diesel and water and stocked up on fruit drinks, before continuing our journey. Few crops can grow on this barren soil, but we passed herds of cattle and goats which seem to thrive on the sparse dry grass. Mopipi was our next destination.

"Mopipi means the Shepherd's Tree," Pierre explained, "so called because it is always green and provides food and shelter for birds, animals, insects and humans when all else has died."

At this spot we had a glimpse of the Boteti River, which our early travellers referred to as the Zouga, and which flows between the Okavango Delta and the Makgadikgadi Pans. Once a mighty river, similar in size and scale to the Chobe or Linyanti, it shows now just a hint of its former glory in the depth and width of the channel it has cut in the sand.

At Mopipi we left the tarred road and headed north across the Makgadikgadi Pans. As we travelled, we could see in the distance, stretching across the horizon from west to east what we would have sworn was an expanse of water, shimmering and glinting in the sunlight. As we came nearer we could see that it was not water but a sea of white, blinding sand, flat and dry. Many an early traveller, including Livingstone, was deceived in the same way.

Lake Makgadikgadi was formed about two million years ago, at the same time as the Okavango Delta, by a shift in the earth's crust which caused a network of rivers such as the Okavango, Chobe and Zambezi to fill an enormous basin in the Kalahari. This formed one of the largest lakes in Africa, estimated to be between 60,000 and 80,000 sq.km. The lake filled to capacity about twenty thousand years ago, forcing the waters to find another outlet to the Indian Ocean, which they did by running north and east, merging the middle and lower Zambezi rivers.

Gradually over the next ten thousand years, through a further shift in the earth's crust, Lake Makgadikgadi dried up, leaving the salt deposits carried down from the river sources to merge with the windblown sand from the desert dunes. This incredible landscape is bordered by Real Fan palm trees and hosts large patches of sparse short, spiky, sand-coloured grass, where former islands stood. There must be nourishment in this, as we came across small herds of cattle and some wild animals; a few wildebeest, zebra and ostriches.

Driving across the salt pans is a unique and fascinating experience. We travelled across the Ntwetwe Salt Pan, where both Holloway's and Thabi's wagons had sunk to their axles and were in danger of capsizing. We must remember that they crossed in October and Holloway mentions that they had had some rain, therefore the sand must have been very soft and muddy. In contrast we were in the dry season. Although Pierre had ensured that all containers and windows were securely closed before we set off, we were soon enveloped in a cloud of fine, white dust, which created a haze even inside the vehicle and got into our hair, our eyes, ears, nose and mouth. Cameras were quickly covered up and we were grateful for the air conditioning which at least kept us at a reasonable temperature. You can only cross these pans with a four-wheel drive vehicle and many a traveller has met with disaster by straying from the barely discernible tracks. The landscape is bleak and flat, just this enormous expanse of white sand as far as the eye can see. In summer the glare from the salt pans can burn the skin and eyes severely; even now, in early autumn, it made us squint and we kept our sunglasses on.

Eventually in the distance, looming on the horizon, we could see a line of Real Fan palm trees which slowly grew bigger. We gradually realised that one tree was far larger than the others.

"Yes, that's Chapman's Baobab," confirmed Pierre, "that is where we are camping tonight."

It was mid-afternoon when we reached the spot, about 100 km from Mopipi. This stretch had taken us three hours to cover, in comparison to our early travellers' three days. There is no proper camp-site here, but we had brought our own supply of water. On looking back, this was the loveliest of the many delightful camp-sites we rested at on our journey. This beautiful baobab is a giant even amongst its own species, with five thick trunks emanating from its single root stem. Set on the flat landscape, with nothing to mar its glory, it has stood there for centuries, a monumental landmark for travellers across the salt pan and a nesting place for birds.

James Chapman, a hunter and explorer, who travelled extensively in these regions, had carved his initials near the base on the eastern side of this tree, possibly in 1854, when he crossed the Ntwetwe Pan, heading east to the Sowa pan. Since then many others have done likewise; such as James Jolly, a hunter, and his companion Oswald Badger, whose initials, carved in the 1870's are still clearly seen.

According to Holloway's diary, he was there on 31st October 1859 for a few short hours before proceeding to the Gutsha Pan and Green's Baobab, as, then as now, there is no water in the vicinity of Chapman's Baobab. Paul Augustinus gives a clear account of his discovery of the carved initials of Holloway Helmore on one of the tree's great trunks, about twenty years ago:

> "During the latter part of my day there, the rays of the setting sun played at a conveniently low angle over its eastern side in such a way that every bump and irregularity was thrown into sharp relief. While examining that section under such ideal lighting, I discerned the distinct shapes of seven letters, the first two of which were indecipherable but the remaining five were easily seen to be..LMORE. Without a doubt it originally spelt out HELMORE." [9]

At sunset, with great difficulty we eventually located these barely discernible outlines. What made Holloway, a quiet reticent man, carve his initials for posterity?

We drove the short distance to Gutsha Pan. Even this early in the dry season, there was no water there, though the soil was muddy and by digging, water could have been obtained. It is surrounded by the Real Fan palm trees which we had seen whilst driving across Ntwetwe. Slightly to the east of this large water-hole stands Green's Baobab, named after the brothers Frederick and Charles Green, hunter/explorers, who crossed this area en route to the Chobe in 1852, but who carved their names on the tree in 1858. The tree is now a national monument. It has many carvings all round its trunk, testimony to the number of travellers who have rested under its branches near the water-hole. Livingstone rested here and, equally important for us, we know that the Helmore/Price party stopped here. Holloway mentions this in his journal for October 31st.

Suddenly Cyril called: "Come and look here." Sure enough, he had found, carved on the trunk:

† 1859

It was quite obvious that either Holloway or Price had carved it. Here and at Chapmans, in this vast wilderness, we were standing where we knew our ancestors had stood, gazing at the landscape which had changed little during the intervening years and admiring these giants among trees, as they had done. We felt very close to them. We could picture the wagons pulled up, the oxen being outspanned and taken to the water to slake their thirst; Lizzie, Willie, Selina and Henry running around in the sand, perhaps tearing their clothes on the camelthorn, and receiving a scolding from their mother, whilst tiny Eliza Price cried lustily, awaiting her evening feed.

We returned to our camp-site and enjoyed a most refreshing shower in a portable plastic unit, washing away the dust that had settled on our bodies and in our hair. The sunset was glorious. Through the branches of the giant baobab the white sand reflected the orange rays of the sun, topped by a brilliantly blue sky streaked with gold. The stars when they appeared were even more dazzling across the vast, unbroken expanse of black, velvety sky. It was 9.30 before the moon appeared, when it cast its ghostly light across the white landscape. The only sounds to break the silence were the cattle, goats and dogs at a nearby cattle outpost and the calling of the small herd boys guarding them. In the distance a jackal barked and, right beside us, the crackling of the camp fire and the clinking of pots as Pierre prepared our supper, made us realize how hungry we were.

Wednesday 5th May

The Ntwetwe Salt Pan stretches further north-east forming a peninsular, but our road took us due north onto a plain of thick grass and camelthorn bush, where springbok and ostriches graze. We spotted some lion spoor,

The weir on the dam that Holloway Helmore built on the Harts River, Lekhatlong, now on the farm Dikathong. Remains of the dam wall built in the 1850's can still be seen.

Kuruman Avenue, which runs alongside the Moffat homestead. Wagons lined up here, ready for departure on the many missionary journeys

A traditional Tswana home, built of mud and thatch. The roof extends beyond the mud wall, supported by poles a little above the top of the wall, to allow for ventilation.

Driving across the Ntwetwe Salt Pan in Makgadikgadi. In the distance, the tallest trees on the Lekhubu (Kubu) Island...

Camping alongside Chapman's Baobab.

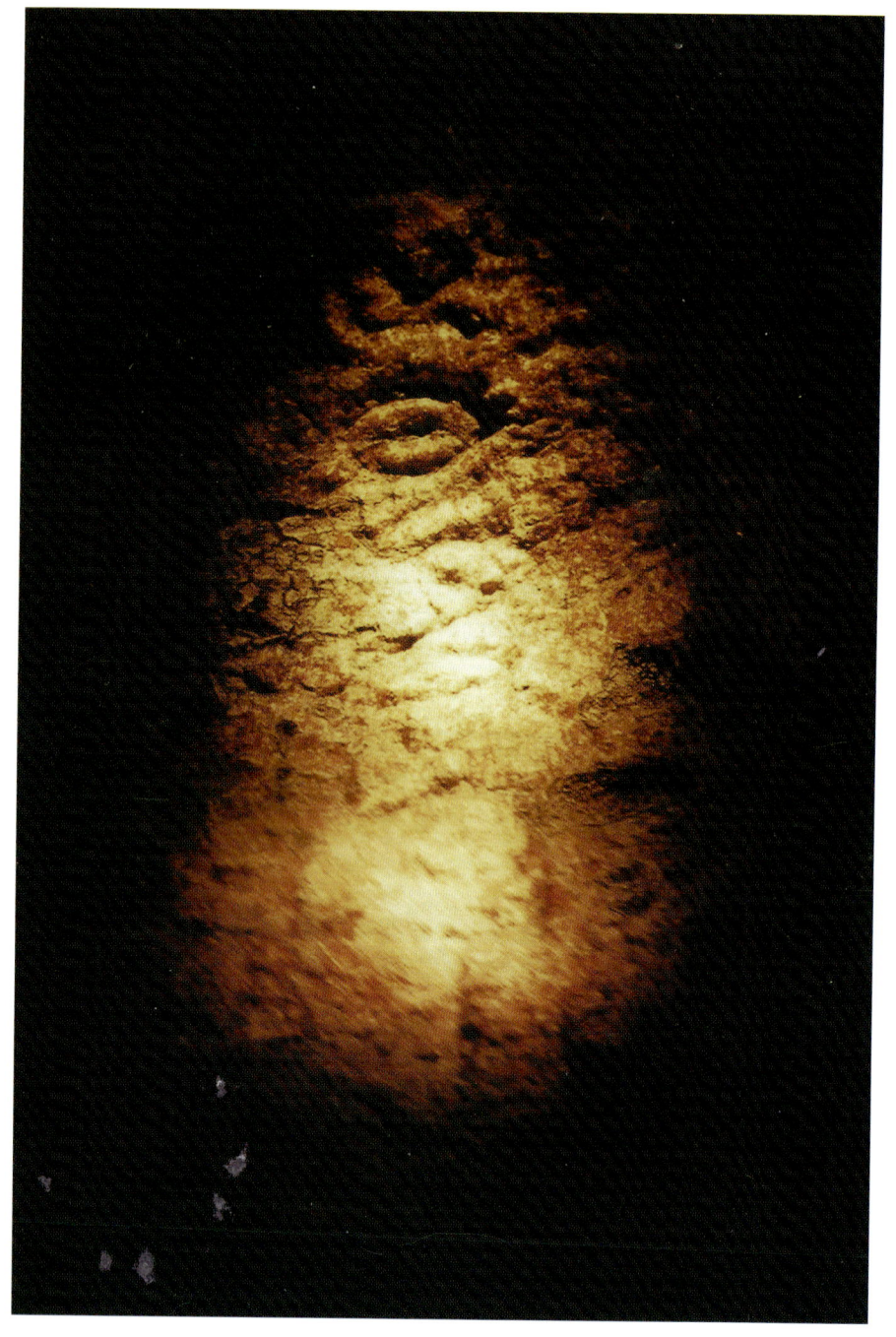

All that remains of Holloway Helmore's name carved on Chapman's Baobab in 1950.

View from the top of one of the Gutscha Hills on Savuti Plain, looking across the now dry Savuti Channel towards the Mababe Plains.

Transport old and new. Oxen are still a vital part of the economy in Botswana and Namibia. Here at Sangwali.

The grave of Chief Sebituane of the Makololo, at Sangwali, which was the first Linyanti.

Chief Bornface ShuFu of the Mavevi with his council, or khuta members, inside the khuta at Sanoyuli

The Kilby party with Chief Bornface ShuFu of the Mayeyi (seated), together with his council and invited advisers. Taken outside the khuta at Sangwali.

Site of the Helmore/Price camp at Malewalewa

though not fresh enough to track, and came across a large flock of rare Lappet-faced vultures at the only water-hole we saw on this vast, sandy plain. This species is number one on the list of the 'Big Six' most endangered large birds in Africa. Ambling along in the dry grass were some Kori bustards, the largest flying bird in Africa, another of the six endangered species. An increasingly familiar sight were the cattle outposts, consisting of a kraal and one or two huts, far from a village, where young herd boys stay to look after the cattle and take them out to graze in the morning, bringing them back at sunset.

At Gweta, a fair-sized town, we turned due west then, shortly afterwards, we turned north again into the Nxai Pan National Park. Here the road was exceptionally rough and bumpy, with deep sand. At one point the Landrover stuck fast, its wheels spinning, necessitating some human power to add to the horsepower.

"How on earth did the Helmores cope with their wagons? Those poor oxen, what a burden, and with no water," Vincent commented.

"It was here that Price's wagon was brought to a standstill, when his front oxen collapsed from exhaustion, and by the morning they had all wandered away in search of water," I responded. "No wonder they were constantly having to create new *disselbooms* and axles, and no wonder it took them so long."

"For them the worst was yet to come," Pierre joined in, "beyond KhamaKhama the bush and trees are denser, the sand just as thick and deep; and remember there are no tracks, nor were there any then. That's why we need to make a detour."

What faith those missionaries had. What endurance and dedication to their duty. Our respect and admiration for them increased as we went along.

We headed for the camp at the Nxai Pan, where we were to camp overnight.

The old town of Maila was in this area. The Helmore/Price party reached Maila on November 5th and had difficulty getting guides to take them further.

"You will find no water beyond this point," they were told. Holloway did not believe them. They had been told earlier that the fountain at

Maila was dry, but when they reached it they had found plenty of water. As we know, however, the local people were right. Their sufferings after leaving KhamaKhama are detailed in Chapter Six. It was at Maila too that John MacKenzie first heard of the disaster that had befallen the missionary party, though he refused to believe it was true.

The grass plains of the Nxai National Park are ideal for springbok and we spotted many herds throughout the park. These graceful creatures, the emblem of South Africa are so scarce there now, it was encouraging to see they are thriving here, in parts of Botswana. There was a lot of game around the water-hole and hovering in the sky we espied a Martial Eagle, another one of the endangered species.

After lunch, our first destination was KhamaKhama Pan, which is in the National Park. It is thought that this site got its name through a large cattle outpost belonging to King Khama III of the BaNgwato.

Here we stood and faced north-west, gazing across the flat, wooded expanse of waterless terrain towards the Mababe Plain and Savuti, across which the Helmore/Price party set out, without guides, on about November 11th. The landscape was indeed bleak, savannah with acacia and camelthorn growing out of fine, grey sand, with areas of mopane near the water-holes, where the soil was more clay-like. There were many dry, bare, grey patches where, as Holloway had said, water could be obtained by digging.

Holloway's journal ended here, on November 10th. He may have carried on writing, but the pages have been lost to us. Were they amongst the papers that some Makololo men strewed across the camp site whilst Roger Price lay, too ill to intervene, after Holloway's death? Here we can do no better than give part of Price's account of this stretch of their journey. Elsewhere we have read their experiences from Anne's and Isabella's perspective.

"We remained at Kamakama a few days to rest our oxen, when we got a fearful thunderstorm, which in about half an hour covered the ground with water about a foot deep. It soon disappeared however, some flowing into hollow places and the rest drunk in by the thirsty ground. When we proceeded again we got out of the region of the thunderstorm in about half an hour, and the country was as dry as it well could be. About two days journey to S.E. of Kamakama we found the last fountain water before reaching the Chobe; a distance of about 250 miles. Hence we had to be entirely dependent on rain water and hence our great difficulties and privations between Kamakama and the Makololo country. You will think it rather hard when I tell you that on one occasion my dear friend and brother Mr Helmore happening to sit in front of my waggon [*sic*] and seeing a small quantity of water spilt on the forechest, asked permission to lick it up. Shortly after that, for nearly a fortnight, every drop of water that we used had to be carried on men's backs for about 20 miles........"[10]

With no roads, limited time, on our own and in the dry season, there was no question of our venturing across this plain. Our plan was to go back to the main tarred road to Maun, thence after a pleasant interlude at Moremi, to follow Livingstone's original attempted route in 1850, which skirted the western side of the Mababe Plain towards the Savuti.

Thursday 6th May

We were up in time to see a golden dawn at 6.30 a.m. Lions were roaring in the vicinity for a long time during the night but nothing else disturbed our peace.

Returning southwards, we made a detour to see the famous Baine's baobabs. We had to cross Kudiakam Pan, another salt pan, its fine, white sand billowing around inside the Landrover. Holloway described this group of baobabs as looking 'very strange,' [November 1st]. They certainly do create an unusual feature, like a cluster of giants on the flat landscape. I counted eight of them, including a comparatively new young tree with its straight, single stem.

Thomas Baines joined James Chapman on a journey from Walvis Bay to the Victoria Falls in 1861, after the visit of the Helmore/Price party. His connection with the Livingstone Expedition is related in Chapter Eight. It was on this journey that he painted his famous picture of these baobabs. Here they still are, exactly as he painted them, even the large old one, with its roots still exposed to the sun and wind, which had in his time already fallen over.

We arrived at Maun early afternoon where we refuelled, again filling all available drums with diesel and water.

"This will need to last us until we get to Katimo Molilo," Pierre said. We studied the map. It was a long way north, through thick sand. However, we had every confidence in our guide. He had already proved to us that he knew what he was doing. At least water would not be a problem for us, since we would be staying at camp sites. In this respect, if nothing else, we were far better off than our missionaries were.

Maun is the main tourist centre for the Okavango Delta, catering for all visitors' needs with plenty of gift and curio shops. It felt quite strange to be in a bustling town again after the quiet emptiness of the bush; was it really only three days since we had left Gaberone?

As we proceeded northwards we found the days were getting hotter; after all we were well inside the tropical zone by then. On the other hand, the nights became quite cold and, though it was still only early May, we were wearing our sweatshirts and were glad of warm sleeping bags. In any event, since we were in malaria country, we covered as much of our bodies as we possibly could in the evening, spraying the exposed parts with mosquito repellent.

Just outside Maun is a settlement of Herero people who fascinated us, particularly the women with their Victorian-style dresses. These were of brightly coloured cotton, with full, ankle-length skirts and billowing sleeves. The elaborate head-dresses were usually of the same fabric as the dress. Tall and graceful, these women made a pleasant picture. The Herero originally came from Namibia, formerly South West Africa. In the nineteenth century they were converted to Christianity by British missionaries and adopted their dress. At the beginning of the twentieth century they were persecuted by the Germans who had colonised the country, and fled across the border into the former Bechuanaland.

We had hoped to drive to Toteng, about 70km south of Maun, but our time was too limited. Toteng is the spot where Chief Lechulatebe had resided with his BaTawana tribe. Livingstone first visited him there in 1849, when he discovered Lake Ngami. At that time Toteng was on the banks of this great lake, which Livingstone estimated to be 'about 70 miles in circumference.'[11] As the waters of the Okavango Delta have shifted, this vast lake has dried up; it did so soon after

Livingstone's visit. In 1962 it reappeared on a smaller scale for about twenty years, but has again disappeared, leaving just a vast area of bush and scrub and sand. The BaTawana people in the middle of the nineteenth century were reliant upon the fish from Lake Ngami. When the lake dried up they moved further north and are now settled in the Maun district. They are the dominant tribe in Ngamiland, their chief being the chief for this area.

Of relevance to our story, Toteng is where Roger Price, with Willie and Lizzie Helmore, were given sanctuary by Chief Lechulatebe after their traumatic departure from Linyanti. There they remained from about mid-July (Price had lost sense of time) until John MacKenzie was led to them by some Bushmen guides on 8th September, 1860.

Lechulatebe and his BaTawana people had reason to hate the Makololo. Lechulatebe's grandfather, Tauana, was the son of the BaMangwato chief Matebe. Tauana had fled north-west after a quarrel with his brother and founded the tribe to which he gave his name.[12] His son Moremi withstood the might of the Matebele, but not of the Makololo. Defeated by Sebituane, he moved to Lake Ngami. His son Lechulatebe, still a child, was captured by Sebituane and brought up by the maYei, who were a subject tribe of the Makololo.

Lechulatebe lived in constant fear of the Makololo and had tried to block Livingstone's attempts to reach the Linyanti, fearing he might sell guns to Sebituane.[13] This is why Mackenzie suspected Lechulatebe of trying to prevent him reaching Linyanti, when he was, in fact, trying to entice him to Lake Ngami to rescue Price and the remnants of the Makololo mission.

Friday 7th May

Proceeding north alongside the Thamalakane River, a two-and-a-half hour's drive took us to the Moremi Game Reserve in the Okavango Delta. Our chosen spot at North Gate Camp was quite secluded, near the ablutions block and beneath the trees for shade. We set up camp and began preparing lunch. A large troop of Vervet monkeys were in the trees, watching our every move. Despite sharp vigilance, before we realised what had happened, our loaf of bread was snatched from the table in the mouth of one small monkey and whisked up a tree. For the next hour we watched helplessly, nibbling our ProVita, whilst the monkeys enjoyed our bread, passing pieces to each other and occasionally adding insult to injury by dropping a morsel at our feet.

The Okavango Delta covers an area of approximately 15,000 sq.km. It contains crystal-clear water in a vegetation of reeds and papyrus, with numerous islands of mainly mopane vegetation. It is fed by the Okavango River, the source of which is on the Benguela Plateau in Angola, an area of extremely high rainfall. The river flows south-east across the Kalahari sand for approximately 1,300 km into a panhandle shaped channel at the north-west corner of Botswana. It then hits a fault known as the Gumare Fault, the southernmost point of the Great Rift of Africa, running at right angles from the Linyanti Swamp. This causes the waters to spread out, creating its characteristically fan-shaped channels. At its south-east end it hits another fault, the Thamalakane, thus forming the river of this name. By this time, due to distribution of the water and the drying effects of wind and sand, only about 3% of the water which entered the pan-handle remains, to flow into the Thamalakane at Maun, and then at its confluence, into the Boteti River. These two latter rivers are thus dry for much of the year, the flood only reaching the Thamalakane River about July, in the middle of the dry season. This is because the Okavango River does not start rushing on its course south until about March or April, at the end of the rainy season, when it is full. It enters the Delta in about June, spreading out at approximately 3 km per day, drowning the low-lying islands and uprooting vegetation. In mid-summer, therefore, the delta is often dry and the best time to visit is from late May to September. The land is shifting constantly and new waterways are forming whilst old ones dry up. Often old rivers or lakes will be dry for decades before suddenly filling up again for a short period until a shift in the earth's surface re-routes the waters.

"Have a taste," said Pierre, scooping up a cupful of water from a stream. It was perfectly clear and surprisingly sweet, not a trace of salt.

"Some of the salts are deposited on the islands, and the reeds in the delta itself act as a filter. What's left is carried away into the Thamalakane River," Pierre explained.

The Moremi Game Reserve is situated right in the delta. Being early May, the water was still low. However, Botswana had had an exceptionally wet summer and the roads were quite muddy. Some parts were submerged, necessitating detours or wading through. The mopane vegetation attracts a lot of elephants, who love the succulent leaves. These lovely trees, which Anne Helmore described so effectively in her letter to Olive of 24th November 1859, quoted in Chapter Six, are much taller here than elsewhere in the Kalahari region, possibly due to the large amount of water and more fertile soil.

We noticed that the light is much softer here than in the Kalahari itself, the blue of the sky being of a paler hue against the dark green of the mopane trees and the clear, blue water. The Okavango Delta's charm and magical qualities has an effect on all one's senses. It is a memorable experience to see its beauty, to hear the silence of the waterways disturbed only by the cry of a bird or an elephant tearing a branch from a tree; to smell the pure air of this vast, unpolluted wilderness and to trail one's hand in the cool, clear waters.

"Watch out for crocodiles," warned Pierre, bringing us back to earth. It was difficult to imagine anything sinister in this paradise but this is the natural world. We were made even more aware of this when we came across the half-rotten carcass of an elephant which had been brought down by a lion a fortnight previously. Our game drive was fruitful. We saw a few herds of lechwe, our first view of these beautiful chestnut and white antelope, which only occur in this corner of Africa.

At sunset, a pair of Namaqua doves started a sweet duet, backed by a chorus of Cape starlings, yellow-billed hornbills, turtle doves and other birds, with the chattering monkeys adding their oratorio to a symphony which lasted for an hour or more. As darkness fell some impala rams started emitting short, sharp barks as they indulged in seasonal ranting. The hippo in the nearby swamps grunted and snorted as they prepared to wade ashore to feed. A herd of elephant crashed about in some trees nearby, breaking off branches and stripping off the leaves, and in the background the crickets chirped their way through the night, as they always do.

Saturday 8th May
This day had been planned as a day of leisure before we proceeded northwards to pick up the missionaries' trail again. We indulged in a rich feast of game-spotting, driving around the Moremi Game Park, with its huge variety of mammals, reptiles and birds, on land and in the water. A hyena wandered into our camp after dark, attracted by the smell of cooking. He returned later, after we had retired to our tents, and started scavenging in our bags until he was chased off by Pierre.

Sunday 9th May
During the night a lion roared nearby and the hippo grunted as they foraged in the reeds, whilst more than once we heard the distinctive whooping and giggling of a hyena. We all agreed, however, that these sounds were far better than the roar of traffic and we awoke refreshed at 5.30 a.m., before dawn broke. By 7 a.m. we were on the road, aiming to get across the Magwikhwe Sand Ridge whilst the sand was still damp. Once the sun has been on it for a few hours it becomes extremely difficult for a vehicle to get a grip. By 11.30 a.m. we had crossed the most difficult part without having to stop and had entered the Chobe National Park by the Mababe Gate. Taking the dry season track and still going north, we travelled with the greener mopane woodland of the delta on our left, contrasting with the acacia scrub land of the Mababe Depression on our right. Along the sand ridge there is some vegetation of acacia scrub, though even this appears bleak and hostile.

The Helmore/Price party had had to cross the Mababe plain. This plain is the massive basin of the vast lake which covered the region thousands of years ago, and which has now dried up; the same lake of which the Makgadikgadi pans were part. They crossed it, as we know, from KhamaKhama, going in a north-westerly direction towards Savuti.

Then, on their return journey from Linyanti, Roger and Isabella Price with the two orphaned Helmore children again crossed the Mababe Depression, but this time they came south towards Lake Ngami, travelling the same route that we were taking, in the opposite direction. Not far from this road, Isabella died on the morning of 5th July, 1860; details of her death have been given in Chapter Seven. Here, in this desolate wilderness, her husband dug a grave and buried her. We paid our silent tribute to this brave young woman as we travelled by.

It was easy to understand the feeling of despair of a man, isolated in this wilderness, not knowing when or from whom help would come, or whether it would come in time for him. Price had seen death strike so many in that party and now his dear wife had died as well. Would he survive? What of the two young children, Lizzie, not quite fourteen, and Willie, just six years old? What nightmares must they have endured, having witnessed and experienced such trauma?

"We'll go for a game drive this afternoon," Pierre informed us after lunch. "Make sure you put on plenty of sun-block and that you have your hats." We did not need reminding; we realised already that it was very hot, dry and barren at Savuti.

Soon after leaving the camp we crossed the Savuti Channel. It was completely dry, of course, but the width and depth of this watercourse gave us the impression of a mighty river when it was flowing. As we drove south, a range of hills appeared; enormous dark, volcanic boulders, breaking the flat landscape.

"These must be the Gubaatsa Hills, the ones Livingstone took his hat off to, but he called them Ngwa,"[14] Chantal observed.

"No, they lie a bit further south" Pierre replied. "These are the Gcocha Hills, not as high as the Gubaatsa." He stopped the vehicle on the track alongside one range. Looking up, we were faced by a formidable wall of sheer rock. "This hill is called Tsongwha. We're going to do some climbing," he calmly informed us.

It was a difficult and exhausting climb. When we had recovered and were able to breathe freely again, we gazed around and gasped in wonder. What a view! The whole of the Savuti Marsh was spread out below us. Although the hill is not very high, it lies on the sand ridge which formed the edge of that vast ancient lake, and therefore creates a greater sense of height. We could see for miles, in whichever direction we turned.

"Cast your eyes that way," said Pierre, pointing in a direction almost due south. "KhamaKhama lies there. We know that our missionaries travelled across this plain from that direction, therefore we must assume that that was their route. That's the Savuti Channel below us. It starts near the Linyanti Marshes, coming right round behind us on the left, where we crossed it, and goes round to end up in the marshes to our right. Do you see that line of sand on the horizon? That's the Mababe Depression. Price said they crossed the Sonta River, which we believe is the Savuti Channel, now dry. If that is so, then they crossed there and came this way and skirted these hills to get to Linyanti."

I could almost see the caravan of four wagons, with the spare oxen and the sheep and goats, wending their way through the bushes, struggling in the thick sand.

What a journey. Two hundred and fifty miles by ox-wagon across this wilderness. We know they left KhamaKhama mid-November and Price said they arrived at the borders of Sekeletu's country at the end of January. Two and a half months, in the intense heat of mid-summer, with constant delays through lack of water; chopping down trees to force a way through for the wagons; oxen and sheep straying.

"But why is it called the Savuti Marsh when it's so dry?" we wondered.

"It's a flood plain," explained Pierre. "When the Savuti Channel fills up it overflows onto the plains."

The Savuti Channel, 100 km long, runs along a fault line and is susceptible to movement. It starts from the Selinda Spillway near its junction with the Linyanti River and travels east, then south, on to the Savuti Marshes in the Mababe Depression. Thus these waterways are all linked; the Selinda coming from the Okavango Delta to the Linyanti Marshes, then these linking with the Savuti Marsh through the channel. Strangely, however, these waterways are not interdependent and the Savuti River especially fills and dries up of its own accord.

We know it was filled with water when our early missionary travellers crossed it. Then in about 1888 it dried up and did not flow again until 1957. It then stopped flowing in 1966 but started again in 1967 and remained until 1979 when it once more dried up. It has had no water since 1982. The flooding and drying out of the marsh and channel has produced an exceptional landscape of yellow, sparse grass, with mainly camelthorn.

After 1888 many acacia trees took root and by 1957 had grown to maturity. When the river flowed again these trees died. There they still stand, a unique vista of dead trees standing stark, black and naked, like sentinels on the landscape. However, it is not just the irregular water supply that has caused this phenomena. Vast herds of elephant inhabit the region. They can be most destructive, pulling off branches and destroying whole trees as they move around, trying to satisfy their hunger.

Climbing down the hill was only slightly easier. There is a rich variety of animals and birds in this southern part of the Chobe National Park and we saw a good deal of them, including a Burchell's Coucal, a medium sized bird with a brilliant contrast of white breast and chestnut back. We saw many Bateleur, usually in flight, a large bird with a scarlet head and legs, long brown wings, and a very short tail. It glides with a rocking, sideways movement.

The day finished on a high note. We were on our way back to camp when we spotted a pack of wild dogs ambling towards us on the sandy track. As we pulled up they veered off the road into the bushes. Pierre turned the vehicle so that we could follow them. We saw them slowly creep out from behind the bushes, one by one and sit down for a minute or two. Then suddenly the leader sprang up and bounded forward, followed by the rest of the pack. A herd of impala which had been grazing peacefully suddenly sensed their danger and ran off in fright, with the dogs in hot pursuit. We followed as best we could in the vehicle, but of course we had to keep to the tracks and could not go as fast as they did, and we eventually lost their trail. They don't run very fast, but they follow their prey relentlessly until they are worn out and then they pounce. The hunt can go on for a long, long time. For this reason they're usually successful. It was interesting to observe the other animals' reaction. All had stopped grazing and all heads were turned in the direction of the fleeing impala and the pursuing wild dogs. The wild dog is the second most endangered carnivore in Africa. We felt privileged indeed to have seen them.

By this time the sun was low on the horizon and the western sky was taking on a golden hue. Pierre turned the vehicle back onto the main track. Suddenly we spotted a large lion ahead of us, walking sedately along the road, in the same direction as ourselves. His belly was bloated; he had clearly fed well quite recently. We travelled alongside him for a good couple of kilometres, he walking steadily alongside, turning his head now and again to look at the Landrover with his sharp, red-rimmed eyes. He was not interested in us as individual people, only as a complete unit in the vehicle. Since he had recently fed well he posed no threat to us, unless we had challenged him or left the vehicle.

Monday 10th May

We left Savuti early to drive the short 30 km distance to the camp site on the banks of the Linyanti River. We were now back on the route that the Helmore/Price party took in January, 1860.

Winding our way through the scrub land of acacia with some silver leaf terminalia, we could frequently smell the sweet scent of the wild sage. We were still on the Magwikhwe Sand Ridge and on this stretch we did experience some difficulty. The track again consisted of very deep sand, fine and grey. Within a short time the Landrover was struggling gamely, its engines revving fiercely, its wheels spinning, until suddenly we came to a halt, unable to get a grip. Everybody had to get out and help. Arms and legs straining, lungs filled to bursting point, we truly exerted ourselves.

"How on earth could oxen pull a wagon through this sand, it's too deep," puffed Chantal as she paused for breath, glancing anxiously over her shoulder at a herd of elephant nearby, who were sniffing the air suspiciously.

"This was tsetse country," I panted, "and the missionaries crossed this part at night to avoid the fly biting the oxen. By doing this, and especially in the wet season, the sand was no doubt firmer."

Three times we stuck on that stretch of sand. We had to scour the surrounding area for fallen branches and twigs to place under the wheels, in order to get a grip; with elephant around, there were enough of these.

Two and a half hours later we arrived at Linyanti Camp on the banks of the Linyanti River. What a lovely spot, scenic and tranquil. The blue of the sky reflects in the water, contrasting with the white water lilies on the surface and the dark green of the reeds shooting up out of the river and along its banks. The banks of the river are lined with trees and undergrowth and across the stretch of water we looked upon the Linyanti Marshes, rich and green, with no doubt many water channels.

It did not take us long to set up our camp, at which by then we were quite proficient. After a light lunch Pierre suggested a short game drive. This was always tempting. However, on taking stock of our dwindling supply of diesel, we agreed it would be safest to conserve it for the morning. We knew we would be unable to obtain further supplies until we reached Katimo Molilo, our next destination, a distance of nearly 200 km. Our problems on the sand ridge that morning had consumed a lot of fuel. In any event a few hours' relaxation in this lovely spot was a pleasant respite. We sat under the trees, listening to the hippo grunting in the river and watching the large variety of birds, many of them, especially the yellowbilled hornbills, pecking upon the ground at our feet, ignoring our presence.

According to our calculations a few short miles into the distance, looking west to north-west across the river, lay the final destination of the Helmore/Price party. To obtain some idea of the final stages of our missionaries' journey, Price in an address in Cape Town in July 1861, had said:

"…… About the end of January 1860 we drew near to the country of the Makololo. When we were within four days of Sekeletu's town, we were detained a week for messengers to be sent to Sekeletu to bring back information whether we should be allowed to come to the town. At last a messenger returned, reporting favourably; and we proceeded, passing through the Tsetse district, fortunately without any danger, as we did it through the night. On arriving at the Chobe, a large river coming from the West, we met numbers of the Makololo, coming as we thought to help us across the river. They helped us across with canoes. This was Saturday; and in the evening we drew out a little distance from the river and encamped for the Sunday. Then for the first time, the Makololo heard the word of everlasting life……. From there we proceeded on Monday morning, and had to cross another river. On Friday afternoon we arrived at the town of Sekeletu which is called Linyanti."[15]

In his letter to Tidman[16] Price further defines their route by saying that about four days' journey from Sekeletu's town they crossed the River Sonta before proceeding across the tsetse belt. This is the Savuti Channel.

They then, he said, crossed the Chobe on 11th February before encamping for the Sabbath. Continuing on the Monday morning they crossed 'several small rivers, branching out into the plain from the Chobe, and in the afternoon arrived at and crossed the River of Linyanti.'

It is clear from both accounts that they crossed three main rivers. The river which Price called the Chobe, as did Livingstone in his *Missionary Travels* is, in fact, now one continuous, vast river with three names. It is known as the Kwando as it flows south from the plains of Angola, then the Linyanti when it forms a 90° curve around the Linyanti Marshes and as far as Lake Liambezi, and then the Chobe. The river Livingstone and Price called the Linyanti was another large river flowing in the Linyanti marshes. (See Livingstone's map on page 43). We must remember that these water courses are changing constantly with the movement along the lines at the southern end of the Great Rift fault.

The Linyanti forms the boundary between Botswana and Namibia and across the river is the Caprivi Strip. The Chobe River is a tributary of the Zambezi, starting at the rapids at Kasane. It takes the backwash from the latter when the river is full, and runs south-west to Lake Liambezi. Here, when all the rivers and Lake Liambezi are full, it joins the Linyanti. In Livingstone's time, Lake Liambezi was full, but it is now dry, and has been since the 1980's.

Here on the banks of the Linyanti, we were within sight of the spot where Sekeletu had his capital when the Helmore/Price party arrived on 14th February 1860. It was moving to gaze across the water, at a scene very much the same as they had gazed upon a hundred and thirty nine years ago.

> "Oh how sanguine our hopes were then! What joy filled our hearts that day when we thought that that was the beginning of a great work among those dark and benighted heathen,"

Roger Price said afterwards, describing their arrival at this river.[17]

They had nearly perished on that terrible journey but they had survived. The Lord had brought them safely to the Makololo. Surely this meant they were destined to fulfil their mission amongst them. Full of hope they had crossed this river, trusting to find Livingstone and the Makololo ready to move out of the marshes to healthier ground. Little did they know what tragedies lay ahead.

The sunset that evening was the best we had yet seen. Suspended like a flaming orb over the river and marshes, the sun cast its reflection on the water, enveloping the whole landscape in a soft, gentle, golden light. As it met the horizon the sky took on the same richly-coloured hue, turning gradually to a deep orange with red and purple streaks. The Evening Star emitted a bright, silver radiance and the trees and bushes cast dark shadows against the fading blue of the sky. Slowly, more stars appeared, bats and fireflies were seen flying around and soon afterwards it was quite, quite dark. There is no twilight period in the tropics, darkness falls quickly once the sun goes down.

Alas, after dark the mosquitoes also become active. Although the tsetse fly has been eradicated and domestic animals are able to graze in former tsetse country, the mosquito scourge, which cost the missionary party so dearly, has still not been brought under control, and in fact remains the biggest killer in Africa. We had insect repellent and, of course, were taking malaria tablets.

As we listened to the hippo snorting as they emerged from the water to begin their nocturnal forage on land, we pondered on our journey so far. We had covered most of the early missionaries' route. Ahead of us lay our final destination, Linyanti. Would we find the answers to our questions?

1 *The Colonisation of the Southern Tswana*, Shillington, p.114
2 *Putting a Plough to the Ground*, K.Shillington, p.315
3 *The Colonisation of the Southern Tswana*, p.53
4 Ibid, p.239.
5 Personal Collection, Mary Moffat to Anne Helmore, 22.7.1859 (Original in the L.M.S. Archives)
6 Personal Collection, Anne Helmore to Olive Helmore, Shoshong, 23.8.1859 (Original in the L.M.S. Archives)
7 MacKenzie, p.113
8 *The Journals of Elizabeth Lees Price*, edited by Una Long
9 Augustinus, p.32
10 LMS Archives, Price to Tidman, 20.2.1861
11 Livingstone to Tidman, 30.4.1851, quoted in Chamberlin, p.148
12 Chapman Part 2, p.178
13 Augustinus, p.57
14 Smith, p.87
15 *South African Advertiser and Mail*, 31 July 1861, in the South African Library, Cape Town.
16 Price to Tidman, Kuruman, 20.2.1861, L.M.S. Archives and S.A. Archives, Cape Town.
17 *South African Advertiser and Mail*, 31 July 1861, in the South African Library, Cape Town.

Chapter Ten
The Linyanti Marshes, 1999
The Search for the Truth

Tuesday 11th May

The missionaries crossed a series of rivers to Linyanti, but we had to proceed northwards to the border to enter Namibia, then drive south along the west bank of the Linyanti River. By making a very early start we managed to get across the sand ridge without the misfortunes of the previous day, despite the fact that the track was very difficult and bumpy, with deep sand. We travelled along the now dry flood plains of Kachekawbe, then turned east along an unmarked track.

On our left was Lake Liambezi, which has had no water since the 1980's. Was this really the same area where Livingstone had waded up to his waist in water in 1853, and which he described in his usual concise manner in his *Missionary Travels:*

"… we proceeded up the bank of the Chobe till we came to the point of departure of the branch Sanschurch."

[*On the map which Livingstone drew, he shows the Sanschurch as coming from Lake Liambezi and travelling east across the plains of Kachekawbe, parallel to the Chobe*].

"We then went in the opposite direction, or down the Chobe, though from the highest trees we could see nothing but one vast expanse of reed, with here and there a tree on the islands.…… We came to a deserted Bayeiye hut on an anthill. Not a bit of wood or anything else could be got for a fire……. After remaining a few days [*in a village of Makololo*] some of the headmen of the Makololo came down from Linyanti with a large party of Barotse to take us across the river……. We were now among friends, so going about thirty miles to the north, in order to avoid the still flooded lands on the north of the Chobe, we turned westward toward Linyanti (lat. 18° 17' 20" E, long. 23° 50' 9" E), where we arrived on the 23rd May 1853. This is the capital of the Makololo and only a short distance from our wagon-stand of 1851."[1]

The area around Lake Liambezi lies in Namibia and the land is being farmed, with the view that it is now permanently dry. The soil along our unmarked track was of clay, firmer but still very bumpy. Eventually, at Kavimba, we linked up with the main gravel road between Savuti and Ngoma Bridge, which skirts the western boundaries of the Chobe National Park. We noticed we were moving into a more affluent area. Bricks were being made from the clay for houses, which were of a more modern style, larger with corrugated iron rather than thatched roofs. There were fields of corn and sorghum, the cattle at the outposts looked healthier and the people were well-dressed.

Later that morning we reached Ngoma Bridge, the border post on the Chobe River, and passed into Namibia. The Chobe is a pretty river, the water is blue with many small islands and baobabs growing along its sloping banks. We had entered the Caprivi Strip, a narrow band of land with four countries meeting at its eastern point; Botswana, Namibia, Zimbabwe and Zambia. Further west on the north side of the River Cuando (or Kwando) is Angola. It is therefore a strategic area and it saw a lot of military activity as South African troops camped here in the recent Angolan wars.

We soon came to Katimo Molilo, the main town in this region, where we had our first sight of the mighty Zambezi River. At this point the mileometer revealed that we had travelled over 4,000 km since leaving Johannesburg. The service station was our first stop, where the thirst of the Landrover was quenched, whilst we duly quenched our own from the refrigerated cabinet alongside the petrol and diesel pumps. After stocking up on necessities, we made for nearby Hippo Lodge, where we camped overnight. Their bar and restaurant is built over the river, with magnificent views in both directions. We watched the fish popping up out of the water, and the birds flitting around in the bushes, whilst nearby a crocodile lay sunning himself on the rocks.

After lunch Pierre took Cyril and I back into Katimo Molilo to keep an appointment with Mr Innocent Mahoto. A minister in the Namibian Government, he is a Makololo. He had previously indicated that he was willing to see us and would attempt to answer any questions we had with regard to that episode in their history when Holloway Helmore and his party were amongst them.

Mr Mahoto was most obliging, well-spoken and informative and we were indeed grateful to him for giving us his time. In our hour-long interview with him we learnt that there have, in fact, been three villages with the name of Linyanti. The first was where Sangwali now stands. This was where Sebituane had his headquarters. The second was about 20 km further east, where Malengalenga is now situated. This was where Sekeletu made his headquarters. There is now a third town with that name 30 km further north, near Chinchimani. If he was right, we needed to go to Malengalenga to try to locate the missionaries' camp site. We knew from Roger Price that it was a bare plain, with just one tree under which they camped. When this was mentioned to Mr Mahoto he told us that as children, they used to sing a song about a tree on that plain. Legend had it that Sekeletu had placed his walking stick in the ground and it grew into a huge tree. "It might have fallen down now," he said. "I believe it was a *Mupoloto* [Sausage] tree." These trees, *Kigelia africana*, are indigenous to the floodplains in this area. They can grow to 15 m high and have dark green foliage with a long, velvety sausage-shaped fruit hanging in sprays.

Without any prompting, Mr Mahoto made an interesting point with regard to Livingstone's reaction to the tragedy that had occurred.

"At first, we are told, he was under the impression that they had died of fever, in spite of the fact that he was told that they had been given an ox that was poisoned," Mr Mahoto said. "But later on, when he discovered that the chief had kept behind the wagon and tent and other things of Helmore, then he realised that truly it was possible that Sekeletu was responsible for the death of the missionaries. Livingstone then suspected Sekeletu of poisoning the ox and was very angry with him."

This was entirely at variance with Livingstone's comments to the London Missionary Society and other correspondents. As we have seen from the evidence related in Chapter Eight, he would not acknowledge that the Makololo had committed these atrocities, alleging that it was Price and, to a lesser extent, Helmore who was to blame. He denied emphatically the allegations that they had been poisoned.

"What did the people themselves feel, did they think the missionaries were poisoned?" we asked Mr Mahoto.

"Oh yes," was the reply. Price had said that after Helmore's death and just before his departure from Linyanti, he was warned by the people that Sekeletu had poisoned some beer and some meat:

"About the same time [after Helmore's death] I purchased beer, because the water was very unpalatable; some of the men cautioned me against drinking the beer, telling me that it was that which killed Mr Helmore. Just before my departure from Linyanti I received 5 oxen from Sekeletu, in return for others he had taken from me, with regard to one of which some of the Makololo said to my men, 'Take care you do not slaughter that blue ox, it has been poisoned by Sekeletu.'..."[2]

We continued to question Mr Mahoto. "Is it possible to identify the poison from what you know of the circumstances under which they died?"

"The tree which contains that poison, I think that the older people say even now, if one takes the liquid of that, they can die. They say how they proved it is poison, they took the liquid from that tree and gave some to some chickens. After that the chickens died. Later they gave it to some dogs and the dogs died. They were making an experiment. So the last thing was to give it to an ox and give the ox to the visitors. This is the story that we get from older people."

"Why do you think Sekeletu was so hostile to the missionaries?"

"Perhaps it was because he thought Helmore would usurp him," was the response. "Perhaps he was afraid the missionaries would stop him dealing with the slave traders, or perhaps he wanted Livingstone and his wife and not Helmore."

The point about the slave traders is a valid one. Livingstone was concerned that Sekeletu was dealing with the Mambari, a band of half-caste Portuguese slave traders, who were very active in the area. At one time, Mr Mahoto told us, Sekeletu sold eighty young boys to the slave traders. Raids would be carried out on the villages, the young boys rounded up and sold for ivory or guns.

"Why did Sekeletu take all Helmore's possessions?" we asked. "Surely that was not normal practice?"

"Maybe he wanted Helmore's gun and ammunition," Mr Mahoto replied. "Then he decided that he would take the wagon and tent and other things as well."

It is clear that in their history, the regard of the Makololo themselves for Sekeletu falls well below that enjoyed by his father Sebituane, who is considered as being a great and good chief.

"Do you know where our ancestors had their camp and where they are buried?"

"Yes, the Headman Shozi who lives at Malengalenga will be able to show you. The graves are next to his house, next to the old *khuta*. There is also a very old maLozi man who lives at Chinchimani who knows a lot of history. His father was a chief and visited all the areas and he used to go with his father."

Alas, in the end, we could see neither of these two old men. Age and infirmity had caught up with them. Headman Shozi would not have been able to remember anything. His mind, we were told, had gone and Mr Kabende, when we called at Chinchimani later that week, was unable to see us at the time. On a subsequent visit Pierre was told that he had, in fact, died.

"What happened to the mighty Makololo after Price, and then Livingstone, left this area? Are there many left now?"

"Yes, there are quite a few," Mr Mahoto said. "We do keep in touch and try to keep our customs and language."

It is perhaps an appropriate point in this narrative to relate the demise of the Makololo. At the time that Holloway and Livingstone were amongst them, living in the marshes had already severely weakened the Makololo, who were dying of fever at a very high rate. A good account of the fate of the Makololo is given by John MacKenzie.[3] Incredibly, after the disastrous Helmore/Price mission the London Missionary Society mooted the idea of making another attempt and Price was asked - and agreed to go, together with MacKenzie and Robert Moffat's son John, who had originally gone to Inyati to open the mission amongst the Matebele. Early in 1862 Price and MacKenzie sent an emissary to Sekeletu to inform him that they intended proceeding north of the Zambezi to Tabacheu [*near Sesheke*] and would welcome any of the Makololo who cared to come and reside with them.[4]

Meantime, Livingstone's old friend, Chief Sechele of the BaKwena, had taken it upon himself to send a party by wagon to the Makololo to demand the return of the missionaries' possessions. They were unsuccessful in this respect, but Sekeletu sent four young men of his tribe back with them, as ambassadors. Price and MacKenzie were both at Shoshong, where they had been sent to work amongst the BaMangwato, when this party passed through on their way back from Sechele. Price's young wife, Elizabeth Lees or Bessie, daughter of Robert Moffat, describes this incident in her journals:

> "This is Wed-Nov 25 [1862]. Roger is away again on a hunt……. Moreover a party of Makololo arrived last night and R[oger] wishes to kill something for them. They have been on an embassy to Sechele - the Bakuena chief - and are now returning. The very man who (under authority) plundered poor dear Husband's things and those of the sainted Helmore, is here with them - a young chief - a fine prepossessing countenance. Those Makololo! They fascinate me in a strange, sad way! I feel as if I must stand and gaze and gaze - and see all those sad, sad things taking place amongst them. They are abt. 20 in number, some fine featured - very - but the slaves - oh horribly plain, poor things! Crushed - abused - oppressed - with great scars and wounds upon their backs. They are encamped just behind our wagons in view as I sit writing. They wear some of the s[t]olen apparel! And have no shadow of remorse or regret (in looks or words) visible! They talk respectfully to R[oger] and seem to feel him an old friend, but make no apologising remarks. R[oger] can return good for evil. I wish him success in hunting."[5]

She goes on to describe how the following day the same young chief came to her "and asked if Missus would not give him a patch for his trousers - trousers which belonged to Helmore…"[6]

Bessie, born in 1839, was of the same age as Olive and Anne Sophia and they had been companions and playmates in their childhood.

The messenger sent by Price and MacKenzie to Sekeletu returned with a positive response. The chief was willing to go with his tribe to Tabacheu. As MacKenzie said, this was no doubt prompted by the fact that his leprosy had got much worse and he thought that the men would have medicine that would cure him.[7] However, the plan faltered. Price suffered a severe attack of malaria, an affliction he was to bear for the rest of his life, and it was clear that he could not return to this region. Other minor setbacks delayed their departure and then, at the end of 1863, Sekeletu died of his leprosy.

There began a short period of infighting for succession of the chieftainship of the Makololo, with scheming and assassinations. These events were watched closely by the Barotse, who had been made subjects and slaves of the Makololo. As the tribe weakened and became more deeply immersed in their internal strife over leadership, the Barotse seized their opportunity and laid their plans.

One night they struck and within a few hours, in every village, the Makololo were seized. The men were all put to death, the women and small children were spared and in turn were made vassals of the Barotse, who from then on became known as the Lozi. Their chief Lotanku took Mamochisane, the daughter of Sebituane and his original successor, as a wife and consolidated the Lozi supremacy once more over the region; a situation which exists to the present day.

Two small parties of Makololo escaped. One sought and received sanctuary with Moselekatse; the other headed across the Mababe plain towards Chief Sekhomi of the BaMangwato at Shoshong. We hear no more of the group who went into Matabele country. The other group were intercepted south of Mababe by a Makololo who had some time previously been given sanctuary with Chief Lechulatebe of the BaTawana, the same chief who had cared for Price and the two Helmore orphans until MacKenzie rescued them. This Makololo was indebted to Lechulatebe and betrayed his own tribesmen by leading them into a carefully-laid ambush, headed by Lechulatebe himself. The men were all slaughtered, though one young lad was spared, his sister having been accepted previously into Lechulatebe's harem. The women and children were herded, with their cattle, to Toteng and there became vassals to the BaTawana.

So ends the story of a mighty tribe, in their time as powerful and strong as the Matabele and the Zulus. The power of these two latter was eventually destroyed by White man's incursion, with their guns and ambitions of Empire, but that of the Makololo was destroyed by the neighbouring tribes, with the assistance of those small but deadly insects, the mosquito and the tsetse.

Are these present-day Makololo, like Mr Mahoto, descendants of those few who escaped to Matabeleland, and the children of the children who were taken to Lake Ngami, who eventually made their way back into the Caprivi Strip? We got the impression that to this day they are accepted but not liked by the other people.

"They consider themselves superior to us," we were told by one of the Mayeyi. "We cannot forgive the Makololo for the way we were treated in the past."

Wednesday 12th May

We had a leisure day, relaxing on the banks of the Zambezi at the lovely Kalizo Lodge, about 30 km east of Katimo Molilo in the Kalembezi district. Since the Zambezi had overspilled its banks here, as it often does at this time of year, we were met by the proprietor's launch and ferried along to the lodge, having left the vehicle and trailer in a safe spot.

Skimming over the vast expanse of this great river, past numerous islands and thick beds of reeds, papyrus and waterlilies, is a most exhilarating experience. The Zambezi, fed from numerous tributaries along its course, teems with life; crocodiles, hippo and an enormous variety of birds and fishes.

About 100 km north of Katimo Molilo, on the plains of Zambia, two rivers merge to form the source of the Zambezi. Its greatest width is 1,360 metres, nearly one mile. At Katimo Molilo the river turns and starts flowing in a south-easterly direction. On it rushes, over the deep rift in the earth's surface, to create the spectacular Victoria Falls; through man-made Lake Kariba; over hills and plains to another deep gorge, the former Kebrabasa. Here, in October 1858, Livingstone stood in despair, realising that the river was not navigable after all. Lake Cahora Basa has now been created on this spot. The cataracts have been harnessed to provide a dam which supplies hydro-electric power to Zimbabwe, Malawi and Mozambique. Still the Zambezi rushes on, through the Lupata Gorge and onto the Mozambique Plains where it spreads out in a wide delta, tumbling over sandbanks until at last it enters the Indian Ocean; a distance of 3,500 km, or 2,200 miles.

Thursday 13th May

A lovely sunrise, to herald what was for us a memorable day and the climax of our quest for information on the missionaries. We returned by

The Linyanti region as it is today.

launch to the vehicle and headed south along the banks of the Linyanti for a 130 km drive to Sangwali.

It was difficult to imagine the marshes which Livingstone and Helmore encountered; the area was very dry and sandy, covered with reeds and thorn bush.

At Sangwali we were met by our host and interpreter, Linus Mukwata, head of the Sangwali Community Conservation office. Our guide had previously arranged a meeting through him with the elders of the Mayeyi tribe. The Mayeyi are of the Bayeyi people. They were living in this area at the time of the Makololo, who ruled over them as they did over the Barotse and all the other tribes. Pierre had told Linus that descendants of Holloway Helmore wished to visit them to find out more about his stay in the area and his subsequent death.

Sangwali is the capital town of the Mayeyi and is where their chief, BornFace Shufu lives. It is a sizeable town, with the traditional round houses made of red sand walls and reed thatched roofs, each enclosed by a thicket fence. In the centre of the town, next to the water pump is the *khuta*, or council hall, which is also the community centre. This long, large building is made of traditional material, with the flag of Namibia flying from a mast. There were a lot of people about and many were already entering the *khuta* building. One very old man approached, leaning heavily on his stick.

"He is 91 years old," said Linus, "and he has walked ten kilometres to be here."

We began to realise what a stir our visit had caused amongst these people. When Pierre had first approached Linus he was assured that the people knew about this period in their history. Stories had been handed down about the visit of David Livingstone, the first European to set foot amongst them with his stories of a new Saviour whom they must worship and a new way of life which he assured them would be better than theirs. They also knew about the missionaries who had followed soon after, but who were not welcomed by the Makololo chief and who they believe were poisoned by him. So, there we were, waiting in the shade of a sausage tree for the *khuta* to assemble and for the signal to be given that they were ready to receive us. We were not kept waiting long before Linus escorted us to the door of the *khuta* building where, following his guidance, as a mark of respect we knelt down on one knee and clapped our hands three times before entering.

Inside the hall many men were sitting on the floor, on reed mats placed on the bare earth floor around the walls. At the end opposite to the entrance, chairs had been arranged in a semi-circle beneath a panelled board, with one in the centre clearly designated for the chief himself. Here the elders who formed the *khuta* or council sat waiting to receive us and after kneeling and clapping we were escorted to a row of chairs in front of them, placed specially for us. We were immediately struck by the relatively smart appearance of all these people, making us feel shabby in our traditional safari gear. They were in European clothes, long trousers, shirts and jackets and many of the elders wore ties; in this heat! Speeches of welcome commenced, each having to be translated by Linus. They assured us of the warmth of their welcome, of how pleased they were that we had come all this way to visit them. They hoped we would be happy and comfortable; we were to let them know if we had any problems. We in turn told them how happy we were to be in their lovely country, explaining the purpose of our visit. They told us that after lunch, at 2 o'clock, they would re-assemble here, when their chief would join them, and they would be happy to answer any questions we might have.

We were back in Sangwali at 2 p.m. and were escorted back into the *khuta* building. Soon after, Chief BornFace Shufu arrived with an escort. All turned towards him as he entered, performing the traditional kneeling and clapping and, of course, we did the same. Young, handsome and upright, dressed in a dark suit and a hat, with a whisk in one hand and a brief case in the other, he made a tall, imposing figure. The chieftainship of this tribe, we were told, is hereditary, though it does not pass automatically to the eldest son of the former chief but to the son considered by the elders to be the most suitable to rule.

We were interested to note that the proceedings started with a prayer, led by a minister from amongst the invited men who sat behind us. The chief then spoke to us through his head *induna* who sat beside him, John Ngambela, who relayed the message to Linus for interpretation to ourselves. His words were warm and welcoming, he asked us the purpose of our visit and when told, he invited us to put our questions to the *khuta* and assembled people, which included teachers, ministers of the church and many elderly men. A secretary sat at the side taking notes and the chief himself made notes as our words were translated.

Each question, after translation, activated a lengthy discussion with all taking part before the answer was finally relayed back to us. The afternoon drew on. For three hours we sat there, fascinated and absorbed in this unique and memorable experience, oblivious to the heat, and to our own increasing thirst.

These people, by searching amongst themselves for answers to our questions, were throwing open to debate their own history, stimulating discussion and more than one argument, which we felt would continue long after we had gone. How we wished we could understand and speak their language. A young student, David Sasa, was amongst them. He was writing a thesis on the history of his people for his PhD at the University of Namibia at Windhoek. His eyes held a constant, excited glint as he absorbed every word, turning in all directions with his tape recorder in his hand. David told us afterwards that the afternoon's proceedings had produced a wealth of material for him about this important period in his people's history.

It is possible to give just a brief outline of the questions asked and the answers we received.

The Mayeyi confirmed what we had been told by Mr Mahoto, that Sangwali is where Chief Sebituane had his capital Linyanti, or Dinyanti as it was sometimes called. This is confirmed by the fact that Sebituane's grave is at Sangwali. After his death the capital was moved to where Malengalenga now stands, which is where Sekeletu was living at the time, though the name Linyanti was retained.

"Do you know where the missionaries had their camp?"

"Yes, we know," they assured us, "unfortunately there are no signs of the camp, but there is something to show where the camp was. We will take you to the place tomorrow."

"Do you know where the graves are?"

"There is nothing to mark the spot," they admitted, "but we know where they are buried."

"What does your history tell you of the way that they died, was it fever, or were they poisoned?"

Their reply was a unanimous, unequivocal assurance that they were poisoned. "Sekeletu," they said, "took an ox and gave it poison and then killed it and gave it to them. When they ate of the meat they died." Roger Price's correspondence and his wife's journal confirms that they indeed received a slaughtered ox soon after arrival, also some beer to drink.

"Why would he want to poison them, after he gave them permission to enter his territory?" we queried.

Two reasons; fear that his authority would be undermined and that he coveted their goods.

"To this day the Makololo do not like anyone else to have more goods than they have. They still want to dominate all the other people in the area."

"How did Sekeletu poison the ox?"

"According to what we know it was taken from a poisonous tree sometimes found growing in mopane. We only know its local name, which is *ucikamacembye*. It still grows around here."

"What about fever? Livingstone said that many of your own people were dying of the fever in the marshes and he said that that is what happened to Helmore and his party."

"Yes, it is true that many were dying of the fever but we are not aware that this is what happened to Helmore. They were poisoned. Price had the fever and he did not eat from the ox and he did not die."

"What did your ancestors think of Sebituane as a chief?"

"He was not a good chief," was the response, "he brought all the Mayeyi together to this region, took away our chief and land and dominated us."

"And what about Sekeletu, was he a good ruler?"

" No, he was very bad. He killed many people. Many he impaled on long, sharp stakes inserted into the rectum, leaving them to die in agony. He sold his own people, as well as those from the other tribes as slaves to the *Mambari* [Portuguese half-castes who were active slave dealers in the area]. Anyone who he thought was richer than he was, he killed. He kept many slaves himself. We will show you tomorrow just how badly he treated his slaves," we were told.

"What do you think of the missionaries coming here? Would it have been a good thing for your ancestors?"

The chief himself, through his head *induna*, responded to this question:

"It was very unfortunate that Sekeletu killed these missionaries. The missionaries gave assistance and helped to create good government. In areas like Zambia, which brought in missionaries, there is good government. If the missionaries had been allowed to come and live here, Sangwali would have been a large important town like Katimo Molilo. Today when people think of this area they think there are bad people who might still poison them because of Sekeletu and the Makololo and they do not come to this area.

We would very much like white people to come and settle amongst us, to bring good government. We hope you will spread the word that we would welcome white people."

It did not seem appropriate to tell them that perhaps it was because Katimo Molilo was on higher, healthier ground, very near Sesheke, that it had thrived as a town.

"We would like to tell you what happened to Sekeletu," the *indunas* then told us. "When Livingstone heard how badly he had treated the missionaries he was very angry and he prayed. And after he had prayed, Sekeletu died. The Makololo were destroyed because of what they did to the missionaries."

"There is a baobab tree near Malengalenga," they continued. "Livingstone carved his name on this tree and said he would be back. Tomorrow we will show it to you."

"Was life better for the Mayeyi people after Sekeletu had died?" was our next question.

"Yes," we were assured, "after Sekeletu died there was rejoicing and dancing and big festivals. We were again able to have our own chief and our own land. There are still a lot of Makololo in the area, however, and they would still like to dominate us."

"Could you tell us your own history; how long have you lived in these marshes and where did your ancestors come from?" we then asked.

A lively and lengthy discussion followed, with many of the elders and teachers, sages, story-tellers and ministers sitting behind us actively participating, while David Sasa eagerly recorded the conversations.

"The Mayeyi have been in this area since the fourteenth century," was the final conclusion. "They originally came from the Central African

Republic. They moved to Zimbabwe, at a place called Wanke, then to Kasane, then through Goha, then Marane, then Nkoyo, then to Grootfontein (it was Savunda). They then fought with the Herero and some of the Mayeyi were killed. The Herero captured many. The tribe then returned to Botswana, they crossed at Kawedumu, into Botswana, crossed the Linyanti and settled at Hankuyu near to Maun. We were in this area when the Makololo came."

Thus, they had moved down through what is now Zambia to Zimbabwe, then from Kasane on the Zambesi they had moved west through the Caprivi Strip into Namibia before moving south-east into the Okavango Delta. According to the *History of Botswana*[8] the Bayei have no relation to any of the other tribes of Botswana. In 1680 they were conquered by the Lozi, who were spreading south to the Zambezi River. Many of them then moved south to the Maun area.

Most of them still live in the Okavango Delta, where they punt their *mokoro* or dugout canoes through the reeds with a long pole. Livingstone mentions the Bayei people in his correspondence and journals. Clearly some were here when the Makololo moved north in about 1830 and conquered them, together with all the other tribes in the area.

"Is life good for the Mayeyi people now?" was the final question.

"Today we are experiencing a lot of problems," they told us. "We used to have a lot of wild animals. The white hunters killed off many animals, they shot them all. The wild animals are our mainstay."

For the first time, then, Chief Shufu himself spoke directly to us rather than through his chief *induna*.

"Please get us sponsors," he appealed passionately. "We need help to develop this area, to improve the life of my people."

These people do indeed have very little. There are two schools and a health clinic at Sangwali, but little else. The area is poor, rural and sparsely populated. Women and children still walk to the pump next to the *khuta* building to draw their water. They desperately need foreign investment, for Namibia itself has not the resources. They are peace-loving and anxious to dissociate themselves from the past actions of the Makololo, which they believe has given them a bad reputation.

"Tell your friends we won't poison them, we welcome them and wish them to come and visit us," was his plea.

As they clearly appreciate, the wild animals are their mainstay. The Linyanti Marshes are now preserved as the Mamili National Park. This area, together with that now occupied by the Muduma National Park further north-west, at one time played host to an immense variety of game of all sorts. Sadly, indiscriminate hunting, until as recently as the 1980's, has decimated the rhino population and considerably depleted the elephants as well as other smaller game. This devastation is now being stemmed and these animals are slowly returning.

Other problems still exist, though. There is a need to overcome the traditional habit of local people burning the bush in order, as they think, to encourage fresh rains, which of course is counter-productive in their attempt to build up the animal population. Another problem is poaching. The Botswana Government is fully aware of the importance of controlling this, and takes heavy action against any suspected poachers. It would help if the Namibian government addressed this serious problem with similar severity before it is too late.

We thanked the *khuta* most sincerely and presented our gifts to the chief: T-shirts, and other similar articles purchased in London tourist shops. These were clearly welcome. The chief paid us the compliment of taking off his own hat and replacing it with a cap emblazoned with the Union Flag. The proceedings were brought to an end with another prayer at 6 p.m.

Despite the fading light, we were escorted to the grave of Sebituane, accompanied by a party of elders. Kennedy Munyandi, a brother-in-law of Chief ShuFu and teacher at the local school, who also speaks English, is responsible for the preservation of the grave and he played host to us. The grave is clearly visible, on high ground, with stone slabs marking its boundaries and heavy logs placed in a criss-cross pattern across the top. It lies at latitude 18° 17'17"S, longitude 23° 38'54"E, about 4 km south of Sangwali. Close by, we were told, is the site where Kruger's house had stood. According to Edwin Smith's biography of Price, C.E. Kruger was assistant magistrate in the Caprivi Strip in the 1940's.[9] It was interesting to see that, despite their hatred of the Makololo, Sebituane's grave is still preserved and cared for. In contrast Sekeletu's, grave, which we saw the following day, is bare and indistinguishable. Perhaps the Mayeyei feel Sebituane's grave could become a tourist attraction. After all, this chief surely takes his place in history amongst the greatest, such as Chaka and Mzilikazi.

By the time we returned to our camp at Nsheshe it was quite dark. This was the first and only time that we had to erect our tents in the dark, not an easy feat, with only the large lamp on the trailer and our torches. However, Linus, who was responsible for running the site, recruited members of his family to assist and in no time we were organised and had a fire going. Sadly, Nsheshe suffered a severe fire soon after we left, but another campsite has been built nearby. The facilities are good and it makes a convenient base for exploring the area.

Friday 14th May

We met our hosts, Linus, Kennedy and the head elder, Chief John Ngambela early next morning outside the *khuta*. Also in the party was a woman elder, who represents affairs related to women in the council. She had been assigned to accompany us in case the ladies in the party needed her. In two packed vehicles we set off for Malengalenga, about 20 km east of Sangwali. We were taken straight to a high, bare piece of ground outside the town, where a party of local people waited to receive us. Linus introduced us to an elderly member of the community, who had agreed to tell us their history and to answer any questions.

Sekeletu, we were told, had been sent by his father to this spot, to administer and protect that area against invaders.

"This is where Sekeletu built his house," our guide explained. "You can see, it is on high ground. It was a large house, about 25m square." He scratched away some soil and just beneath the surface he exposed some red bricks, lying distinctly in the light grey indigenous sand. "These bricks were made of sand and straw which had to be carried by slaves all the way from Namaschascha" [*which is situated just south of Kongola, 25 km from Malengalenga*]. "He also used slaves to build a canal across the floodplain from the Linyanti River, about 10 km to the east, to another waterway immediately to the west of the town as a defence against the

Matabele," the old man continued. Did he use this soil to create the mound on which he built his house, we wondered.

About twenty yards away, parallel to the site of his house we were shown a large bare area. "This," our guide said, "is where Sekeletu was buried after he died of leprosy." There was no sign to indicate that a chief was buried there, no trees or building within sight, just the bare, hollowed out bit of earth.

"There are still guns buried in this soil," our guide said, "guns that Sekeletu bought by selling our people as slaves to the *Mambari*."

"Who sold him the guns?" we asked.

"Germans," was the reply. "They came from the west." This is true. Chapman, for example, came to this region from Walvis Bay on the western coast. It must be said that there were also parties of traders and hunters making their way north through the Kalahari desert to this region. A comment by Chapman further confirms the old man's assertion. After Livingstone had opened up the west coast in 1855, Chapman said, Sekeletu ceased dealing with traders from the south in the hope that Livingstone, as promised, would bring greater riches from the west and the east.[10]

We asked about fever. "Yes, there was a lot of fever, many of our own people died of fever in the marshes." They still do, despite the wide use of prophylactics. Again, the question was asked as to whether Sekeletu tried to poison the missionaries and if so why.

"He poisoned some beer and gave it to them to drink and he also poisoned an ox and gave them the meat to eat," was the reply, "he feared that they would take away his power over the people."

"Is there any truth in the story that after Isabella Price had been buried on the Mababe Plains, some Makololo came and dug up the body and removed the head, or face, and took it back to their chief?" we asked.

"No," our guide responded, "we have not heard that story." No one has been able to substantiate this story, which was told to Price at Lake Ngami, and which naturally caused him considerable distress. Perhaps it was merely hearsay, or an attempt to further blacken the Makololo.

After Sebituane died, we were again told, Sekeletu, who was living in this area, made his town the new headquarters and again called it Linyanti. The third and present town of Linyanti lies about 30 km north of

Malengalenga. We were taken to another spot about 1 km from Sekeletu's house and grave which, our guide said, was where he had built his *khuta*, or *kgotla*.

We were shown the stump of an old tree alongside where the *khuta* had stood. "This is where Sekeletu placed his walking stick into the ground, which then grew into a large *mupolota* tree, for which the Yeyi word is *wutsoro*," our guide told us. "When Sekeletu died, the tree died." This must have been the tree which Mr Mahoto sang about as a child.

The co-ordinates which Livingstone took when he arrived at "the capital of the Makololo" on 23rd May 1853 was latitude 18°17'20"S, longitude 23°50'9"E.[11] It was, he said, very near to the spot where their wagon stood in 1851 when he and Mary first came to this region. We took co-ordinates on this spot, which read latitude 18°17'5"S, longitude 23°47'7"E. In Smith's biography of Price, he says:

"In 1899 the Rev. Louis Jalla was taken by the local chief Mamisi (who said he was living when Helmore and Price arrived) to the site of the old township, and was shown the position of the graves near a big tree in a large plain, far from a village. In 1940 C.E. Kruger, assistant magistrate in the Caprivi Strip, reported that the place was named Mushukuka and occupied by the headman Shozi. A man named Maplanka pointed out a *mupolota* tree as the burial place. Shozi said this was where the missionaries' wagons stood."[12]

During our interview with Mr Mahoto at Katimo Molilo we had enquired as to where Mushukuka was. He told us that Malengalenga was at one time earlier last century known as Mushukula, not Mushukuka.

There is, then, continuity through the generations of this story. All this confirms that our hosts were right and we were on the site of Sekeletu's capital, the second Linyanti.

"Now, can you show us where the Helmore party had their camp?" we asked.

"Over there," our hosts pointed. Approximately a hundred yards away from the site of Sekeletu's *khuta* was a field, now farmed by our elderly guide. "This," they said, "is where the party had their camp."

Was it really the site of the Helmore camp? Roger Price wrote a detailed letter to Olive Helmore, in which he mentions that their camp was about half a mile distant from Sekeletu's town.[13] He had also said it was very near the *kgotla*. That fits in with this field.

We had reached our ultimate destination. Here on this field, on 14th February 1860, Holloway Helmore and his party had stopped their wagons for the last time, weak, exhausted but triumphant. Despite all the hardships and rigours of a terrible journey, they had arrived, all still alive and full of hope that they could make a new home amongst those people of whom Livingstone had spoken so favourably.

We surveyed a bare field, recently ploughed but barren of crops. Parched and hard, it contained just a few strands of dry grass and straw, scattered like flotsam on a sea of grey soil, which had over the centuries been submerged as the Linyanti River overflowed its banks. Already at ten on this May morning, the sun was scorching. What would it have been like in January, when our missionaries arrived in their layers of thick Victorian clothing? Only one tree was to be seen nearby and in the distance was a line of trees and bushes, bordering the Linyanti River. Nearby there was a row of bushes growing alongside a channel which, though now dry, was clearly a water course; an ideal spot for a campsite.

We asked whether there had been a tree on this piece of ground in the past. Our young student friend, David Sasa, had been listening with excited eagerness and interest. He now came forward and said that this piece of ground had belonged to his grandmother and as a child he had helped to plough the ground.

"I used to often pick up pieces of pottery like this in the soil," he said. He held out some shards. Immediately we started scouring for more fragments and others joined in the search. We collected sufficient to send away for analysis to ascertain the origin of the clay from which they were made. David pointed to a short tree stump, now covered with leaves.

"I can remember this tree stump," he said. "I always had to plough around it, it was much higher when I was a child. If only I knew then what had happened on this field!" Was this the *mupolota* tree that was pointed out to Kruger? If so, could the graves be on this spot? It is unlikely that we can ever be certain, as Livingstone had written contradictory comments to Tidman:

> "There, without a tree within a hundred yards to mark the spot, he rests from his labours, as good and as devoted a missionary as ever left England......."[14]

If we found the location of the camp, we can be certain that the graves are in close proximity, as Price could not have laid them to rest at any distance. He conducted all but one of the burials himself, even though he was very weak with fever and could not have walked far:

According to Isabella Price's journal, of their party of twenty one people, eight were buried in the Linyanti marshes in 1860, next to each other, in the order that they had died:-

2nd March	Molatsi, Bechuana driver of the Price's wagon
7th March	Henry Helmore, aged 3 years 10 months
9th March	Eliza Price, aged 5 months
11th March	Selina Helmore, aged 8 years
11th March	Thabi, Bechuana teacher from Lekhatlong
12th March	Anne Helmore, aged 48 years
19th March	Setloki, Bechuana driver of loose oxen and sheep
21st April	Holloway Helmore, aged 44 years

Alas, no cross marks the spot where they lie, they must rest in peace in their remote graves.

Those brave people had taken on a most difficult undertaking, despite all their misgivings, knowing that their chances of survival were slim. They had accepted as their Christian duty the decision of the London Missionary Society directors. Such emotional thoughts were going through our minds as we stood on that bare patch of ground.

We were recalled to the present by our guides and our accompanying group of Mayeyi people, who were waiting patiently in the hot sun. They were anxious to take us on to our next excursion, to view the large old baobab at Mbilajwe, approximately 8 km north east of Malengalenga. Our hosts had placed much emphasis on this baobab, anxious that we should see it. Livingstone, they told us, had carved his initials on this tree, with the promise that he would be back. However, we could find no trace of Livingstone's initials on this tree. Those pointed out to us were:

D.... M... S[or L], 1869

This does not fit into Livingstone's movements. After his brief visit to Linyanti in 1860 after the Helmore party deaths, he again returned to the east coast, never to visit this region again. As we know, Sekeletu died in 1863. After the overthrow of the Makololo by the maLozi, Sesheke became the new capital and Linyanti was abandoned. By this time many hunters and traders were traversing the region and it is difficult to determine who it was who may have carved his initials on this ancient baobab; was it Martinus Schwartz, a Dutch elephant hunter? Whatever the significance of the initials, the tree, which is preserved as a monument by the Mayeyi, is well worth a visit. Its trunk has split in two and is hollow inside, providing a convenient nesting place for birds, or shade from the sun for a few minutes for anyone willing to climb into it. A wonderful view of the surrounding countryside can be enjoyed from its higher branches.

Here another elderly man from the village again offered to tell us what he knew of the Helmore tragedy. The same stories emerged, and the same insistence that they were poisoned, that they did not die of fever.

"What sort of poison did he use?" we asked him. Our friends offered to show us a specimen of the tree from which it was extracted. They eventually tracked down a magnificent Euphorbia tree, known locally as *ucikamacembye*. Shaped like a giant candelabra, it emerged to an enormous height from a clump of mopane bush and, when cut, its succulent stems exuded a thick, sticky, white fluid.

"Don't touch the fluid," our guide warned us. "It's highly toxic and will blind you."

Perhaps now is the time to look at and weigh up all the known facts in the debate about the cause of deaths in the missionary party, in an effort to answer one of our questions.

It is probable that most, if not all of the party suffered from fever. We know that Lizzie and Willie were taken ill on the journey and that the Prices were badly bitten by mosquitoes at the Zouga (see Helmore's journal entry for October 22nd); also that they both had fever whilst at Linyanti. Roger Price was to suffer recurrent bouts of malaria for the rest of his life.

We must remember that at that time it was universally thought the fever was produced by vapours rising from the rank vegetation of the marshes, hence 'mal aria.' It was only towards the end of the nineteenth century that scientists in France, Britain and Italy proved that mosquitoes infected humans with the disease. James Chapman gives a graphic account of the problems with mosquitoes at Lake Ngami. Writing in 1856, he said:

"……But nothing is so painful to the traveller at this season as the tortures from the mosquitoes. Their numbers are overwhelming, there is no escape, and ordinary remedies are here of no avail. You are bitten into a fever, and rise next morning with face and forehead disfigured. Often we steamed ourselves in the smoke of cattle dung in a closed hut, almost to suffocation, without relief; some enter somehow and escape the fumes. We were often driven out of our wagons, and the mosquitoes visited the Lake in such clouds that they nearly obscured the setting sun. The sufferings from them are enough to bring on fever without the aid of malaria, and we first mistook their buzzing at night for the croaking of frogs. Cattle, horses and sheep also suffer from them, and ours fled into the desert, lowing and bellowing, and were often not recovered till late the next day. The only relief we had from the terrible plague was cold air or a gust of wind."[15]

Livingstone frequently talked about the unhealthy region in which the Makololo were living. Although they were safe from the spears of the Matabele, a more insidious killer was at work amongst them, weakening and destroying them. Livingstone himself had his first attack of fever there in 1853[16], followed by eight further attacks before he set out for the west coast.

Nevertheless, the allegations that they were given poison must be seriously considered. There is a full account of Roger Price's version of events in Appendix B, in the form of a talk given in Cape Town in August 1861. Price claimed that he was warned by the Makololo people themselves not to eat of an ox or drink the beer that was sent to them from Sekeletu, because it was poisoned. Price's fellow missionaries, Moffat and Mackenzie preferred to reserve judgement on this issue, rather than accuse Sekeletu of murder. Following Livingstone's opinion that it was without doubt fever, the allegations were quietly set aside, especially when plans were set in motion to make another attempt to establish a mission station on the Zambezi.

Chapman, who was hunting and trading in the area at this time, substantiates Price's assertion that they were poisoned. Chapman's diary entry for 31st March 1862 records:

"...... People who come from Linyanti tell the sad story of the missionary catastrophe in exactly the same way as Mr Price did on his arrival in the Colony.... Mr Price may be correct, I have had proof enough of the Makololo's brutal character and treachery and will never seek further intercourse with them... From a late refugee from those parts we learnt particulars unknown to Mr Price. It was not the ox that was poisoned, but some beer or other drink presented to the missionaries. Sekeletu was afraid to go near the party, but now and then sent to see how the poison was acting. He was consoled for his anxieties by a handsome present from the worthy Doctor [Livingstone], whom he easily convinced of his affectionate treatment of the missionary party.[17]"

A little later he says:

"Refugees from Linyanti say the missionaries were poisoned because the chief believed Livingstone would never return.[18]"

We must bear in mind that the Makololo had made many enemies, and that the BaTawana, of whom Lechulatebe was chief, had been driven from their land by Sebituane. Sebituane was a tyrant, even by nineteenth century African standards, but he treated his subjects fairly, exercising qualities of good leadership and he had the respect and devotion of his own people. His successor Sekeletu on the other hand, was a cruel, despotic chief, hated by the Makololo themselves to this day.

As we know, Livingstone did not arrive on the scene until August 1860, four months after Helmore's death and nearly two months after the survivors had left the area. The reasons for his delay have already been dealt with in Chapter Eight. He subsequently made no effort to obtain the facts from Price, the only person who could have explained the circumstances of the deaths. He diagnosed fever from a pre-conceived notion and from what the Makololo told him. He would not accept that the Makololo could use poison and strongly repudiated Price's allegations. "The spear, and not poison, is their weapon" he declared.[19] He had forgotten that in 1853 he acknowledged that it was possible for the Makololo to provide poisoned beer, or *boyaloa*, to guests. "These were brought by women, and each bearer took a good draught of the beer to show that it was not poisoned.[20]" It is possible that the Euphorbia tree pointed out to us by our hosts was known to Livingstone. In writing about poisons generally, he mentions the milky juice of the tree 'Euphorbia arborescens' as being used by the natives to poison the water holes in order to kill animals for meat. "It does not, however, kill oxen or men." he wrote. "On them it acts as a drastic purgative only.[21]"

Either Livingstone naively accepted without question the version of this whole tragedy given to him by Sekeletu and his people, or he would not admit that he was responsible in any way for the tragedy. When he wrote his report to the London Missionary Society he was confident that it was fever:

"The poignancy of my unavailing regret is not diminished by remembering that at the very time when the friends were helplessly perishing we were at a lower and much more unhealthy part of the river, and curing the complaint so quickly that in very severe cases the patient was able to resume his march on foot a day or so after the operation of the remedy.[22]"

Livingstone went on to give his rather traumatic remedy, which he stated he had been using himself in known cases since 1850. For interest, this is quoted here:

"Fever Powder - Take a Resin of Jalap and Calomel of each eight grains, Quinine and Rhubarba of each four grains. Mix well together, and when needed, make into pills with spirit of Cardamoms. Dose from (10) ten to (20) twenty grains. The mixture keeps best in powder. If the violent symptoms are not relieved in from four to six hours by the operation of the pills, a dessert spoonful of Epsom salts may be taken. Then quinine in four or six grain doses completes the cure. It is usually given till the ears ring or deafness is produced."

Traumatic as it sounds, it is a pity he had not imparted his remedy to Helmore earlier. As we know, Livingstone had left some of this medicine in his wagon at Linyanti when he set out for the west coast in 1853.[23]

On our return to Britain we consulted the experts. Dr Sasha Barrow of the Royal Botanical Gardens, Kew, identified the species as *Euphorbia ingens*. Her opinion is:

"The latex of *Euphorbia ingens*, as with many other species in this genus, is very acrid and is used both as a poison and medicinally....... According to one record, 'one drop [of the latex] in the eye causes blindness.' The latex of *Euphorbia ingens* is also used as a fish poison. The branches are thrown into a pool, and any fish present are quickly paralysed and so rise to the surface where they are easy to catch. Apparently, the fish can be safely eaten after being caught by this method.

Relating the above information to the tragic case of the poisoned missionaries, the latex of *Euphorbia ingens* is caustic and toxic, and it could cause stomach pains, diarrhoea and vomiting if enough was consumed in the beer, but it seems doubtful that it could have caused death. Certainly, death could not have been caused by eating the meat of oxen that had fed on *Euphorbia ingens*."

This is similar to Livingstone's observations.

We also approached Dr John Frean of the South African Institute for Medical Research, providing as many details as we could glean from the documents with regard to symptoms. In consultation with his colleagues, he reached the following opinion:

"The descriptions of the illness are scanty and non-specific and I can only speculate on the possible causes, keeping in mind that the party may well have been exposed to several potentially fatal illnesses, amongst which may have been some form of poisoning. Other possibilities include trypanosomiasis [*sleeping sickness, usually from tsetse fly*] and typhoid (or enteric) fever. The association of tsetse flies (and mosquitoes) with disease transmission had not yet been recognised, which may account for their lack of mention.

However, I think on balance that the most likely explanation regarding at least some of the members of the party is that they died of malaria. Most of the symptoms and signs described by Mr Price, although non-specific, could fit this diagnosis. Severe prostration, vomiting and diarrhoea can occur in acute malaria. Typhoid tends to have an insidious onset, with constipation rather than diarrhoea early in the disease. Postural hypotension (producing giddiness), headache, and back and body pains are also typical of, but not unique to, malaria. The apparent absence of overt fever and rigors is difficult to explain, but the moist skin (indicating sweating) which was mentioned, would be expected to occur at times in acute malaria. Isabella's journal, however, mentions fever several times. A wish for a cold sheet would seem to indicate a high temperature. A 'regular' pulse presumably could mean 'slow', which would fit more with typhoid fever than with malaria, in which it would be quick, as described (Rev Price's report).

The most telling evidence for malaria, and against poisoning, is in the timing of the deaths. Six out of seven deaths occurred over a period of about seven weeks, with the last (that of Isabella Price) more than two months later. This pattern is not consistent with acute poisoning, but it could fit very well with malaria. The baby, at about 5 months of age, would presumably not have been exposed directly to poison in meat or beer. The fact that some of the party survived despite having been ill, is in keeping with the variable severity of malaria."

These latest findings are similar to the conclusions reached by Edwin Smith after his comprehensive research on this subject in his autobiography of Roger Price.[24]

However, it was common practice for tribes in this area at that time to administer poison to their enemies. Sekeletu we know was hostile to the arrival of these missionaries to his country. As we were told more than once, he poisoned them because he feared he would have his authority taken from him. This is a credible story. These men and their families were useless to him. We know that he was waiting for Livingstone and his wife Mary to settle amongst them.

Although, therefore, malaria is the most likely cause of death for the people who lie buried in those fever-ridden marshes, there is sufficiently strong evidence that Sekeletu did administer poison to them in the hope that they would eventually die or return to their own land. One must take seriously the allegations of even the descendants of the Makololo. This is the conclusion to the first question we had set out to answer.

The pieces of pottery were given a thorough analysis by Professor Leon Jacobson of the McGregor Museum at Kimberley. They were all found to have been of local clay, or of clay found further west in Namibia. No samples could be identified as having come from Kuruman. This test was, therefore, inconclusive and a more thorough archaeological investigation of the field would be necessary. Documents and co-ordinate readings, however, confirm the Mayeyi view that we have found the site of the camp, which was our second quest.

We know within an area of about half a square kilometre where the graves are but, alas, we cannot be sure exactly where they were buried; this last question remains unanswered.

Saturday 15th May
With cheerful waves from Linus and Kennedy we set off for the return to Katimo Malilo, and from there we turned eastwards. Our mission accomplished, we allowed ourselves a pleasant respite in the Chobe National Park. The difference between this park and the quieter Mamili, which we had briefly visited the previous day, is quite marked. Being a popular venue for European tourists, the Chobe is far more crowded. Its attraction is, nevertheless, justified. It teems with wildlife, especially elephants.

Sunday 16th May
Crossing the border at Ngoma Bridge into Zimbabwe, we travelled about 70 km along the tarred road, parallel to the Zambezi River. About 15 km from Livingstone, on coming around a bend in the road, we saw on the horizon ahead of us what appeared to be a huge white cloud of smoke, rising high into the air.

"That's the Victoria Falls," Pierre said, "that's the spray as it tumbles over the edge of the cataract. A little nearer and we'll be able to hear it." *Mosi oa Tunya*, the smoke that thunders. The natives had named it aptly.

On his first visit to the Makololo in 1851, Livingstone had been told of a huge waterfall, about 210 km from Linyanti as the crow flies. Though his curiosity had been aroused he set off for the west coast in 1853 without inspecting them. It is probable that even then he had an inkling of their importance. Chapman was in the area in August 1853, at the same time that Livingstone was at Linyanti. Chapman had arranged for local men to take him and his companions, Thompson and Campbell to inspect the falls. They were about to step into the boat when they were told that Livingstone had ordered that they should not proceed, owing to unrest in the area caused by the Matabele.[25] Chapman was to regret his decision not to have proceeded, had he done so he would have been the first European to bring this magnificent natural spectacle to the attention of the world, not Livingstone. In any event, neither of these men were the first Europeans to have actually seen the falls. Portuguese traders and slave dealers were already well aware of their existence.

Livingstone finally visited the falls on his return from the west coast, as he was about to embark on his journey east. On 15th November 1855, accompanied by Sekeletu, he gazed upon them and named them "The Falls of Victoria" - the only English name, he said, that he ever affixed to any part of the country.[26]

Tuesday 18th May

Our journey was drawing to an end. We were on the road very early for the long drive south. The tarred road is good and there was nothing to hamper our progress as we shortened the 500 km distance to Bulawayo, driving hard, hour after hour.

Bulawayo, the *place of slaughter* as the Matabele or Ndebele called it, is a large sprawling town, retaining much of its Colonial atmosphere, but with a very high crime rate. We drove on to the Matoba National Park, just south of Bulawayo, where we spent the night.

Matoba was the home of the ancient tribes the Torwa and then the Rozwi, before they were conquered by the Matebele who, as we know, moved up from the south after skirmishes with the encroaching Boers. It seemed fitting that we should end our pilgrimage here, the heart of Matabeleland, where that other great chief Moselekatse held court. It was to this area that the other party of young missionaries were sent, in an effort to keep the peace between the Matabele and the Makololo in order that the latter could move out of the marshes. The party consisted of Robert Moffat's son John Smith Moffat, Thomas Morgan Thomas and their wives and the widowed William Sykes. Robert Moffat accompanied them. They had left Kuruman immediately after the Helmore/Price party set out, in July 1859 and arrived three months later, in October. They did not endure the same hardships that their brethren did on their route. Lung-sickness, however, had broken out amongst their cattle and rather than risk taking this killer-disease to the Matabele, Moffat sent ahead and asked Moselekatse for some of his oxen to be sent to the frontier to assist them. Rather than send oxen, the old chief sent teams of his powerful warriors to pull the wagons. These warriors struggled valiantly; 80 men pulling the wagons three at a time for eleven miles a day, then returning for the others.[27] The pace was painfully slow and in the end oxen had to be brought in.

Moselekatse was by then a sick old man and still reluctant to accept the missionaries. He feared that the Boers would follow in their wake. Alas, it was not the Boers but the prospectors and empire builders who eventually followed. At last, on December 16th 1859, he pointed out to them a piece of land at Inyati, about 60 km north of Bulawayo, on which to build the first mission station. This mission was more successful in establishing itself than its Makololo counter-part, but nevertheless it had its share of problems. Death, which had already struck in Kuruman taking Mrs Sykes, her baby and the Moffats' first infant, now took Mrs Thomas and her baby. There were personality clashes in the tiny, isolated community. Sykes and Thomas could not agree on many aspects of missionary policy, resulting in the latter finally leaving the London Missionary Society and setting up his own station nearby. Christianity did not take root easily amongst the Matebele and Moselekatse's resistance to their teachings added to their problems. On the positive side, on 15th April 1860, Livingstone Moffat was born; the first white child to be born in what was to become Rhodesia.[28] However, Emily Moffat suffered continual ill health and eventually the Moffats had to return to Kuruman.

Moselekatse died in 1868, just four years after Sekeletu and was buried in these hills. His son Lobengula eventually succeeded him and had his capital at Bulawayo. In the 1870's the British were becoming increasingly interested in this land and its presumed wealth. Cecil Rhodes finally wrangled a mining concession in 1888 and this was the beginning of the end for the Matabele. Lobengula died of smallpox in 1894, bereft of his kingdom, a fugitive in these hills of Matoba.

Wednesday 19th May

Our arrival in Johannesburg in the evening rush-hour ended our journey. We had covered 6,500 kilometres; over 4,000 miles.

We had accomplished our mission. We now have a new respect for those early missionaries, gained from a deeper understanding of the hardships they endured. Further, it is comforting to know that the seeds sown by them did come to fruition. Christianity is well established in the Caprivi Strip and although Holloway Helmore and Roger Price were at Linyanti for a mere few weeks, the memory of their visit has endured.

1 *Travels and Researches 1858,* p.194ff
2 Cape Archives, S.A. Advertiser and Mail, 17.8.1861
3 Mackenzie, p.243ff
4 MacKenzie, p.239ff
5 *The Journals of Elizabeth Lees Price*, p.94ff
6 Ibid, p.96
7 MacKenzie, p.240
8 *History of Botswana*, Tjqu and Campbell
9 Smith, p.88
10 Chapman, Part 1, p.158ff
11 *Travels and Researches*, 1858, p.195
12 Smith, p.88
13 Personal collection, Roger Price to Olive Helmore, 1.12.1861 (Original in the L.M.S. Archives)
14 L.M.S. Archives, Livingstone to Tidman, 25.2.1862
15 Chapman, Part 1, p.179
16 LMS Archives, Livingstone to Tidman, 24.9.1853
17 Chapman, Part 2, p.34
18 Ibid, p.37
19 *The Dark Interior*, Oliver Ransford, p.173
20 *Travels and Researches*, 1937 ed., p.49
21 *Travels and Researches*, 1858, p.189
22 L.M.S. Archives, Livingstone to Tidman, Chicova, 10.11.1860
23 L.M.S. Archives, Livingstone to Tidman, 25.2.1862
24 Smith Appendix B
25 Chapman, Part 2, p.61
26 *Travels and Researches*, 1937 ed., p.264
27 Matabele Journals (2), p.196
28 The Harvest and the Hope, Briggs/Wing, p.70ff

Appendices
Sources
Index

Appendix A

Palmyra Lodge
Lotlakani
Sept. 28 1859

My very dear Emily

I write this in a pretty little hut 14 ft. by 18, built by your Brother. The walls are of Palmyra wood and it is thatched with Palmyra leaves, so it answers literally to the name we have given it, Palmyra Lodge, and though rough looking on the outside, it forms a delightful shelter from the scorching rays of the sun. I should tell you that it is 'Hartebeest' shape, and has a window at each end with thin calico as a substitute for glass. I only wish I were in a hut of similar description but of larger dimensions north of the Zambesi instead of being still 200 miles south of it and the prospect of another six weeks journey, but I must be patient and leave fearing for the future to record the mercies of the past.

I wrote last from the Bamanwato town and the letters were sent by the guide to the care of Sechele. I hope they will be delivered safely but I am afraid there will be some delay.

The last stage of our journey has been without exception the most trying time of travelling I have experienced in Africa. The heat as you are aware is most oppressive at this season of the year before the rains commence. We are also within the Tropics and on a journey more exposed to it than in a house. The heat during the day is intense, 102° in the shade, it causes in one faintness and giddiness but the early mornings are still thankfully cool. We may expect rain this month and are longing for it as those only can long who have travelled through dry and scorched wilderness where there is no water.

The country we have travelled through from Letloche to this place has been for the most part destitute of water and uninteresting in its aspect. Our poor oxen were at one time 4 and at another 3 days without drink, it was quite painful to see how tame they were rendered by thirst, they crowded round the waggon licking the water casks and pushing their noses down to the dishes and basins and up to our faces as if asking for water. We suffered very much ourselves from thirst, being obliged to economize the little we had in our vessels, not knowing when we should get more. We had guides but they either could not or would not give us any information. We half suspect they were instructed to deny us the water.

Tuesday the 6th was one of the most trying days I ever passed. About sunrise the poor oxen which had been painfully dragging the heavy waggons through the deep sand during the night, stopping now and then to draw breath, gave signs of giving up altogether. We had not gone as many miles as they were inspanned hours.

Holloway now resolved to remain behind with one waggon and a single man while I and the children and the rest of the people went forward with all the oxen thinking that we should certainly reach water by night. We had had a most scanty supply the day before. The men had not tasted drink since breakfast, until late in the evening we divided a bottleful among 4 of them. There now remained 5 bottles of water. I gave H(olloway) 3 and reserved 2 for the children, expecting that we should get water first. It was a sorrowful parting for we were all faint from thirst and of course eating was out of the question. We were afraid even to do anything lest exercise should aggravate our thirst.

After dragging slowly on for four hours the heat obliged us to stop. The poor children continually asked for water. I put them off as long as I could and when they could be denied no longer doled the precious fluid out a spoonful at a time to each of them. Poor Selina and little Henry cried bitterly. Willie bore up manfully, but his sunken eyes showed how much he suffered. Occasionally I observed a convulsive twitching of his features showing what an effort he was making to restrain his feelings. As for dear Lizzie you may fancy her, not a word of complaint, she did not even ask for water but lay on the ground all the day perfectly quiet, her lips quite parched and blanched.

About sunset we made another attempt and got on about 5 miles. The people then proposed going on with the oxen in search of water, promising to return with some to the waggon, but I (insisted upon) their resting a little and then making another attempt that we might possibly get near enough to drive on to it. They yielded, tied up the poor oxen to prevent their wandering and laid down to sleep, having tasted neither food nor drink all day. None of us could eat. I gave the children a few prunes in the middle of the day, as they were slightly acid, but thirst took away all desire to eat. Once in the course of the afternoon Willie, after a desperate effort not to cry, suddenly asked me if he might go and drain the bottle. Of course I consented and presently he called out to me with such eagerness that he had found some! Poor little fellow, it must have been little indeed for Selina had drained them already. Soon after he called out that he had found another bottle of water. You can imagine the disappointment when I told him it was cocoanut oil melted by the heat.

But this is a digression. I must go back to our outspanning at half past 9 o'clock. The water was long since gone and as a last resource, just before dark, I divided among the children half a teacupful of wine and water, which I had been saving for myself in case I should feel faint. They were revived by it and said how nice it was although it scarcely allayed their thirst. Henry at length cried himself to sleep and the rest were dozing feverishly. It was a beautiful moonlight night but the air hot and sultry. I was in front of the waggon, unable to sleep, hoping that water would arrive before the children awoke on another day.

About half past 10 I saw some persons appearing. They proved to be two Bakalahari bringing a tin canteen half full of water and a note from Mrs Price saying that, having heard from the men we had sent forward of the trouble we were in, and being themselves not very far from the water, they had sent us all they had. The sound of water soon roused the children who had tried in vain to sleep and I shall not soon forget the rush they made to get a drink. There was not much, but enough for the present. I gave each of the children and men a cupful and then drank myself. It was the first liquid that had entered my lips for more than 24 hours and I had eaten nothing.

The Bakalahari passed on after having deposited the precious treasure, saying that though they had brought me water they had none for themselves. They were merely passing travellers. I almost thought them angels sent from heaven.

All now slept comfortably excepting myself. My mind had been too much excited for sleep and now a fresh disturbance arose. The poor oxen had smelt the water and became very troublesome. The loose cattle crowding about the waggon looking and snuffling and pushing their noses towards me as if begging for water.

At 2 o'clock I roused the men telling them that if we were to make another attempt to reach water, no time was to be lost. They were tired, faint and very unwilling to move, but at last they got up and began to unloose the oxen and drive them off. I remonstrated but in vain, they had lost all spirit. I was obliged to let them go, but they assured me I should have water sent as quickly as possible, and the cattle should be brought back again after they had drunk. They knew no more than I did the distance to the water.

I felt anxious at the thought of their leaving us spending another day like the last, but they had not been gone more than half an hour, when I saw in the bright moonlight a figure at a distance coming along the road. At first I could not make it out, it looked so tall but on coming nearer, who should it prove to be but my servant Kionecoe, 18 years of age, carrying on her head an immense calabash holding about a pailful of water. On learning of our distress she volunteered to assist us. She had walked 4 hours. A young man had set out with her but he had driven on the sheep the day before a great distance without either food or water and became so exhausted that he lay down under a bush to rest and on she came alone in the dead of the night, in a strange country infested with lions, bearing her precious burden. Oh how grateful I felt to her. Surely woman is the same all the world over. She had only lived with me since June, was but an indifferent servant and had never shown any particular attachment to the children, but this kind act revealed her heart and seemed to draw us more closely together, for her conduct since has been excellent.

I made a bed for the girl beside me on the forepart of the waggon and the children having now slaked their thirst with the deliciously cool water, we all slept till 6 o'clock. I made coffee and offered some to Kionecoe and the young man who had now come up. At first they declined it, saying the water was for me and the children. I had now the happiness of seeing the children enjoy a meal of tea and biscuits and then once more filling up my two bottles, I sent the calabash with the remainder of its contents to Holloway, who by this time stood greatly in need of it. ... ...
I afterwards found we were about the same from water.

Another hot day had now commenced and I had still only the 4 bottles of water, so thinking employment the best thing for the children I made them take off their shoes and stockings and outer garments and sit upon the bed and I gave them a bag of buttons to assort and string.

About now a horseman rode up leading a second horse with two water casks and a tin canteen in his pack. This was a supply for Holloway, sent by our kind fellow travellers Capt. and Mrs Thompson, who had heard of our distress from the Prices. The man said that an ox was coming with a supply for me. I begged for a little from the tin to make coffee promising to make it good when my supply arrived and while we were preparing the coffee, up came the pack ox sent by Mr Price with two water casks for me, and soon after some Bakalahari arrived with a calabash, so we had now an abundant supply and my heart overflowed with gratitude to the Father in Heaven who had watched over me and mine, as over Hagar of old, and sent us relief.

I related this and other instances of God's care to the children the day before and exhorted them to pray to their Heavenly Father and rest assured that he would send them help. They now referred very sweetly to the subject, saying "it was just as I had said." I could not but wish that the simple experience they had now had might prove a valuable lesson through life.

We could now wash our faces and hands, a luxury we had not enjoyed since Sunday. Mr. and Mrs T(hompson) rode up to the waggon in the afternoon to see if they could be of any further assistance and brought a little milk for the children. I forget if I told you in a previous letter who Mr and Mrs T are. They are, I have been told, related to families of high rank. Mrs. T, I believe is a daughter of Admiral (left blank). Mr T. was an officer in the Crimean army. He had a sunstroke which obliged him to quit the service and try a year's travelling in Africa for the recovery of his health. They are both very young. They were accompanied by a surgeon of the name of Palgrave, who intends presenting his discoveries into the interior, in company with a Dr Holden who seems to be making a scientific tour. It has been very pleasant to meet occasionally with agreeable educated fellow countrymen and has tended greatly to alleviate the feeling of solitude while travelling through the uninhabited wilderness. Now, however, we have separated. Mr T's party have gone to the lake and go on to Walwich Bay for England. The two medical men we may possibly meet again at the Zambesi.

Excuse this digression. A span of oxen passed me in the middle of the night going to fetch H(olloway) and at about half past 9 o'clock on Wednesday night, a span arrived for us. We waited 2 hours thinking H's waggon might come up but hearing nothing of it, we started and I sent a note and a can of water for him by some Bakalahari, which they faithfully delivered.

We travelled 3 hours on, then one of the hind oxen laid himself down and refused to stir, so we outspanned for 2 hours and had just taken a slight breakfast when Mr Price came to meet us and in another hour we reached Logaganeng, where Mrs Price had kindly prepared a substantial breakfast.

H(olloway) did not come up till the evening and as the water of these wells was rather salty we moved on next day one hour to the deep well of "Nkaune." We formed quite an interesting encampment there on the dry salt pan, surrounded by bushes. On one side were Mr Thompson's 2 waggons, cart and 2 tents, at a short distance Dr Holden's 2 waggons and his tent between them, on the other side Mr Price and Thabe's waggon and our own 2 and tent.

Our next halting place was Banchukura. Here was a steep well of 12 feet with water dripping from the rocky sides. One of the men said it reminded him of God's bringing water from the rock for the Israelites of old.

There were now several days again without water, but as we knew about the distance we could arrange accordingly. We cooked a quantity of provisions and filled available vessels with water, so we did not suffer.

This time it was Mr Price's turn to be in trouble through the wandering of his oxen, so we had an opportunity of returning his kindness to us. About a mile from this place (Lotlakani), the axle of our larger waggon broke and down it came on one side, so we had to get out and walk. Here was another instance of divine care, for had this happened during one of those long stages without water, or even the day before when we were 20 miles from water, how different it would have been.

We were greatly disappointed on arriving here to find instead of the nice fountain we expected, nothing but a dense mass of mud. It required a whole day's hard labour to clear away the mud so as to obtain sufficient water for the cattle. Most of them had by this time been 3 days without drink.

We were now brought to a stand, partly by the fatigue of the poor oxen, but chiefly by Mrs Price's circumstances. On Friday last, September 30th, she was made the joyful mother of a sweet little girl. Everything has gone on most favourably and we hope in about 10 days to be able to resume our journey.

Oct. 8th.

An Englishman has just come in from the Lake on his return to Natal. I shall send this by him. I fear there will not be time to write any more letters.

Selina and Willie are (?poorly) from the heat. Henry is hearty enough and a sensible, loving boy. Dear Lizzie is growing quite a fine girl, handy and clever as a little woman, yet playful and active as a child. She talks Sechuana now fluently, as dear Olive used to do. Willie does not manifest much energy. I think the heat does not suit him. He often asks when we shall be at home. H(olloway) sends fondest love, his health keeps remarkably good, notwithstanding such constant hard work. Indeed, we are all very well, though we feel the heat.

End of letter.

Original in the Transvaal Archives, Pretoria, Ref.A.551

Appendix B

The South African Advertiser and Mail, Cape Town
17th August 1861

MR PRICE AND THE MAKALOLO
On Thursday evening, the annual social meeting of the Congregational Church Sabbath School Teachers, was held in the Barrack-street Schoolroom. The Rev. W. Thompson occupied the chair; and addresses were delivered by the Rev. Dr Adamson, Rev. Mr Stewart, Rev. Mr Price, Rev. Mr Morgan and Mr A. McDonald.

The Rev. Mr Price said: —

Fully aware that we are met together to further the interests of Sunday Schools connected with the Congregational Church in Caledon-square, I feel sure that you will excuse me when I bring before you certain facts connected with the Makololo Mission.

It will be remembered that soon after the report of the death of the Missionaries was made public, I stated that their death was not caused by fever but poison. I have not made reference to this before the public since I arrived here, and some have thought that I have given up the idea, but it is still my conviction; having the facts before me I cannot avoid the conclusion; but briefly to refer to some things stated:

On our arrival at Linyanti we were told that Sekeletu was out hunting, and that he would not return for three days. This naturally surprised us, because he had heard of our approach. The next day, he sent us an ox; on the third day he came with a large number of men, and brought some beer. Soon after our arrival, about a fortnight, one after another became sick and died, and passed from a scene of pain to that of joy and bliss. These deaths having taken place, what was the cause of death?

My attention was first drawn to it by certain Makololo who told our Bechuanas that during the time that Sekeletu was said to be out hunting he was in his own house and that the ox which was sent on the second day after our arrival, was poisoned by his own hand.

I am not supposed to be able to explain the mode of poisoning, but suffice it to say that it is a custom which prevails in the Interior. On the third day the king himself visited our encampment with a large retinue, bringing large quantities of beer with them. This beer was declared to be poisoned also, and this with his own hand. This news was first communicated by a man (Mapalayana) who is in constant attendance on the chief. When this was told me, I was unwilling to believe it, and the more so because the chief and his people had also partaken of the beer. The Bechuana, however, laughed at me for disbelieving it on that account because they said that that was a common practice among the Bechuanas. One man having enmity against another would put him to death; he dare not do it openly; but makes a pot of beer, and mixes poison with it. He invites his friend to partake with him of the beer; the one knows what he has taken, and takes another medicine which causes him to vomit; the other, not having any suspicion, allows the poison to work through his system and by and bye sickens and dies. This difficulty being removed, I was led to look more thoroughly into what had taken place.

Immediately after the arrival of the post from Moselekatse's country, about the middle of April, Mr Helmore, who was then comparatively well, had occasion to go to the town to see Sekeletu, to ask for messengers to send back to Moselekatse, which were promised. Mr Helmore there partook of more beer, he returned to his wagon ill, he became much worse, and in a few days died. About the same time I purchased beer because the water was very unpalatable. Some of the men cautioned me against drinking the beer, telling me that it was that which killed Mr Helmore. Just before my departure from Linyanti I received 5 oxen from Sekeletu, in return for others he had taken from me, with regard to one of which some of the Makololo said to my men: 'Take care you do not slaughter that blue ox, it has been poisoned by Sekeletu.' These facts are corroborative of the testimony given by Mapalayana and others, that these deaths were not caused by fever.

In addition to these facts, in proof that these deaths were caused by poison and not by fever, I must state first the favourableness of the season during which we were at Linyanti. Generally, during the summer months, the whole of the plain of Linyanti is covered with water, even in the town itself they have sometimes to cross from one part to the other in canoes.

At such times we may naturally expect that there would be much fever, the people being almost steamed by the evaporation of these stagnant waters. But during the summer of 1859/60 there was no rain in the country, and hence the cause of fever was absent. There was none, or at least very little, water within a mile and a half of the town of Linyanti. During the first few days after our arrival we were all particularly struck with the healthiness of the place; there was none of that oppressive feeling which we had sometimes had in the neighbourhood of large pools, where there was much rank vegetation. Generally during the unhealthy season, fever prevails among the inhabitants of Linyanti, but during the time that we were there, there was little or no sickness.

I happened to have with me a man (Konati) who had visited Linyanti with Dr Livingstone. After my return to Kuruman that man was asked by Mr Moffat if the sickness which they had this time was like that which they had on the former occasion, he replied no, *botleku bo sele lela* (another sickness altogether).

Again, by taking into consideration the symptoms which prevailed among the sick in our party, I came to the same conclusion. I have witnessed several cases of what is called African fever. I have suffered from it myself, and also from the sickness we had at Linyanti, and hence am able in some degree to compare the two. The symptoms of the African fever, as far as I have been able to observe, are a great fullness in the whole system, obstinate constipation, dry hot skin, quick pulse, giddiness, etc. The prevailing symptoms among our party were great giddiness, severe pain and weakness in the spine and lower extremities, followed in a very short time by an entire prostration of the whole frame, diarrhoea, and in some cases very severe and prolonged vomiting, also so severe that the stomach rejected almost everything. Different from African fever, the skin was moist, and the pulse regular.

I attended Mr Helmore during his last illness, and I can safely say that I could not discover any fever in him. In African fever I have not seen much pain suffered; but some of my friends suffered pain of the most excruciating character. There was also the utmost indifference to everything that transpired; the dearest friends might be taken away and not the slightest notice taken of it, I have not sufficiently studied the medical art to say whether these things indicate poisoning; but be this as it may, the testimony of the Makololo remains the same. And the treatment we received from the Makololo are in keeping with this. If they had been blameless why have deprived us of almost everything we had, why have sent us away with scarcely anything to eat? I have, on a former occasion referred to the taking of our goods, and need not refer to it again. Some will say perhaps that it is the custom among native tribes, when a white man or any other dies in their country, all his property goes to the Chief; this may be so, although I am not aware of it, but still it remains for such parties to say why Sekeletu deprived me of almost everything I had. Not even satisfied with this, the Makololo must needs give orders to their Bushmen, who were to be our guides, to take us straight into the Tsetse fly, and then to run away. They thought that then we must either die or abandon what we had left, and in either case they would have the undisputed possession of the whole.

I may here mention a fact which I have on a former occasion referred to, though not in this connection. When we parted with Mr Moffat at the Bamangwato, he told us that as soon as he arrived in Moselekatse's country he would despatch messengers to Linyanti, and requested us to impress on Sekeletu's mind the importance of receiving these messengers well. This we told Sekeletu on our arrival, and this he promised to do. About the middle of April, however, when these messengers arrived, they were not allowed to cross the river at all, but were turned back at one of Sekeletu's farthest outposts, the letter bag was taken from them and delivered to us. Sekeletu professed to be sorry that they were gone back, and promised that he would send messengers to Moselekatse. When afterwards I asked him to fulfil this promise, he simply said that he was not going to send his men to be killed by Moselekatse. When I met Mr Moffat, after my return from Linyanti, almost the first question he asked me was if we had received the letters he sent. I replied yes, but that his messengers were not allowed to come to Linyanti. Then he gave me the account of the messengers, which was this: that when they got to the borders of Sekeletu's country they were prevented from going farther, they could not obtain anything to eat, although half starving, but having delivered up the post bag, had to return immediately with the message, that the missionaries had not arrived, but that as soon as they did arrive Sekeletu would send messengers to Moselekatse; when at that very time seven were in their graves. Now I would ask any body who has had experience of the native tribes, if this is the course that would have been taken by any except those who had a purpose to answer. Had the Makololo been blameless they would have said to Moselekatse's messengers, return at once and tell Moffat that his friends were dying and that he must come and take them away as soon as possible. This fact to my mind, and to the minds of others who have had ten times the experience that I have of native tribes, is one of a most suspicious character, and is, I think, a strong proof of foul play.

Before concluding, I would just avert to certain reports which came from the Victoria Falls. At the Bamangwato I fell in with a native Christian, one well reported of by the German Missionaries; he had come from the Falls and had seen several of the Makololo, some of whom told him that the white men had gone past Lechulatebe's, that he had poisoned them, and that they had proceeded to Linyanti to die. Others said that when the white men arrived at Linyanti, they encamped near an old kraal where there was witchcraft, that they were warned against this but they would not listen, and hence the death of so many. This report is only of importance because the Makololo attributed the death of the mission party, not to fever, but to another cause. It is a native report and you must take it for what it is worth. All I claim for it is, the same credit that you give the other reports, founded entirely on native testimony.

There are before the public statements from Dr Livingstone which are a direct contradiction of what I have stated both this evening and on a former occasion. Now, all I claim for this report is, that it should be looked upon as of equal value to that on which the statements referred to are based.

Original in the South African Library, Cape Town.

Appendix C

Letter written in Sechuana by Chief Sekeletu to Lord John Russell, Foreign Secretary, in September 1860. Translation in Chapter 8.

"Go itumetse Sekeletu mahuku a lokualo lo lo thileñ, nu Naga e mo paletse ka go tsabana le Mosilikatsi – Oa bona botluku yo vegolu kua o teñ – go hela bathu – go hela likhomia a ga si botluku yona bo 00 Naga ki eoana ea Bhori li ea Mpakane ki nago e emtle kua bathu ba ka agela ruri – Mi nka aga hau ki le nosi Ha ki aga ki le nosi le go ro bala gankitle ki [? Robala] go eona. Ha MaRobert o kabo o tlileki gona nka itumelañ, gobane Mosilikatse o ka mo lesa, le roua, ka e le nuana oa Molekane oa gae – Mosheta – Mi Sekeletu oa re go Morena oa Makoa, Mpa bana va gago go aga le na mi ki tla ba khao – Ganan naga va ka aga mo go eona.

Tsela kua Bophirimo yoa Letsatsi ka yenu Monare o e phuntse mi tsela kua bophirimo yoa letsatse oa e plunya Le Ena Morena la tusa Sekeletu ka go roma Mokhoro oa tsepé – A ga o ka tlaolele bana ba gae go aga le ena ba bua taba le ena yale tsela e phimyegele rure – Ki gona go robala ga Mothu Naga e ae e gopolan ki a maloba mi lichaba tsa Batoka ha a loga – ki naga ea mechoeri – Banagoa le bona ba yala Maloba ba a roka.

A go ba tsalano le bena ka metla ka melta – re utluane monate.

    Go bua ( ) Sekeletu

Sources

Manuscript Sources

The bulk of the documents which were used in the research for this book are in the archives of the old London Missionary Society, now under the auspices of the Council for World Mission. These are housed in the library of the University of London's School of Oriental and African Studies.

Material from the personal collection of the author has also been extensively drawn upon. Most of these documents, however, are copies made by the Helmore family before the originals were deposited in the London Missionary Society Archives.

A cache of Helmore papers and letters are in the Transvaal Archives, Pretoria, South Africa, also in the South Africa Archives, Cape Town.

Reference was also made to the British Library, the Public Records Office at Kew and to Dr Williams Library, London, where a comprehensive range of non-conformist records is held.

Printed Sources

Abbreviated references to printed sources are as under:

Augustinus	*Botswana - A Brush with the Wild*, Paul Augustinus, 1992, Acorn Books C.C., Randburg, South Africa
Chamberlin	*Some Letters from Livingstone - 1840-1872*, Ed. D.Chamberlin, 1940, Oxford University Press, London
Chapman	*Travels in the Interior of South Africa*, James Chapman, Ed. Edward Tabler, Parts 1 and 2, 1971, Balkema, Cape Town
Dickson	*Beloved Partner, Mary Moffat of Kuruman*, Mora Dickson, 1989, Botswana Book Centre/Kuruman Moffat Mission Trust
Jeal	*Livingstone*, Tim Jeal, 1973, Heinemann, London
Mackenzie	*Ten Years North of the Orange River*, John MacKenzie, 1971, Frank Cass & Co. Ltd.
Matabele Journals	*Matabele Journals of Robert Moffat*, Volume Two, edited by J.P.R. Wallis, 1945, Chatto & Windus, London

Narrative	*Narrative of an Expedition to the Zambesi and Its Tributaries, 1858-1864*, David and Charles Livingstone, 1865, John Murray, London
Northcott	*Robert Moffat, Pioneer in Africa*, Cecil Northcott, 1961, Lutterworth Press, London
Seaver	*David Livingstone, His Life and Letters, George Seaver*, 1957, Harper and Brothers, New York.
Smith	*Great Lion of Bechuanaland,* Edwin W. Smith, 1957, Independent Press Ltd., London
Travels and Researches	*Missionary Travels and Researches in South Africa*, David Livingstone, 1858, J.Murray, New York,
Zambezi Expedition	*Zambezi Expedition of David Livingstone, The*, Vols I and II, edited by J.P.R. Wallis, 1956, Chatto & Windus Ltd., London

Reference was also made to:

A Church of the Ejectment - The Story of Rother Street Congregational Church, Stratford-upon-Avon, 1912, Alexander Barber
Colonisation of the Southern Tswana, The, 1870-1900, Kevin Shillington, 1985, Ravan Press, Johannesburg
David Livingstone: The Dark Interior, Oliver Ransford, 1978, John Murray (Publishers) Ltd., London
Harvest and The Hope, The: A Story of Congregationalism in Southern Africa, D.Roy Briggs and Joseph L Wing, 1970, The United Congregational Church of Southern Africa, Johannesburg
History of Botswana, Tjqu and Campbell
Isabella Price, Pioneer, Maud Isabella Slater, 1931, The Livingstone Press, London
John MacKenzie of Bechuanaland, Anthony Sillery, 1971, A A Balkema, Cape Town
Journals of Elizabeth Lees Price, The, Ed. Una Long, 1956, Edward Arnold
Memoir of the Rev. Thomas Helmore, M.A., Frederick Helmore, 1891, J. Masters & Company, London.
Putting a Plough to the Ground, ed. W.Beinart, P.Delius and S.Trapido, 1986, Ravan Press, Johannesburg - Essay 'Irrigation, Agjriculture and the State: The Harts Valley in Historical Perspective' by K.Shillington
Travels and Researches in South Africa, David Livingstone, ed.Hugh Schonfield, 1937, Herbert Joseph Ltd., London
Zimbabwe, Botswana and Namibia, Deanna Swaney, 1995, Lonely Planet Publications, Victoria, Australia

Index

Anderson, William, 12
Arundel, John, 3, 6

Baines, Thomas, 78, 177-8, 227
Bakwena, 121, 123, 204-5 (*see also* Sechele)
Bamangwato, 64, 120, 122-4, 142, 166, 167, 207, 226, 229, 245, 273, 283, 284 (*see also* Sekhomi)
Barotse (*maLozi*), 44, 55, 62, 64-5, 240, 246, 249, 254
Batawana, 44, 165, *origins of*: 228-9, 263 (*see also* Lechulathebe)
Batlapin, 9, 12, 14, 18, 20, 21, 25, 34, 44, 49- 50, 85, 100, 192, 200 (*see also under chiefs*: Gasebonwe, Jantjie, Mahura, Matimo, Mothibi, Tyso)
Boers,
  conflict with tribes: 12, 37, 45, 47-52, 117, 204-5, 269
  Great Trek: 31-2,
  threat to missionaries: 32, 35, 40, 48-9, 100-1, 104-5, 200
  Boer War: 199, 203,
Borigelong, 18, 20, 21-23, 30, 35, 38, 50, 100 (*see also* Mothibi)

Carl, *son of* Thabi, 106, 108, 154, 167
Chapman, James, 44, 53-4, 65, 177, 211, 227, 257, 262-3, 268
Chapman's baobab, *link with missionaries*: 210-11, **217**, **218**
Clarendon, Lord, 74, 175, 181

Ellis, William, 9, 16

Freeman, Joseph, 35-6, 37, 38,

Gasebonwe, 30, 38, 50 (*see also* Batlapin)
Grey, Sir George, 54, 84, 101
Griquas, *origins of*: 12, 14, 16, 32, 44, 120, 122, 200 (*see also* Waterboer)

Griquatown, 9, 11, 12, 13, 16, 17, 18, 21, 23, 26, 41, 44, 103

Hamilton, Robert, 20, 23, 201
Helmore, Anne, 3, 6, *marriage*: 7, *arrival in the Cape*: 9, 10-12, *at* Lekhatlong: 13, 14-19, *leaves* Lekhatlong: 19, Borigelong: 20-3, *return to* Lekhatlong: 23, 26-31, 33-4, 41, 52, 53, 56-7, *in England*: 59-61, 66, 70, 75, 77, 81, 84-5, *return to Africa*: 85-6, **89**, 99, 103-5, *departure on* Makololo *mission*: 106, 108, 119, 129, 140, *letter re journey*: 141-5, 146, 148, 151, 152, *death of*: 154, 157-8, 166, 167, 186-7, 191-2, *author's findings*: 198, 199, 200, 201, 202, 205, 208-9, 226, 231, 260, *account of sufferings*: 273-9
Helmore, Anne Sophia (*daughter*), *birth*: 26, 27, 30, 34, 41, 61, 71, 84-5, **97**, 100, 140, 141, 168, 191, 198, 205, 245
Helmore, Emily (*daughter*), *birth*: 34, 84-5, 100, 141, 168, 191-2, 201
Helmore, Emily (*sister*) *see* Stuart, Emily
Helmore, Emma Elizabeth (Lizzie), *birth*: 33, 34, 61, 84-5, 106, 112, 135, 136, 140, 142-4, 145, 155, 157-8, 160-1, 163, 166-9, 191-2, 229, 232-3, 246, 262, 274, 279
Helmore, Frederick, 4, 5, 7, 31, 56, 60
Helmore, Henry Charles, *birth*: 57, 85, 106, 142, 148, *death*: 152, 157, 169, 260, 274-5, 279
Helmore, Holloway, i, *childhood*: 3-4, *early years*: 5-6, *ordination*: 7, *marriage*: 7, *arrival in the Cape*: 9, 10-12, *takes over* Lekhatlong: 13, 14-16, *conflict over* Lekhatlong: 16-18, *leaves* Lekhatlong: 19, *at* Borigelong: 20-3, *returns to* Lekhatlong: 23, *life at* Lekhatlong: 25-34, 35-7, *building of dam*: 38-40, 41, 46-7, *trouble with* Boers: 47-52, *success of mission*: 55, 56-7, *return to England*: 59-61, 66, *setting up of*

Makololo *mission*: 70-1, *plans to head* Makololo *mission*: 75, 76, 77, 78, 81, 82, 83, 84-5, *arrival in Cape*: 85, 86, **87**, **88**, 99, 100, 103-5, 106, *departure for* Linyanti: 106-7, *journal of journey*: 108-140, 142, 143, *walked 30 miles for water*: 144, 145, 146, 147, 148, *arrival at* Linyanti: 151, 152, 154, *death of*: 155, 156-8, *taking of his goods*: 159, 161, 162, 163-4, *events leading to tragedy*: 170, 176, Livingstone's *involvement*: 178-183, 184-8, 190-2, *author's findings*: 197, 198, 199, 200, 201-7, 208-9, 210-12, 225, *thirst on Mababe Plain*: 226-7, 232, 236-8, Mahoto's *account of tragedy*: 241-4, 245, Mayeyi's *account*: 249-254, *location of camp*: 258-60, *poison/fever investigation*: 261-7, 269-70, 274, 276-9, Price's *poison allegation*: 280-4

Helmore, Olive (*daughter*), *birth*: 19, 21, 22, 27, 30, 34, 41, 61, 71, 84-5, 86, **96**, 99-100, 105-7, 140-5, 167-8, 191, 205, 208, 231, 245, 259, 273, 279

Helmore, Olive (*mother*), 4, 7, *death*: 27

Helmore, Porter, 4, 5, 7

Helmore, Selina, *birth*: 41, 84-5, 106, 142, *death of*: 154, 157, 169, 260, 274-5, 279

Helmore, Revd.Thomas (*father*), 3-5, 7, *death*: 27

Helmore, Thomas (*brother*), 4, 5, 7, 31, 56, 60

Helmore, William Holloway (Willie), *birth*: 53, 84-5, 106, 107, 135-6, 141-2, 155, 157-8, 160-1, 163, 166-9, 191-2, 198, 229, 232-3, 246, 262, 274-5, 279

Hughes, Isaac, 9, 11, 13, 18, 21, 23

Inglis, Walter, 26, 33, 51-2

Jantjie Mothibi, 14, 17-18, 21, 22, 25, 34, 39, 47, 50, 85, 99, 106, *death of*: 200 (*see also* Batlapin)

Kebrabasa Rapids, 67, 170-5, 180, 182-4, 247
Kionecoe, 108, 154, 167, 276
Kirk, John, 78, 174-5, 177, 179-80, 182, 183-4, 186
Kok, Adam, 12

Kolobeng, 35, 37, 41, 46, 47-8, 63, 80, 204-5
Konati, 147, 149, 152, 167, 282
Kramer, Cornelius, 12
Kuisang, 108, 167
Kuruman, i, 6, 13, 16, 18, 19, 20-1, 23, 25, 26, 27, 30, 35-6, 38, 44, 48-9, 55, 63, 71, 72, 76, 80, 81, 83, 84, 86, **98**, 100-1, 103-5, 106, 108, 115, 122, 160, 161, 163, 167, 168, 176, 178, 180, 200-2, 203-4, **214**, 269, 282 (*see also* Moffat, Robert)

Lechulatebe, 35, 44, 161, 163, 165-8, 186, 228-9, 246, 263, 284 (*see also* Batawana)
Lekhatlong, i, 9, 11, Helmore's *missionary begins*: 13-14, *new town built*: 15, *missionary conflict*: 16-19, 21-3, Helmore's *missionary*: 25-34, 35-6, Freeman's *report*: 37, *dam*: 38-40, 46-7, 48, 51, 52, 55-7, 75-6, 86, 99, 106, 167, 192, *fate of*: 199-200, *remains of dam*: 199-200, **213**

Lingkomi, 108, 128, 167
Linyanti, ii, Livingstone's *first visit*: 41-2, 44, 45, Livingstone's *second visit*: 53-5, 60, 63, 66, 67, 68, 76, 81, 83, 100, 101, 102, 104, 105, 106, *arrival of* Helmore *party*: 150-1, 155-6, 158, 162, 163, 164, 165, 167-8, 170, 176, 178, 179, 180, 182, 183, 184-6, 188, 191, 197, 202, 229, 234, 236-7, *river system*: 238-9, 240, 242-3, 249, 251, 254, 255, 256-7, 258-9, 260-1, 262, 263, 265, 268, 270, 280-2, 283, 284 (*see also* Malengalenga *and* Sangwali)

Livingstone, Charles, 78, 176-7, 179
Livingstone, David, i, 21, 26, *marriage to Mary Moffat*: 30, *moves to Chonuane* 33, *discovery of* Lake Ngami: 34-5, 37-8, *reaches* Makololo: 41-6, Kolobeng *sacked*: 47, *commences trans-Africa journey*: 53-5, *news of arrival at Tete*: 60, *returns to England*: 61, *involvement in* Makololo *mission*: 62-76, *discovers* Victoria Falls: 66, *resigns from* London Missionary Society: 74-5, *Zambezi expedition*: 78-84, **90**, 99, 101-2, 103, 104, 105, 121, 122, 124, 134-5, 136, 138, 139, 151-2, 156, 158, 162, 168, Kebrabasa *obstacle*: 170-6, *exploration of the Shire*:

177, *relations with crew*: 177-8, *reaches Lake Nyasa*: 178, *escorts* Makololo *back to Barotseland*: 179-80, *with* Sekeletu: 180-3, *reaction to* Linyanti *deaths*: 184-8, *aftermath of failed mission*: 189-191, 192, *author's findings*: 204-5, 209, 212, 227-9, 233, 238, 240, 242-4, 247, 249, 252-3, 254, 257, 258, 259, 260, 261, 262, 263, *cure for* malaria: 264-5, 266, *Victoria Falls*: 268, 282, 284

Livingstone, Mary (*formerly* Moffat), 26, 30, 37, 41-2, 45-6, 48, 54, 61-3, 65, 68, 69, 70, 76, 78-81, 86, **91**, 99, 100, 101-2, 103, 105, 162, 170, 176, 178, 181, 182, 185, 189, *death of*: 190, 191, 204, 243, 258, 266

London Missionary Society, ii, 3, 6, 9, 10, 12, 13, 16, 22, 23, 30, 35, 40, 45, 46, 47, 60, 61, 62, 68-9, *plans for* Makololo *mission*: 70-6, 78, 79, 80, 81, 84, 100, 107, 158, 188, 191, 201, 202, 242, 244, 260, 264, 269 (*see also* Tidman)

Mackenzie, Bishop Charles, 74, 184, 189-90
MacKenzie, Ellen, 100, 106, 161, 163, 166, 167, 207
MacKenzie, John, 73, 81, 86, **95**, 103-4, 106, 161, *account of rescue of survivors*: 163-7, 168, 207, 226, 229, 244-6, 263
Mahoto, Innocent, ii, *interview with*: 241-4, 246, 251, 258
Mahura, 14, 40, 50-1 (*see also* Batlapin)
Makololo, i, 35, 37-8, 41, *history of*: 42-5, 53-5, 62-8, *plan for* Makololo *mission*: 70-3, 75-7, *preparations for* Makololo *mission*: 78-84, 85, 99, 102-4, 105, 140, *description of*: 151, 156-8, *theft of goods*: 159-60, 161, 162, 163, 165, 167, 168, 170, 171, 174-5, 176, 178, *return of porters by* Livingstone: 179-80, 181, 182, 183, Livingstone's *view of tragedy*: 184-8, 189, 190-1, 192, 226-7, 229, 237-8, 240, *interview with* Mahoto: 241-4, *decline of*: 244-6, 247, 249, 252-4, 257, 261, 262-4, 267, 268, 269, 280-1, 283-4 (*see also* Sebituane, Sekeletu *and* Mahoto, Innocent)
Makgadikgadi, *geographical features*: 209-10, **216**

malaria (African fever), 37, 44, 53, 55, 62, 63, 64, 149, 152-5, 178, 181, 239, *mosquitos*: 262-3, 282 (*see also* poison/fever debate)
Malengalenga (*formerly* Linyanti), **224**, 242, 244, 251, *visit to*: 256-60
Malmesbury, Lord, 175-6
Mamili National Park, 255, 267
Mamochisane, 53-4, 246
Matabele, 37, 42, 50, 54-5, 63, 65, 70-3, 75, 76, 78, 83-4, 85, 101, 103, 105, 157, 162, 185, 229, 244, 246, 257, 262, 268-70 (*see also* Moselekatse)
Matimo, 49-50 (*see also* Batlapin)
Matlaba, (*Barolong chief*), 49-50
Mayeyi (*or Bayeiye*), ii, **222, 223**, 229, 247, 249, *interview with*: 250-6, 260-1, 267
Moffat, Bessie (*see* Price, Elizabeth Lees)
Moffat, Jane (Jeannie), 30, 86, 108, 167-8, 202
Moffat, John Smith, 72-3, 79-81, 85, 100, 104, 106, 108, 124, 187, 244, 269
Moffat, Mary, 6, 26-30, 37, 46, 71, 79-80, 85, 86, **93**, 106, 122, 167, 168, 201-2, 207
Moffat, Robert, 6, 13, 20-1, 25, 26-30, 35, 36, *relationship with* Moselekatse: 37, 38, 42-4, 51-2, 54-5, 56, 65, 70-2, 75, 76, *concerns about* Makololo *mission*: 79-84, 85, 86, **92**, 100, 101, 103, 104, 105, 106-7, 108, 115, 124, 126, 162, 167-8, 176, 181-2, 190, 201-2, 207, 245, 263, 269, 282, 283-4 (*see also* Kuruman)
Molatsi, 152-3, 157, 167, 260
Monatse, 152, 167
Moriegi, 108, 128, 135, 140, 167
Moselekatse, 37, 42, 44-5, 50, 55, 65, 70-2, 75, 78, 79, 82-3, 100, 101-2, 181-2, 186, 246, 256, 268, *death of*: 269, 281, 283-4 (*see also* Matabele)
Mothibi, 9, 13-14, 21, 23, *death of*: 30, 38, 41 (*see also* Batlapin)
Murchison, Sir Roderick, 62, 74

Ngami, Lake, 34-5, 37, 41, 44, 46, 100, 134, 160, 163, 165, 168, 204, *geographical features*: 228-9, 232, 247, 257, 262

Okavango Delta, *geographical feature*: 230-1

Oswell, William Cotton, 34, 41-2, 44-6, 121, 134

Philip, John, 3, 6, 9-10, 11, 12, 13, 16-18, 21, 132

Poison/fever debate, 158, 242-3, 252, 257, 261-7, Price's *account*: 280-4 (*see also* malaria)

Pretorius, Commandant General, 49-51, 100-1

Price, Elizabeth Lees (*formerly* Moffat), 30, 108, 168, 188, 207, 245

Price, Isabella, 73, 86, **94**, 101-3, 105, 106, 107, 108, 114, 126, 131, *birth of baby*: 133, 136, *quotes from her diary*: 145-9 *and* 150-6, 157, 158, *death of*: 160, 166, *author's findings*: 197, 209, 226, 232-3, 252, 257, 260, 262, 266, 275, 278, 279

Price, Roger, 73, 81, 86, **94**, 103-4, 105, *departure for* Linyanti: 106, 108, 109, 113, 117, 119, 121, 122, 123, 124, 126, 127, 128, 129-30, 131, 132, 134, 135, 137, 138, 139, 140, 142, 145, 146-7, 149, 150, 152, 153, 154, 155, 156, 157-8, *account of disaster*: 159-62, *rescue by* MacKenzie: 163-7, 168, 170, 178, 179, 182, 186-8, 191, *author's findings*: 197, 202-7, 208, 212, 225, *thirst on Mababe Plain*: 226-7, 229, 232-3, 234, 236-8, 242-3, 244-5, 246, maYeyi's *account*: 252, 257, 258, *site of camp*: 259-60, 262-4, 266, 269-70, 277-8, *allegation of poison*: 280-4

Read, James, 17-18
Ross, William, 21, 26, 40, 57, 99, 106
Royal Geographical Society, 62, 73, 74 (*see also* Murchison, Sir Roderick)
Russell, Lord John, 177, 181, 190

Saboknena, 108, 167
Sangwali (*formerly* Linyanti), 242, *visit to*: 249-256
Savuti, *geographical features*: 234-5, **219**
Schreiner, Olive, 11
Sebituane, 35, 37, *his story*: 42-5, *death of*: 46, 53-5, 63-5, 103, 189, *grave*: **221**, 229, 242-3, 246, 251-2, *site of grave*: 255-6, 257, 263 (*see also* Makololo)

Sechele, 33, 34, 37, 47-8, 50, 53, 101, 118-20, 122, 124, 134, 204-5, 244-5, 273 (*see also* Bakwena)

Sekeletu, *his origins*: 44, *and* 53-4, 55, 62-3, 65-6, 76, 81, 83, 150, 151, 152, 155, 156-8, *plundering*: 159-60, 162, 163, 176, 180-1, 185-7, 188, 189, 190, 237-8, 242-3, 244, *death of*: 245, 251-3, 256, *site of grave*: 257-8, 261, 263, 266-7, 268, Price's *charge of poisoning*: 280-4 (*see also* Makololo)

Sekhomi, 114, 120, 122-6, 207, 246 (*see also* Bamangwato)

Sekwebu, 66-7, 69, 179

Setloki, 108, 113, 116, 140, 155, 167, 260

ShuFu, Bornface, ii, **222**, 249-50, 253, 254-5 (*see also* Mayeyi)

Stuart, Charles, 36, 41, 56-7, 205

Stuart, Emily (*formerly* Helmore), 4, 7, 19, 27, 30-1, 32, 33, 34, *marriage*: 36, 41, 56-7, 59-60, 84, 129, 145, 168, 191, 208, 273

Sykes, William, 73, 81, 86, 100, 106, 108, 202, 269

Taung, 14, 33, 40, 49, 50, 100, 200
Thabi, 13-14, 17, 22-3, 25, 99, 106, 108, 109-10, 111, 118, 121, 123, 125, 127, 128, 132, 133, 135, 136, 137, 138, 140, 143, 147, *death of*: 154, 162, 167, 210, 260, 278
Thomas, Thomas Morgan, 81, 86, 106, 108, 269
Thompson, William, 39, 57. 63, 69, 79, 102, 145, 280
Thornton, Richard, 78, 177
Tidman, Arthur, 16, 33, 45, 46, 48, 56, 60, 63, 67, 68, 69, 72, 75, 76, 78, 81-2, 99, 144-5, 182, 184-5, 188, 190, 237, 260 (*see also* London Missionary Society)
Tyso, 13, 25 (*see also* Batlapin)

Waterboer, Andries and Nicolaas, 12-13, 16-18, 21, 200
Wright, Peter, 9, 10, 11, 13, 17-18, 21, 22, 55

Zambezi River, *course of*: 247

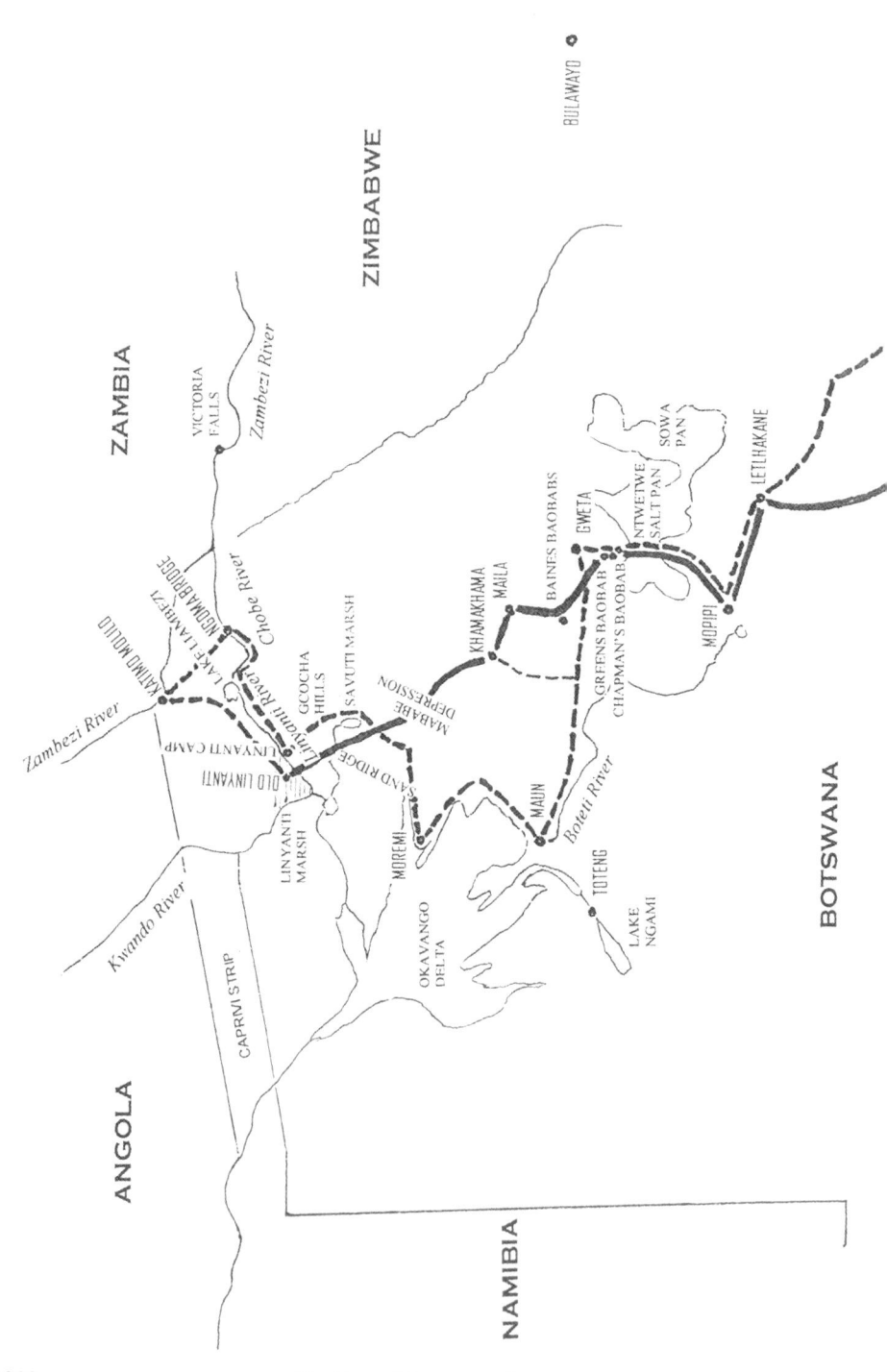

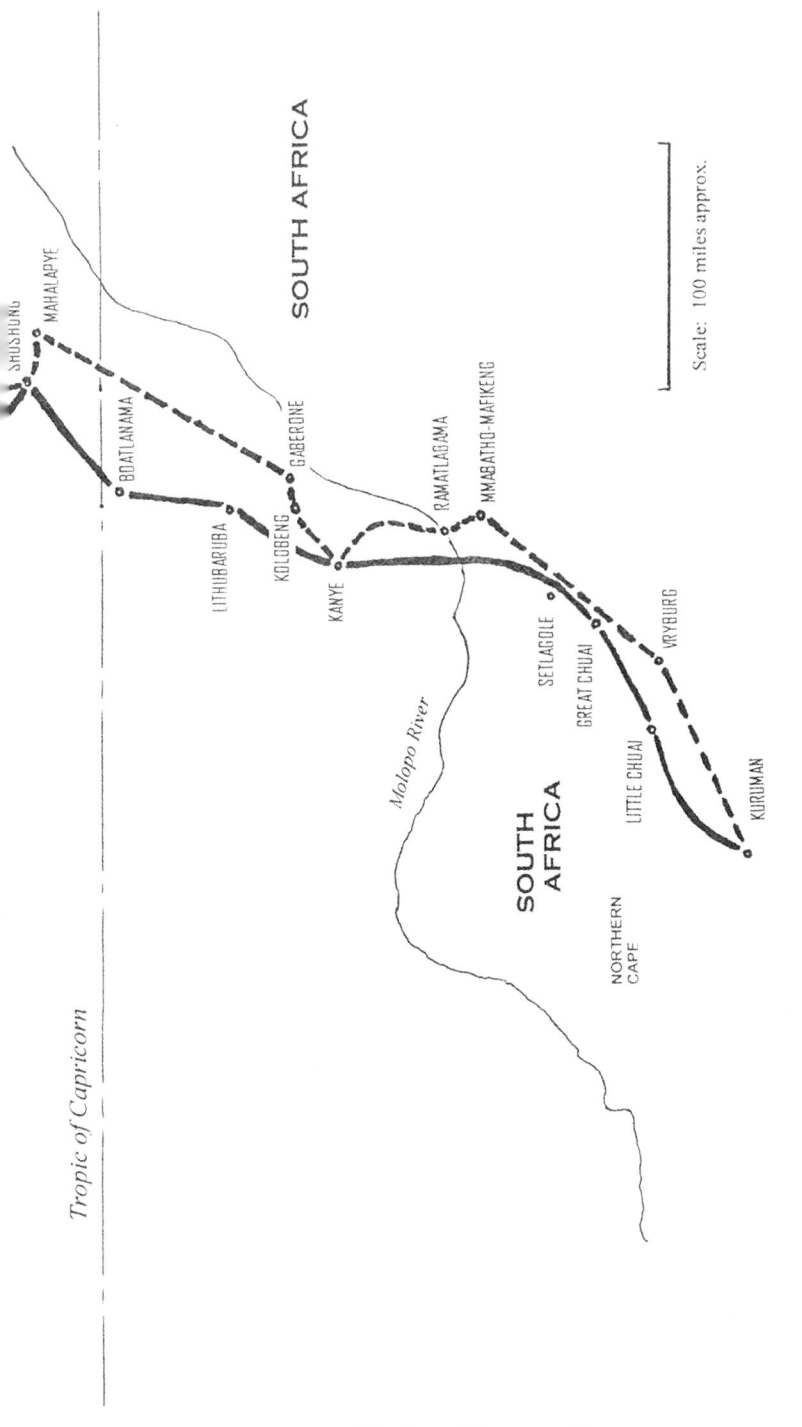

Part of Northern Cape, Botswana and Namibia, showing the route from Kuruman to the Linyanti. Helmore/Price route, 1859/60: ——— *Kilby party route, 1999:* - - - - - -

No Cross Marks the Spot